The Jesus of Faith

Theological Inquiries

*Studies in Contemporary
Biblical and Theological Problems*

General Editor
Lawrence Boadt, C. S. P.

PAULIST PRESS
New York • Ramsey • Toronto

The Jesus of Faith

A Study in Christology

Michael L. Cook, S.J.

PAULIST PRESS
New York • Ramsey • Toronto

Acknowledgments
The Publisher gratefully acknowledges the use of the following materials: Excerpts
from *Jesus—Word and Presence* by Peter C. Hodgson, © 1971, Fortress Press.
Reprinted with permission of Fortress Press. Chapters 1 and 2 reproduce, mostly
verbatim, the greater portion of Michael Cook's article, "The Call to Faith of the
Historical Jesus: Questions for the Christian Understanding of Faith," from
Theological Studies 39 (1978) 679–700. Reprinted with permission of the Editor.

Library of Congress
Catalog Card Number: 80-84510

ISBN: 0-8091-2349-5

Published by Paulist Press
545 Island Road, Ramsey, N.J. 07446

Printed and bound in the
United States of America

Contents

FOR POPPA
whose loving and gentle ways
first taught me what it means
to call God
ABBĀ

CHAPTER ONE

Jesus and Faith:
The Question of Continuity

A. THE BASIC PROBLEM

"The question of the relation between Jesus and faith affects the heart of christology, and indeed the prime datum of Christian dogmatics as such. It is the cardinal point of the whole account of what Christianity really means. For there is no doubt that what makes a Christian is faith in Jesus Christ. And the one basic problem of christology is precisely the meaning of the statement, 'I believe in Jesus'."[1] The very name 'Jesus Christ' is already the problem, for it is not simply a proper name but a combination of a name that refers to a particular historical person, Jesus of Nazareth, and a confession of faith about that person, viz. that he is the Christ of God. Between that historical person and that confession of faith there lies the event that for Christians is both decisive and problematical, Jesus' death and resurrection. The fundamental task of Christian theology from within the Christian faith itself is to "demonstrate the intrinsic basis and justification of christology in the person and history of Jesus."[2] The key question is that of the continuity (including both identity and difference) between the Jesus of history and the Christ of faith.

It should be noted that this problem is both old and new. It is

---

1. Gerhard Ebeling, "Jesus and Faith," in *Word and Faith* (Philadelphia: Fortress, 1963) 201.

2. Juergen Moltmann, *The Crucified God* (New York: Harper & Row, 1974) 84. Moltmann aptly remarks on p. 107, n.2: "History comes about in a person, and a person comes into being in his history."

as old as the disputes in the first five centuries of Christian history over the proper relationship between the humanity and the divinity of Jesus. It is new insofar as the question today is framed in terms of contemporary historical consciousness. For many, if not most, theologians today, to think theologically is to think historically. Admittedly, this is an intellectual framework that has arisen from the development of historical-critical methods principally in the nineteenth century. We bring to the biblical texts a question that was not in the minds of the first-century authors, but which remains a legitimate and necessary question insofar as it touches the roots of our contemporary understanding of reality. It is not enough to demonstrate the truth of Christian faith from within. We must also "demonstrate that it is relevant to the present-day understanding of reality and the present-day dispute about the truth of God and the righteousness of man and the world."[3] The Christian faith makes claims that have consequences, both present and future, for the whole world. It is of the very nature of that faith, and hence a hermeneutical necessity, continually to engage that world in the spheres of its own legitimacy. This was true for the Fathers of the Church who engaged the hellenistic mind. It is true for us today who must engage an increasingly secularized and historicized world.

A basic assumption of this book is that one cannot do christology today if one seeks to avoid the historical questions. This is true not only because of the modern state of the question, but also because Christianity is deeply rooted in history and hence is historical in its very nature. The approach taken here is thoroughly historical in that it moves from the origins of Christian faith in the Jesus of history through his fate on the cross to the early Church's proclamation. It could be called 'developmental' as long as that word does not connote a progressivist notion of quasi-organic evolution toward perfection which is really a historicist variation on the fixist notion of *semper eadem*.[4] It is essential to realize that historical phenomena involve zigs and zags, regressions (insights lost), lapses, reversals, re-

---

3. Ibid.
4. See in this connection the remarks of Paul Misner, "A Note on the Critique of Dogmas," TS 34 (1973) 690–700, commenting on the position of Jean-Pierre Jossua, O.P.

discoveries, new departures: in a word, real change. Not only can origins be understood in terms of later deveopments, but later developments can be criticized in terms of origins. This is the famous hermeneutical circle: when we interpret a text, we find that the text in turn interprets us. In the final analysis, continuity is grounded in the concrete life of the Church, a living body that hands on, not a dead letter from the past, but a living and vibrant reality—which is the true meaning of tradition.

Another important assumption is that historical consciousness is not simply reducible to historical-critical method. By historical consciousness I mean quite simply that one cannot take a standpoint outside of history in order to understand. We always stand within history and our human knowing consists basically in viewing the world and ourselves in it from a certain perspective. *Christian* faith can be called one such perspective because we stand under the cross. Hence, while striving to remain within historical consciousness as the unavoidable and inseparable condition of knowing anything in this world, it is important to make a clear differentiation between 'history' and 'faith'. On the one hand, faith itself is an historical phenomenon, which is to say that it properly belongs *within* the historical process as the appropriate and indispensable stance of human beings confronted with a world that has 'not-yet' arrived at its consummation. Without some form of faith commitment, being human at all is not possible as we shall see. In this sense, faith is constitutive of the human precisely *as* historical. On the other hand, faith is not reducible to history as that word is used by contemporary historians. History in this sense is a human science and/or art with very specific methodological rules. As will be seen, it is not a question of some theory or other about the nature of history but rather of an analytical description of what historians do when they actually do history. Much of the confusion between historians and theologians arises from the use of the word 'history' on different levels. There are certain things that an historian, by reason of his method, cannot call history, e.g., virginal conception, nature miracles, resurrection. This is not to make a judgment one way or another about their actuality, but simply to say that such judgments are beyond the limits of historical-critical methodology. An historian can deal with the phenomenon that shortly after Jesus' death certain of his disciples claimed that he was alive and with the effect of this claim upon subsequent history. But, the historian cannot verify the truth or falsity of the claim itself. Whether or not Jesus was actually raised from the dead simply transcends the criteria of assent to which the historian subscribes. Its verification lies in a different dimension. If actual, such events are at best 'meta-historical'—a word to which we shall return. But, when theologians invoke a 'special' kind of history, particularly when they use terms like 'salvation-history', then in my opinion they simply confuse the issues linguistically.

In the light of these two assumptions, viz. that Christianity is essentially historical, in such wise that it would become something else if it were divorced from its historical roots, and that—contrary to the widespread positivism of the nineteenth century—historical consciousness cannot simply be reduced to historical-critical method, the rest of this chapter is devoted to an articulation of the proper relationship between history and faith. To get an overview of the problem, I will first consider the name of Jesus as the ultimate Christian symbol. Then, in this context, I will turn to the more particular problem of the necessary and hence legitimate role that history plays in relation to Christian faith. Finally, as a preparation for the chapter on Jesus' earthly ministry, I will examine the possibility of making historical judgments given the nature of our sources, i.e., the basic criteria that have been developed in the history of biblical criticism.

B. The Primacy of Jesus

There is a growing consensus among contemporary theologians[5] that the proper starting point for any christology today must be from

---

5. I am particularly influenced by the following four theologians, who in the books mentioned represent four essential elements that must be integrated in any adequate christology, viz. incarnation, resurrection, cross, and historical Jesus. Piet Schoonenberg, S.J., *The Christ* (New York: Herder and Herder, 1971). Wolfhart Pannenberg, *Jesus—God and Man* (Philadelphia: Westminster, 1968). Juergen Moltmann, *The Crucified God.* Peter C. Hodgson, *Jesus—Word and Presence* (Philadelphia: Fortress, 1971). Hodgson draws heavily upon the approach and insights of Martin Heidegger and Gerhard Ebeling. Ebeling has had a great influence on my own thinking as he was the subject of my doctoral dissertation, *The Jesus of Faith: A Study of Gerhard Ebeling's Christology* (Berkeley: Graduate Theological Union, 1974; available through University Microfilms, Ann Arbor).

below, i.e., from the human and historical. Actually, the alternatives 'from above' and 'from below' are not adequate to the problem. It is not being proposed that we now substitute a general theory about what it is to be divine with a general theory about what it is to be human. Both are equally abstract and both presuppose that we already know what it is to be divine or human. What is being proposed is that an adequate christology can only begin from the concrete, personal existence of Jesus of Nazareth. Juergen Moltmann outlines the problem well in his chapter, "Questions about Jesus,"[6] by proposing four questions as possible starting points for a christology, viz. (1) Is Jesus true God? (2) Is Jesus true Man? (3) 'Are you he who is to come?' (4) 'Who do you say that I am?' The first two are rejected because they begin with a general theory about the divine or the human, as mentioned above. The third is closer to the reality of Jesus because it comes out of the concrete, historical experience of the Jewish people awaiting their Messiah but it is colored by the kind of false expectations of that Messiah which Jesus himself had to counter in his ministry. For Moltmann, the fourth question is the proper starting point for a christology precisely because it is open to the future. Here it is not we who question Jesus but Jesus who questions us. In my opinion, this corresponds to the fact that for the Evangelists the question of who Jesus is is, on the level of *praxis,* inseparable from the question of who we are, i.e., christology is inextricably intertwined with discipleship.

Moltmann describes Jesus as one who was singularly open to the future: his center (and therefore his identity) was in his Father whose Kingdom he proclaimed as coming. This has implications for any christology that proposes to be an answer to the question of Jesus' identity. "If he exists for the sake of the one who is to be, then his question and his openness to the future are greater than all the answers which believers and non-believers can give."[7] The *reality* of this future will not be discovered in any closed reality, whether that be of 'purely' subjective experience or of a 'purely' objective system. With regard to the latter, any system of thought—Aristotelian, Thomistic, Hegelian, *et al.*—which would consider itself 'adequate'

6. Moltmann, *Crucified* 82–111.
7. Ibid. 106.

to answer the question, particularly to the exclusion of any other possible approach, is simply refusing to recognize the limits of its own presuppositions and methods. This future will be discovered or 'unveiled' (*a-lētheia*) finally, not in any limited system of the human mind, but only in the very process of coming to be, concrete and contingent as it is, which Moltmann characterizes as the liberation of creation itself.

What is said about the limited nature of systems applies to the New Testament as well. The debate over the unity of the New Testament, i.e., whether the subject-matter (*die Sache*) is to be found primarily in anthropology (Rudolf Bultmann) or in christology (Eduard Lohse), is seen to be vacuous. Christology and/or anthropology receive definite meaning and interpretation from the concrete, personal existence of Jesus. The tension between the earthly and the eternal, the particular and the universal, the temporal and the eschatological finally comes down to the tension between who Jesus is and what we say about him. What is constant and irreplaceable in the New Testament is the name Jesus; what is variable and interchangeable are the titles, the diverse attempts to bring to expression the mystery of this person within changing contexts. It is almost a commonplace today to point out that there is a development of christology within the New Testament from a more Palestinian Jewish to a more Hellenistic Gentile milieu.[8] The very title "Christ" moves from being a proclamation of Jesus' messiahship to being a part of his proper name. What all this means is that Jesus in his personal reality and identity continually transcends any attempt that we make, whether in the New Testament or in the subsequent history of the Church or in the present day, to bring to expression the mystery of his personhood. Jesus is not *simply* "Christ."

What I propose is that the ultimate Christian symbol is the name Jesus ('Yahweh saves'). Symbol is to be understood here not in the steno or literal sense of a one-to-one correspondence between sign and thing, but in the tensive or evocative sense of embodying

---

8. See especially Reginald H. Fuller, *The Foundations of New Testament Christology* (London: Collins, 1965).

more than can simply be articulated rationally.[9] As Avery Dulles puts it: "Unlike historical or abstract truth, mystery cannot be described or positively defined. It can only be evoked."[10] Symbol has power to evoke because it addresses itself to the whole person, to the imagination, the will, and the emotions, as well as to the intellect, and because it is deeply rooted in human experience and human history. That is why one cannot simply invent true symbols. They must emerge from the depths of human consciousness and will last only as long as they continue to evoke those depths. Dulles refers to Suzanne Langer's description of the cross as a "charged" symbol.[11] It evokes a whole range of meanings that speak to the most profound depths of human experience. But, it is even more poignantly the personal experience of a man who was condemned as a blasphemer, executed as a rebel, and died as one cursed by God (Gal.3:13).[12] Christian symbols have a peculiar power precisely because they are rooted in history. If one severs this relationship to history, one ceases in my opinion to be distinctively Christian.

If Jesus is the 'ultimate' or 'primordial' symbol of Christian faith, then experience of him, mediated symbolically as is all human experience, is as primary for the Christian of today as it was for Peter, Andrew, James, and John. The process of bringing the experience to expression, reflecting upon it with the powers of reason, taking a stand toward it in terms of personal commitment must always be seen as integrally necessary but subordinate to the primacy of Jesus himself. We must always return to the symbol and, in Paul Ricoeur's terms, experience it anew with a second or post-critical naiveté.[13]

---

9. See the discussion of this in Norman Perrin, *Jesus and the Language of the Kingdom* (Philadelphia: Fortress, 1976) 22–23, 29–32. The distinction between a steno and a tensive symbol comes from Philip Wheelwright, *Metaphor and Reality* (Bloomington: Indiana U. Press, 1962).

10. Avery Dulles, S.J., *Myth, Biblical Revelation, and Christ* (Washington: Corpus, 1968) 1.

11. Ibid. 4–5. Cf. Suzanne K. Langer, *Philosophy in a New Key* (Cambridge: Harvard U. Press, 1942).

12. Moltmann, *Crucified* 126–153.

13. Loretta Dornisch, by way of introduction to Ricoeur's essay on "Biblical Hermeneutics," offers a useful summary of his theory of symbolic knowledge in "Paul Ricoeur on Biblical Hermeneutics," *Semeia* 4 (ed. John Dominic Crossan; Missoula: Scholar's Press, 1975) 14–16.

C. The Relationship between History and Faith

Given the primacy of Jesus as the basic frame of reference for doing christology, we can now turn to the more particular problem of the necessary and hence legitimate role that history plays in relation to Christian faith. As indicated above, this is a subordinate but indispensable dimension to the total process of responding to this Jesus. In order to clarify the dimensions of the problem, I will first consider what historians mean by the word history, then three major positions that theologians have taken on the relationship between history and faith, and finally the solution that I propose which is fundamental to understanding the method of this book.

(1) *A description of history.* Van A. Harvey, in his very fine and still useful book *The Historian and the Believer,* describes the problem as a confrontation between the modern historian's principles of judgment and the Christian's will to believe. His concern is with the stance of the historian, with what he calls a certain morality of knowledge, or ethic of assent. He is not concerned with theorizing about history but with an analytical description of how historians go about justifying their claims, what kinds of judgments they make and what kinds of assent they solicit.[14]

He begins with an analysis of Ernst Troeltsch which is worth quoting. Troeltsch

> argued that critical historical inquiry rests on three inter-related principles: (1) the principle of criticism, by which he meant that our judgments about the past cannot simply be classified as true or false but must be seen as claiming only a greater or a lesser degree of probability and as always open to revision; (2) the principle of analogy, by which he meant that we are able to make such judgments of probability only if we presuppose that our own present experience is not radically dissimilar to the experience of past persons; and (3) the principle of correlation, by which he meant that the phenomena of man's historical life are so

---

14. Van A. Harvey, *The Historian and the Believer* (Toronto: Macmillan, 1966; paperback edition, 1969) xi–xii, 33–34.

related and interdependent that no radical change can take place at any one point in the historical nexus without effecting a change in all that immediately surrounds it. Historical explanation, therefore, necessarily takes the form of understanding an event in terms of its antecedents and consequences, and no event can be isolated from its historically conditioned time and space.[15]

Each of these principles raises problems for traditional Christian belief, which Troeltsch saw as basically incompatible with his view. For example, the principle of criticism raises questions about the certitude of faith, the principle of analogy about the uniqueness of past events, and the principle of correlation about the possibility of supernatural intervention.

These questions can only be dealt with once we have a clearer notion of the historian's craft. Harvey describes it as involving autonomy, assessment, and sound judgment. Autonomy refers to the will to truth, the conviction of the historian that one must think for oneself and not accept sources as authoritative uncritically. The task of the historian is to confer authority on sources through critical method. Assessment refers to the will to communication, the recognition that history is a matter of public knowledge (as distinct from belief or opinion) and so demands logical candor and the giving of reasons to justify one's claims. The best analogy is the law-court: what sort of case does one make to defend a certain claim? This leads into an analysis of the structure of argument which on the level of form is similar in all justificatory argumentation. One formulates a question, considers the various likely candidates, chooses a particular candidate based on the evidence, and eliminates the alternatives. The evidence involves drawing a conclusion from certain data based on warrants which are usually implicit but offer further reasons for moving from data to conclusion. This is not unlike the ancient syllogism except that there is no logical necessity to the conclusion. It

---

15. Ibid. 14–15. Harvey refers to Ernst Troeltsch, *Gesammelte Schriften* II (Tuebingen: J.C.B. Mohr, 1913) 729–753 and to his article "Historiography" in *Encyclopedia of Religion and Ethics* (ed. James Hastings; New York: Scribner's, 1914) VI 716–723.

can be challenged on the basis of other evidence and so require a qualification or else the warrant might require further backing. More interesting than the formal structure of argument, however, is the recognition that history is a field-encompassing field, i.e., it is "made up of diverse kinds of arguments making use of correspondingly diverse data and warrants. . . ."[16] The historian, like the lawyer, makes a diversity of claims. He appeals to such sciences as epigraphy, archaeology, etc. He seeks to reconstruct the original situation and to assess accurately the principal agents. He interprets the meaning of the events in a larger context. In all of this, the historian must have a sense of sound judgment. He must recognize that there are levels of judgment here that call for a different quality of assent. The texture of that assent may range all the way from simple fact to very broad generalization. The degree of probability, and hence the appropriate qualifications, will shift accordingly. This is a very brief summary of what Harvey develops at much greater length but it will suffice for our purposes here.

The recognition of the complex nature of historical argument, its field-encompassing character, means that the historian's present standpoint in relation to the past must be conceived as a critically interpreted standpoint. It is not reducible simply to 'scientific' knowledge although science does help us to distinguish the possible from the impossible. There are some things we simply cannot accept as real and so we correctly retain the right to disbelieve or to be skeptical about certain kinds of reports from the past. In fact, the scientific revolution has become so much a part of the furniture of our minds that we frequently take for granted knowledge that would have been unintelligible two thousand years ago. On the other hand, it is important to recognize the uniqueness of every event. It is the task of the historian to enter imaginatively into the past and to understand the events in terms of their concrete context (principle of correlation). Yet, it must be recognized, especially as one moves from simple fact to the more complex questions of motives, purposes, or desires, that this is an imaginative reconstruction in which one sets up certain hypotheses about the situation and the principal

---

16. Ibid. 55.

agents. Such hypotheses can only be confirmed on the basis of the evidence so that the final judgment may range from a high degree of probability to a low degree of possibility (principle of criticism). Finally, the basic presupposition, however one justifies it philosophically, is one of common sense, viz. that human beings have enough in common that a contemporary historian can truly enter into the situation of someone who lived two thousand years ago (principle of analogy).

Having established by means of this analytical description what he calls the morality of historical knowledge, Harvey then seeks to engage the three major theological positions which he characterizes as traditional belief, dialectical theology, and the new quest of the historical Jesus. To this we now turn.

(2) *Three schools of thought.* Harvey K. McArthur[17] sees three "schools" which characterize the present scene. First, there is the "Historical-Certainty School" which insists upon the identity of faith and history, i.e., that historical knowledge one way or another is directly constitutive of faith knowledge. Without historical certainty there is no faith. However, such certainty may be based not only on historical research itself (Joachim Jeremias) but also on the infallibility of scripture and/or the authority of the Church (fundamentalism) or even upon one's personal experience in faith insofar as one claims fact on the basis of subjective experience (subjectivism). Given various nuances, this position corresponds to traditional belief. Second, there is the "Immune-From-Historical-Research School" which maintains for theological reasons a dichotomy or opposition between history and faith. It is illegitimate from the nature of faith to base that faith on the contingencies of history, i.e., the absolute quality of faith must not in any way be dependent upon the relative, probability character of historical research. This position corresponds to dialectical theology. Third, there is the "Historical-Risk School" which insists upon neither identity nor opposition but some kind of interrelation between history and faith. This position recognizes the tentative, probability character of historical research, but affirms that faith must be open to all the ambiguities of history insofar as

---

17. Harvey K. McArthur, "From the Historical Jesus to Christology," *Interpretation* 23 (1969) 190–206.

faith is tied to a concrete, contingent historical event. It corresponds to the new quest of the historical Jesus. With this brief summary in mind, let us see how these three positions stand up to the morality of historical knowledge.

The problem with traditional belief is not the desire for certainty but the falsifying influence that belief can have upon the critical ideal of assent. Many of the things that I might wish to believe passionately as a Christian, e.g., virginal conception, nature miracles, resurrection, are precisely those things which can elicit little or no assent on the basis of critical historical method. One cannot appeal to eyewitnesses as authoritative in themselves because autonomy demands freedom from extrinsic authorities and a certain toughness of mind that leaves no witness unexamined, no authority unquestioned. One cannot appeal to faith to establish a matter of fact for assessment demands reasons to justify a claim and such an appeal shatters the possibility of such an assessment. Finally, one cannot seek to elicit a heavy assent to that which cannot bear it for sound judgment demands a certain quality of mind, a balance that recognizes that such assent depends upon degrees of probability and that consequently does not seek a heavier assent than the evidence can bear.

While it may be argued that dialectical theology seeks not so much to set up an opposition between history and faith as to ensure the freedom of both insofar as the so-called Protestant principle of the two Kingdoms allows God to be God and world to be world (thus ensuring its autonomy and responsibility), nonetheless it does set up an intolerable inconsistency that is tantamount to opposition. Here, in my opinion, the problem is not with the concept of history as these theologians would applaud the morality of historical knowledge here set forth as a legitimate effect of their own radicalized concept of justification by faith. The problem is rather with the concept of faith itself. In their efforts to secure for faith absolute independence from the contingencies of history, the dialectical theologians are faced with an insoluble dilemma. On the one hand, they want to maintain what has always been considered essential to Christian faith, viz. that it is tied to a concrete, contingent historical event of the past. On the other hand, they want to maintain that faith is completely independent of any historical knowledge. If that is so, why not drop any reference to a unique act of God in Christ and simply speak in existential terms of the meaning of human existence? That is the criticism of Rudolf Bultmann made in various ways by Karl Jaspers, Fritz Buri, Schubert Ogden, *et al.* If indeed God acts to redeem us in a past historical event, then faith must in some sense be dependent upon historical knowledge. That is the position of the new quest.

The basic concern of the new quest is the decisive importance of the historical Jesus for Christian faith. Ernst Kaesemann has outlined the fundamental presuppositions. First of all, he accepts the result of the old quest that no life of Jesus, no biography that would involve exterior chronological or interior psychological development, is possible. On the other hand, he refuses to allow this fact to lead to defeatism and skepticism with regard to the earthly Jesus. It is possible, even given the kerygmatic nature of the sources, to recover authentic pieces of historical material. This raises the question of criteria to which we shall return later. Moreover, it is necessary to do so both because of the danger of docetism—if there is no connection between the exalted Lord and the earthly Jesus, then we are in danger of committing ourselves to a mythological Lord—and because of the intention of the Evangelists in writing gospels which is to maintain the identity of the exalted Lord with the earthly. This points to the crucial issue of the whole new quest, which is "the question of the continuity of the Gospel within the discontinuity of the times and within the variation of the kerygma."[18]

James M. Robinson gave the new quest its name in his programmatic essay, *A New Quest of the Historical Jesus.* It is important to consider his position a little more fully because of the crucial distinctions and criticisms it has received from both Van Harvey and Norman Perrin.[19] He begins with a review of the conclusions reached by 1959, viz. that the original quest was impossible because of the kerygmatic nature of the sources and illegitimate because of the "at-

---

18. Ernst Kaesemann, "The Problem of the Historical Jesus," *Essays on New Testament Themes* (London: SCM, 1964) 46.

19. James M. Robinson, *A New Quest of the Historical Jesus* (London: SCM, 1959). Compare Harvey, *Historian,* 179–196, and Norman Perrin, *Rediscovering the Teaching of Jesus* (New York: Harper & Row, 1967) 230–234.

tempt to avoid the risk of faith by supplying objectively verified proof for its 'faith'."[20]

For Robinson, the *possibility* of a new quest resides in "a new concept of history and the self." Modern historiography, while not denying the validity of "the objective, factual level upon which the nineteenth century operated" (names, places, dates, occurrences, sequences, causes, effects), focuses upon "a whole new dimension in the facts, a deeper and more central plane of meaning" (the distinctively human, creative, unique, purposeful, which distinguishes us from nature).[21] The task of history is to grasp the acts of intention and commitment in which the self actualizes itself, and hence to grasp the selfhood therein revealed. Such an approach is formally analogous to the kerygma's interest in Jesus' history and selfhood.

The *legitimacy* of a new quest derives from "man's quest for meaningful existence." This again is formally analogous to the kerygma's interest, which is not to prove faith but to confront us with existential decision. The Evangelists themselves "undoubtedly insisted upon the relevance of history for faith."[22] Whereas the original quest tried to drive a wedge between the Jesus of history and the Christ of faith, the modern approach sees that one cannot be isolated or separated from the other. Rather, it seeks to differentiate in order to mediate an encounter with Jesus distinct from an encounter with the kerygma. Modern historiography gives us a second avenue of access to Jesus (*via historica*) besides the kerygma (*via kerygmatica*). Like the original disciples, who had their factual memory as well as their Easter faith, we are allowed today to see "the flesh of the incarnation." To proclaim Jesus 'in the flesh' is to proclaim the meaningfulness of all human life in the flesh. That concern of the kerygma necessitates and hence legitimates a new quest. To establish a continuity between Jesus and the kerygma is not to prove the kerygma true, but rather to prove "that the existential decision with regard to the *kerygma* is an existential decision with regard to Jesus," i.e., that

---

20. Robinson, *New Quest* 44.
21. Ibid. 28.
22. Ibid. 77–78.

the kerygma is faithful to Jesus when it identifies *"its* understanding of existence with Jesus' existence."[23]

The first and most fundamental objection raised by Harvey at this point concerns the question of methodology, viz. can the new quest really claim to have attained a new methodology which would seem to imply new canons of assessment?[24] Harvey very astutely distinguishes between the final aim of history and formal criteria. What could be called new here is the important and indispensable emphasis upon the true aim of history, its humane significance which can profoundly affect one's own understanding of existence. But such an aim cannot dispense with the logic of rational assessment. In fact, it depends upon it if one is to be talking about facts at all. Moreover, the emphasis upon meaning is only one model of history, particularly useful in interpreting religious and philosophical texts, but it is not the only legitimate kind. The aims of history can be as diverse as the questions people can ask.

When Robinson seeks "the solution of typical problems,"[25] he shows a striking similarity to the position that Harvey will take, viz. that Jesus embodies a meaning complex. The focus is on the message of Jesus. If we operate below the terminological level, we will discover an underlying unity of meaning between Jesus and the kerygma. The terminological difference is seen in the fact that Jesus' message is eschatological while the kerygma is christological. This even includes a doctrinal difference, but when one moves beyond this initial comparison to the deeper level of meaning, one finds an underlying similarity in such paradoxes as: in death, life; in suffering, glory; in

---

23. Ibid. 92–94

24. Harvey, *Historian* 178–187. Compare Perrin's three objections to Robinson's approach in *Rediscovering* 232–233, all of which come down to the importance and priority of the historical-critical method: the difficulty of thinking that modern historiography can mediate an 'existential encounter' with Jesus, the necessity of establishing the facts before one interprets them, and the assumption of the identity of the historical Jesus and the kerygmatic Christ rather than the demonstration of it through historical-critical method.

25. Robinson, *New Quest* 120–125. Compare the approach of Herbert Braun, "The Meaning of New Testament Christology," in *God and Christ: Existence and Province* (ed. Robert W. Funk; New York: Harper & Row, 1968) 89–127, who sees anthropology (one's self-understanding before God) as the constant factor in the New Testament and christology as the variable.

judgment, grace; in finitude, transcendence. "It is this existential meaning latent in Jesus' message which is constitutive of his selfhood, expresses itself in his action, and is finally codified in the Church's kerygma."[26]

Robinson's interest in "Jesus' transcendental selfhood," manifest in his approval of Ernst Fuchs' analysis of the existential decision of Jesus, is where Harvey radically parts company with him. In fact, his use of the term 'selfhood' pinpoints the central problem of a new quest. Bultmann himself warns that 'self-understanding' must be distinguished from 'self-consciousness', and he accuses Ernst Fuchs and Gerhard Ebeling especially of confusing the two. 'Self-understanding' refers, in this context, to the understanding of existence of which Jesus, in his words and deeds and even in his fate, was the bearer. 'Self-consciousness', on the other hand, refers to Jesus' own appropriation of that understanding, his own attitudes, the decisions which he himself made—all of which must be inferred from his words and deeds. Harvey[27] criticizes Robinson sharply at this point for wanting to put the heaviest kind of historical assent on that which can least bear it. The most difficult and tenuous kind of historical judgment is that which tries to infer motives from one's action and speech, and even worse, the self underlying those motives. We know how difficult that is in our own case, let alone in the case of someone else, even if we have a great deal of historical material about the person. It is even more difficult in the case of Jesus, for we have no writings from him, no chronology of his life, and hence no real way of knowing if he ever changed his mind, especially when he was confronted with death. While this criticism is valid—we have no resources for entering into the interior states of Jesus' mind—I would offer the caution that the above distinction between 'self-understanding' and 'self-consciousness' can be made too rigid and artificial if it implies that one's words and deeds tell us nothing at all about the person who is speaking and acting. In fact, it is only through words and deeds that interpersonal relations are possible at all. This is part

---

26. Robinson, *New Quest* 123.

27. Harvey, *Historian* 187–194. For a fine discussion with Bultmann on the subject, see Gerhard Ebeling, *Theology and Proclamation* (Philadelphia: Fortress, 1966), especially the section of the Appendix entitled "Psychologizing Interpretation of Jesus?" 124–130.

of the limitations of the human condition, but also of its possibility. It is not Jesus' interior states of mind, but the impact that he had on those around him that tells us who he is. In this sense, the new quest has an interest in the *person* of Jesus which is both possible and legitimate.

Another central problem of a new quest, which is the final objection that Harvey proposes,[28] is that the two avenues of access to Jesus (*via kerygmatica* and *via historica*) either demand an *a priori* reduction of history to the role of confirming faith or leave open the possibility that history could disprove faith. It is one of the firmest convictions of all the new questers that history cannot prove faith, but it would seem that the second horn of the dilemma must be accepted in this sense, that a disparity between Jesus and the kerygma—while not necessarily disproving faith—would at least radically change the character of faith. As Ebeling puts it: "If Jesus had never lived, or if faith in him were shown to be a misunderstanding of the significance of the historical Jesus, then clearly the ground would be taken from under Christian faith."[29] At least Christian faith would have an object different from the one it has always proclaimed. Is this not in fact what Bultmann has done by shifting the object of faith from Jesus to the kerygma? The problem again is with the nature of faith. If one holds with the dialectical theologians that faith involves absolute certitude, then the dilemma is insoluble. We will return to this.

Harvey sees the positive significance of the new quest not to lie in any attempt to get at Jesus' selfhood but in the recognition that Jesus, like the kerygma, is the bearer of a message, that he embodies a meaning complex. This seems to give support to the "left-wing" critics (Buri, Ogden) and thus to raise again the problem of whether Jesus is only the symbol of a timeless truth. In order to avoid that consequence, Harvey next develops a perspective theory of history. His position offers a possible solution to the problem of the relation-

---

28. Harvey, *Historian* 194–196. See also Van A. Harvey & Schubert M. Ogden, "How New is the 'New Quest of the Historical Jesus'?" in *The Historical Jesus and the Kerygmatic Christ* (ed. Carl E. Braaten & Roy A. Harrisville; Nashville: Abingdon, 1964) 197–242.

29. Gerhard Ebeling, *The Nature of Faith* (London: Collins, 1961) 46.

ship between faith and history. I will make use of his position in order to clarify the alternative that I propose.

(3) *A proposed solution.* Harvey offers a brilliant analysis of perspectivism[30] which it is not necessary to go into in detail here. The basic issue is whether one takes seriously the fundamental distinction between facts and their interpretations. Hard perspectivism seeks to make a virtue out of the necessity of selectivity. It so identifies a particular interpretation with the facts that it results in historical relativism: one perspective is as good as another. This is disastrous in Christian apologetics when appeal is made to distinctively Christian presuppositions, such as unique events, for which no historical assessment is possible. Even in disagreements among Christian biblical scholars, appeal must be made to the common experience of the human condition. The question is one of meaning (what are we talking about?) and the answer must be justified on the basis of the normal human canons of assessment. Soft perspectivism, on the other hand, recognizes that events are disclosure situations, i.e., the same event can have diverse meanings. As Harvey puts it:

> The difference between the believer and the unbeliever is not whether a given event occurred; rather, the difference lies in the way the event is interpreted, the significance attributed to the event. . . . Any given historical event, so to speak, makes claims in several different directions, and not all of them are mutually incompatible. Moreover, these in-

---

30. Harvey, *Historian* 204–245. See especially his discussion of soft perspectivism (234–242) in relation to H. Richard Niebuhr's proposal that there are two kinds of history: external, in which the historian takes a sort of 'I-it' stance as a disinterested observer (e.g., as one might observe the blindness of another person), and internal, in which the historian takes a sort of 'I-Thou' stance as an involved participant (e.g., as the blind man himself). He makes three important modifications to this position (239ff): (1) the division is too restrictive; there are not just two possible perspectives but a plurality of inner and outer histories; (2) in order to assess various perspectives, one must be able to transcend one's own perspective and enter into an 'alien' internal history without making it one's own or communication is impossible (note that understanding is not the same as agreement here); and (3) perspectives are field-encompassing involving a complexity of standpoints: factual judgments, value judgments, assumptions about human nature, etc., which allow for agreement on one level of judgment and disagreement on another; hence, a Christian perspective will contain much that is not specifically Christian.

terpretations presuppose that there is some 'given' to be interpreted and, as we have seen, it is just this insight we presuppose in the rough distinction between fact and interpretation.[31]

For Harvey, faith can be described as a response to a disclosure situation, to a certain meaning perceived in an historic event. If so, his concern then becomes to relate the once-for-all character of revelation to the wider structures of human existence. For this, he employs the notion of paradigmatic events which he describes as the fusion of concreteness (particular) and wider meaning (universal). Such events are revelatory insofar as they capture the imagination of the community in such wise that they alter their way of looking at reality. "The more fundamental the meaning, the more the event becomes capable of being transformed into myth, where 'myth' does not mean a false story but a highly selective story that is used to structure and convey the basic self-understanding of a person or a community. A pattern is abstracted from the event and becomes the formalized parable that is used to interpret larger tracts of history and experience."[32] Such myths can be called 'religious' insofar as they offer insight into the nature of reality itself. A religion, then, can be described as a symbolic perspective that makes total and universal claims based on certain dominant images. In the field of comparative religions, this is a useful way to approach the question of why religions differ on the phenomenological level. But, does this get us to the level of what is *distinctively* Christian? Do Christians make claims about uniqueness that cannot simply be covered by comparative descriptions?

Harvey recognizes that Judaism and Christianity "are preoccupied with history in a way that most other religions are not."[33] What should be mentioned in this connection, however, is the decisive centrality of faith. As Ebeling puts it: "the view that the fundamental religious relationship is 'faith' is by no means a general element in the language of religion, but rather belongs to a limited area in his-

---

31. Ibid. 252.
32. Ibid. 257.
33. Ibid. 265.

tory."[34] It is not a religious word of universal occurrence, but comes from the Old Testament and obtains "its central and decisive significance" in Christianity. It is faith that ties the Judaeo-Christian heritage to history in a way that is not true of other religions. The problem I have with Harvey is not his analysis of history but his notion of faith, a notion that relativizes the uniqueness of Christianity.

There are four meanings of 'Jesus of Nazareth': (1) actual: Jesus as he really was; (2) historical: Jesus as he can be rediscovered through historical-critical methods, which involves a certain consensus among scholars; (3) perspectival: the memory impression of the early Christian community, which was highly selective but which has some real correlation with the historical Jesus; (4) the Biblical Christ, the transformation and alteration of the perspectival image under the influence of later theological interpretations. Harvey develops the perspectival image of Jesus as crucial for his solution to the problem. The concrete lineaments of this image will concern us in the next chapter. What is important to note here is that we are always dealing with an "interpreted Christ" but that historical knowledge allows us to differentiate two avenues of access (compare Robinson above), that of the memory impression and of the Biblical Christ. The methodological consequence, which I would agree with, is that the historian can compare the one with the other, differentiate the different levels of development in order to write a history of the tradition, and criticize the one in the light of the other. The theological consequence, which I would distinguish, is that the conditions of belief today require us to approach the faith historically. Harvey recognizes that the content of faith can as well be mediated through myth as through history. He acknowledges the validity and profundity of the Christian faith over the past two millennia which was largely ignorant of the latest developments in historical-critical method. But he insists, quite rightly, that we live in different circumstances. Insofar as this is taken to mean that we cannot ignore the results of biblical criticism, and that our faith is seriously conditioned by those results, I agree. But, the danger I see in Harvey's position

---

34. Ebeling, "Jesus" 207. Compare his analysis in the chapter entitled "The History of Faith" in *Nature* 19–30.

is that he tends to reduce faith to a dimension of historical knowledge.

On the level of historical knowledge, Harvey quite rightly insists: "The situation is not so much that the Christian has access to realities to which the non-Christian does not, or that the Christian believes that certain entities exist which the non-Christian finds doubtful. The situation is, rather, that both Christian and non-Christian are confronted with the *same realities* but interpret them differently."[35] That different perspectives can be taken on historical facts is clear. But, for Harvey, faith is simply one of the possible perspectives. He distinguishes this, to be sure, from simple belief about a contingent fact remote from present experience. The important thing is the significance that a past event can have for us in the present, the adequacy of the perspectival image of Jesus for interpreting the very nature of reality. He thus describes the certitude of faith as follows: "Faith finds its certitude, its confirmation, in the viability of the image for relating one to present reality."[36]

The obvious objection, once again, is that this seems to reduce Jesus to a symbol of some timeless truth. Harvey is correct in saying that one cannot play symbol off against event in that way. The notion of paradigmatic event is precisely that the universal occurs only in the concrete particular. It is not so much the content of a teaching, which can indeed be abstracted and considered in itself, but the kind of existential self-knowledge which is indissolubly connected with the embodiment of a great truth in a particular person, e.g., Socrates embodies the love of truth, Lincoln a passion for union, Jesus the righteousness of God, etc. In this sense, the one who embodies the truth is always indispensable; he belongs ineradicably to our historical consciousness and cannot be dispensed with once we have grasped the content of his message.

Harvey finally calls his position a "radical historical confessionalism." It is certainly true that one can engage Jesus on this purely historical level and that the image evoked can have a powerful impact on the contemporary consciousness. Harvey's position is true as

---

35. Harvey, *Historian* 284 (italics mine).
36. Ibid. 283.

far as it goes but does it go far enough? The net effect is to reduce
Jesus to the level of a great teacher, unique in his own way as are
all human, historical persons, but not radically different from Socrates or Lincoln or any other historical figure who has had a profound impact upon human experience. Christians have traditionally
claimed more, viz. that Jesus is one in being with the divine—something that cannot be said of any other human being. We will return
in later chapters to the legitimacy of such claims. But, for the moment, the point is that Harvey's position is in the final analysis re-
ductionist. He fails, I think, to make use of one of his own principles:
not only is history a field-encompassing field which makes a great
diversity of claims, but faith makes a great diversity of claims among
which are historical claims.

The alternative solution that I propose follows the basic line of
Norman Perrin.[37] Basically, he introduces a third dimension to Martin Kaehler's distinction between *der historische Jesus* (history) and
der geschichtliche Christus (faith). There are three different kinds of
knowledge. First, there is "historical knowledge" which is essentially
descriptive. This is the kind of knowledge established by scientific
methodology. It is 'neutral' in the sense that it is open to any critical
observer and is thus subject to revision. Second, there is "historic
knowledge" which has two dimensions: the meaning a past event can
have in its own context and the meaning it can have insofar as the
past assumes direct significance for the present, i.e., 'speaks to our
condition' (compare Harvey above). Such knowledge in this second
sense, as we have seen, can be highly selective, depending upon the
perspective taken but it is still open to any critical observer as part
of the total phenomenon, whether the observer personally takes the
same stance or not. This distinction is important for it overcomes the
dichotomy between fact and meaning that troubles the position of
Kaehler and, later, of Rudolf Bultmann. Such a dichotomy is a mystery to secular historians and it arises from the tendency to identify
'historic' and 'faith' knowledge. Thus, there is thirdly "faith knowledge" which, unlike the first two, is not open to any neutral observer.

---

37. Perrin, *Rediscovering* 234–248. I would, however, disagree with his use of
the term 'separate' (240) in reference to the three kinds of knowledge—distinct, yes;
separate, no.

It is particular (as grace both for the individual and for the group which shares it) and concrete (as recognition of the 'special worth' of only one person, viz. Jesus). These two dimensions indicate that faith knowledge is essentially interpersonal, an 'I-Thou' relationship. Moreover, it is also transhistorical insofar as it introduces the idea of God's activity and it may or may not be related to historical/historic knowledge.

Perrin sees this threefold distinction as a clarification of Bultmann's position which he places in the center as over against those on the right (Jeremias), who tend to see historical knowledge as somehow directly constitutive of faith knowledge, and those on the left (Jasper, Ogden, *et al.*), who tend to reduce, in one way or another, faith knowledge to historic knowledge. However, Perrin seems to move beyond Bultmann and closer to the new quest insofar as he sees both a positive and a negative role that historical/historic knowledge plays in relation to faith knowledge.

For a Christian, the primary relationship to Jesus is one of faith which arises in response to proclamation. Proclamation here must be understood in an inclusive sense: it not only refers to Word and Sacrament in a more strictly ecclesial sense but to any human experience which can contribute to a religious 'awakening' on the part of an individual. Such experiences evoke in us a "faith-image" of Jesus which is constituted by a mixture of historical reminiscence, myth, legend, idealism—the complex mixture of needs that comes to expression as religious experience. This is to say again that faith makes a great diversity of claims. Historical knowledge, including both the 'historical' (fact) and 'historic' (meaning) dimensions and clearly distinct from faith knowledge, has a *subordinate but indispensable* role to play here insofar as it contributes to the formation of this faith-image.

Positively, it can be *a* source (but not the only or major source) for the necessary content of faith. What would our faith-image of Jesus be like if we had only the letters of Paul? The genius of the Evangelists was that they rooted their own proclamation of the risen Lord in the words and deeds of the earthly Jesus and thereby gave concrete content to that proclamation. For example, Luke makes the theological point that the risen Lord is the same person whom the disciples knew prior to his death by appealing to the experience of the earthly Jesus: he was one who walked with them on the way and explained the scriptures to them, who sat at table with them and broke bread for them (Luke 24:13–35).

Negatively, history can act as a *check* on false or inappropriate faith-images. Each age tends to create Jesus in its own image. The best answer to those today who would coopt Jesus into various revolutionary movements is an appeal to historical/historic knowledge.[38] This negative function strikes me as the most important because it means that we can have some critical control on excesses and possible misdirections or deviations, especially within Christianity itself. For example, if salvation through faith, even based on interpretation of the New Testament itself, has taken on an exclusivist connotation so that only those who belong to a particular 'in-group' can be saved, then such a notion needs to be rethought in the light of Jesus' own ministry to the outcast as a direct confrontation of the exclusivist notions of his day. This negative function assumes primary importance in our understanding of the relationship between Jesus' own understanding of faith and contemporary Christian understanding of faith.

Directly, history can be relevant to faith insofar as we can stand in a relationship to the teaching and person of Jesus similar to the memory-impression of the early Church, i.e., a believer in any age can hear the message of Jesus proclaimed into his or her situation. This is valid though misleading if one were thereby to reduce Jesus only to what we can know of him through historical-critical method. Such knowledge, indispensable as it is, must always remain *subordinate* to faith knowledge. Hence, a basic principle of this entire book is put well by Reginald Fuller: "The church's Christology was a response to its total encounter with Jesus, not only in his earthly history but also in its (the church's) continuing life."[39]

The implication of the above assertions is twofold: on the one hand, Jesus 'as he really was' cannot simply be identified with the figure of Jesus as reconstructed by critical historiography; on the other hand, the Jesus of history whom faith affirms cannot be sep-

---

38. An excellent example of the effectiveness of this approach is to be found in Martin Hengel, *Was Jesus a Revolutionist?* (Philadelphia: Fortress, 1971).

39. Fuller, *Foundations* 15.

arated from such work. There is no immunity from historical research nor is there immunity from doubt through historical certainty. McArthur's criticism of the "Historical-Risk School," viz. that the absolute quality of faith becomes dependent upon the relative, probability character of historical research, misses what is to me the vital point: faith itself, *qua* historical, is the risk.[40] Faith does not give us the kind of certainty that would either remove all doubt and risk from the commitment one makes or remove one from involvement in the historical in making the commitment. Yet, it does give us certainty, the kind of certainty that allows us to trust in a promised future. It is the appropriate and indeed necessary stance in a 'not-yet' world, i.e., in a world that is itself historical as it moves toward its future consummation.

Nor should this surprise us, for it is *analogous* to the common experience of every human relationship. It is only by appeal to analogies derived from ordinary human experience (ordinary language) that we can begin to understand what the word 'faith' means, so let us look more closely for a moment at what I would consider to be the prime analogate: 'I-Thou' relations. Interpersonal relationships and therefore, I submit, being human at all would be impossible without some form of a faith commitment that allows us to affirm the other even though all the evidence is not, nor ever can be, 'in'. When two people meet one another they go through a kind of historical–critical process in getting to know one another (name, background, interests, etc.), but if they are to move beyond a merely superficial relationship to something more deeply human there comes a point at which they must be able to make a faith commitment to one another. A person will have reasonable grounds for making such a commitment on the basis of what is known about the other person, but the commitment itself transcends the kind of ev-

---

40. What I am opposing here is the idea that faith has an absolute quality over against and in opposition to any involvement in the human and historical. It is true that for Bultmann faith is a risk in the sense of a naked step into the abyss, but it possesses an absolute quality over against the human and historical in that it is its own verification (as an experience of the activity of God inspiring one to affirm the God who gives life in the face of the overwhelming abyss of Jesus' death on the cross). It is my contention that faith is a risk precisely because it draws us ever more deeply *into* the human and the historical. In other words, God is to be found not in opposition to but at the very center of our humanness *qua* historical.

idence which would prove to oneself or to anyone else that such a commitment should be made. The moment of trust is a moment of transcendence, a willingness to step 'beyond' what can be strictly proved and make a fundamental affirmation of the goodness of another person. As such, it is a great risk to oneself because it is at that very moment that one is the most vulnerable.

Moreover, once the commitment is made, a kind of historical-critical process continues to be operative in the relationship. Should the initial commitment prove to be false or misguided by what is learned subsequently, such knowledge can either destroy or at least radically alter the character of the relationship. It is in this sense that faith must always be open to, and will always be seriously conditioned by, the results of biblical criticism. It is not that I wait breathlessly for the latest results. My commitment is a firm one, but it is also a living one, and that implies room for growth. My relationship to Jesus, my image of him, is far different today than it was twenty-five years ago. There are many reasons for that, not the least of which is a personal study of biblical criticism.

This common experience of every human relationship can be said to be analogous to *Christian* faith insofar as that faith affirms God's activity as the freely given origin that makes the relationship possible. However, this should not lead to a dichotomous way of thinking. Christian faith is a particular gift given freely to those to whom it is given, but on a deeper level the divine activity makes not just Christian faith but *any human faith* possible. The whole of creation is gift. Hence, it would be a mistake to see the divine as being in competition with the human, somehow alienating us from our humanness; rather, it is union with the divine that makes our humanness possible at all.[41] We still return to this when we consider Jesus' unity with God. For the moment, the important point is to see that faith in whatever form it may be experienced is not peripheral to the human condition, an epiphenomenon, something super-added to human nature; some form of faith is, I submit, *constitutive* of what it is to be human. It properly belongs *within* history, and in this sense is an historical phenomenon, but at the same time it is that which

---

41. Schoonenberg, *Christ* 7.

enables us to transcend the inevitable limitations of scientific historical knowledge.

In conclusion, the particular gift that is Christian faith allows
one to affirm the divine activity as identifiable with the person of Jesus, an affirmation that in itself is simply beyond the limits of historical-critical methodology but which at the same time makes the
concern of the new quest for the person of Jesus eminently justifi-
able. Faith must always be interpersonal—a willing response to a
loving word. If Jesus is God's Word, then encounter with him—
whether mediated historically or mythically or mystically—is indispensable to the nature of Christian faith. Historical knowledge is a
subordinate but necessary medium to image forth this Jesus to whom
we respond in faith. Thus, Jesus himself is and always has been decisive for Christian faith. As Willi Marxsen puts it, christology begins at the point where the relationship to Jesus is one of faith (and,
following Gerhard Ebeling, this occurs in the earthly life of Jesus: we
are always dealing with the response of believers) and it develops at
the point where the believer proclaims Jesus.[42] The function of this
proclamation is to mediate Jesus' self-understanding—a self-understanding that is not detachable from Jesus himself. The fact that only
Jesus of all men and women down through the ages has evoked such
a relationship of faith in its religious sense points to his uniqueness.

The implications of all this will be the concern of the rest of this
book. We have sufficiently considered for our methodological purposes the legitimacy of history in relation to Christian faith. We must
now turn to the distinct question of the possibility of making histori-

---

42. Willi Marxsen, *The Beginnings of Christology: A Study in its Problems*
(Philadelphia: Fortress, 1969) 44–57, asks why the primitive community did not separate the preaching of Jesus from Jesus. He seeks to locate the beginnings of christology in the call to faith of the historical Jesus as Ebeling analyzes it (we will consider
this in greater detail later) and the development of christology in the shift of Jesus'
first followers from preaching his message to preaching his person to others. If there
is to be continuity between the two, then such proclamation must remain true to Jesus, i.e., mediate *his* self-understanding. Hence, Marxsen locates the "break" between
proclaimer and proclaimed prior to Easter: "The break lies at the point where a believer proclaims Jesus' words and deeds." Ibid. 70. While critical of Marxsen's understanding of the resurrection and of the initial and later stages of christological
development, I would endorse as basically valid the point that the beginnings of christology lie in the historical ministry of Jesus and that the development of christology
occurs when his followers seek to preach him to others.

cal judgments given the nature of our sources. What are the basic criteria that have been developed in the history of biblical criticism? Only then will we be in a position to investigate the results of the method in Jesus' earthly ministry and the impact that such results have on the christological problematic as a whole.

D. The Basic Criteria for Jesus-Research

It is not necessary to offer an extensive analysis of the history of biblical criticism here.[43] I only wish to highlight those workable hypotheses that have formed something of a consensus among biblical scholars on the basis of the results they produce and which form the basic presuppositions for what follows.

The most enduring result of the old quest of the historical Jesus (1778–1906)[44] is in the area of source criticism. Once it was recognized that John was inferior to the Synoptics as an historical source because more dominated by theological and apologetic interests, there was a drive to discover the purest and most immediate documents that would get us back to the Jesus of history. This led to the development of the two-source hypothesis, viz. that Mark and Q (a source common to Matthew and Luke but independent of Mark) were used by Matthew and Luke along with their own special sources (M and L) in composing their gospels. Although Wilhelm Wrede eventually demonstrated that Mark too is dominated by theological and apologetic interests and therefore cannot simply be used as an historical source, the literary relationships established for the Synoptics remains even today the best hypothesis and it does help to establish the history of the Synoptic tradition. Basic here too is the recognition that whereas in the rest of the New Testament, especially

---

43. For a readable overview of the various movements within biblical criticism, see the series "Guides to Biblical Scholarship" published by Fortress Press of Philadelphia (ed. Dan O. Via, Jr.), especially William A. Beardslee, *Literary Criticism of the New Testament* (1970); Edgar V. McKnight, *What is Form Criticism?* (1969); and Norman Perrin, *What is Redaction Criticism?* (1970). For the method developed here, see especially Perrin, *Rediscovering* 15–53. Also, Fuller, *Foundations* 15–22, and Joachim Jeremias, *New Testament Theology I: The Proclamation of Jesus* (New York: Scribner's, 1971) 1–41.

44. For an interesting and informative account from Reimarus to Wrede, see Albert Schweitzer, *The Quest of the Historical Jesus* (London: A. & C. Black, 1954).

in Paul and John, the present and the future tend to overshadow the past, in the Synoptics the past dimension is dominant in the proclamation.[45] This makes the Synoptics the primary resource for the historical Jesus although there are certainly elements in John that have a strong claim to historicity. Another useful resource, especially in reconstructing the parables, is the Gospel of Thomas. Perrin suggests, as a working hypothesis, that it is independent of the Synoptic tradition.[46]

The outstanding achievement of the nineteenth century was the development of source criticism, but by definition it was limited to the documents at hand. Form criticism as applied to the New Testament (1918 on) asked the further question of whether we can get behind the written documents to a period of oral tradition. The basic presuppositions (developed by Hermann Gunkel in his work on Genesis in 1901) are that there is a preliterary oral tradition prior to the written documents, that this tradition normally circulated by means of small independent units (pericopes), and that these units could be classified according to their formal patterns as determined by the reasons (various needs within the community) for their preservation. This last indicates that a history of the tradition could be written which would reflect the developing life situations. Most broadly, one can distinguish the life situation (*Sitz-im-Leben*) of Jesus, the early community, and the author of the Gospel. Within the early community, one can distinguish the more Palestinian from the more Hellenistic tendencies. For this latter, linguistic features are particularly important, especially the use of Aramaisms as Joachim Jeremias in particular has studied them both philologically and environmentally, seeking always to reconstruct the original context of Jesus' ministry.

Karl Ludwig Schmidt began the form-critical era of the New Testament with his book *Der Rahmen der Geschichte Jesu* (1919), which gave the final blow to dependence upon the Marcan framework. He isolated the individual units (sayings and narratives which he considered as belonging to the oldest tradition of Jesus) from the

---

45. Perrin, *Rediscovering* 233–234, referring to Ernst Kaesemann.
46. Ibid. 35–37. For an excellent use of the Gospel of Thomas in reconstructing the parables, see John Dominic Crossan, *In Parables. The Challenge of the Historical Jesus* (New York: Harper & Row, 1973).

framework, i.e., the connecting links and "bridge passages" (*Sammelberichte*) which the Evangelist provided out of his own interests and those of the early Church—its life, its worship, its apologetic and missionary concerns. What this means, in effect, is that no biography of Jesus is possible, neither an external chronological sequence of events nor an internal psychological development. The framework can tell us something about the life of the early Church, but only the single episodes can tell us about the life of Jesus.

Martin Dibelius in *Die Formgeschichte des Evangeliums* (1919) concentrated upon the narrative material in the Synoptics. He placed great historical reliability on the earliest forms and so later, in his book *Jesus* (1939), he was able to write a rather full and confident account of the earthly Jesus. Rudolf Bultmann in *Die Geschichte der synoptischen Tradition* (1921) did the first form-critical study of the entire Synoptic tradition, both discourse and narrative material. He built upon the conclusions of Schmidt and Dibelius, but he used form-criticism not simply as a means of literary classification of a developing tradition but as a basis for judgments of historicity. Unlike Dibelius, he is extremely skeptical about the historical reliability of the sources. He is skeptical, above all, of the narrative material. He will allow that many of the sayings most probably go back to Jesus but we can never be absolutely sure.

Here one is confronted with the methodological problem created by form-criticism's stress on the role of the early Church in transmitting, shaping, and even creating material about Jesus. According to Bultmann, it is possible to cut away certain developments that originated in Hellenistic Christianity and to get back with reasonable certitude to the Aramaic speaking Palestinian Church. It is further possible to distinguish different layers of the Palestinian material insofar as it reveals special interests of the Church as it develops in different contexts, so that an oldest layer can more or less be determined. But, how do we know whether this oldest layer really goes back to Jesus or simply to the Church at a level we can no longer trace? Thus, in the introduction to his book *Jesus* (1926), which seeks to examine what can be known historically of Jesus, he can say: "Whoever prefers to put the name of 'Jesus' always in quotation marks and let it stand as an abbreviation for the historical phenomenon with which we are concerned, is free to do so."[47] That historical phenomenon is the complex of ideas in the oldest layer of the Synoptic tradition. Jesus has been named as the bearer of the message; Bultmann admits that there is an overwhelming probability that he really was, but we cannot know for sure and in the final analysis it makes no difference for, as we have already seen in treating the dialectical theologians, faith cannot in any way be dependent upon such historical knowledge.

It is a tribute to Bultmann that some of the finest critical work on his positions has come from among his own students. At one end of the spectrum is redaction criticism[48] which calls into question the form-critical assumption that the Synoptics are not strictly literary works but popularizations (*Kleinliteratur*) and that the Evangelists are not true authors but only collectors and compilers. This assumption was an almost inevitable by-product of concentrating almost exclusively on the individual units of the material. In New Testament studies today the emphasis seems to be almost exclusively on this dimension of authorship. But we must not forget the other end of the spectrum represented by the new quest of the historical Jesus which was inaugurated by Ernst Kaesemann in 1953. We have already seen the fundamental presuppositions which he outlined. Our concern now is to explore the criteria which have developed for making judgments of historicity given the nature of our sources.

The basic assumption is that the gospels are kerygmatic and confessional. They have arisen out of the needs of the early communities and their primary purpose is to proclaim Jesus as Christ and Lord in the light of the resurrection. The form-critical view is correct that they are directly and immediately sources for knowledge of the early Christian communities. Any and every saying and/or action *could* simply be the product of those communities, e.g., through Christian prophets speaking in the name of the Lord or through the develop-

---

47. Rudolf Bultmann, *Jesus and the Word* (New York: Scribner's, 1958) 14.

48. The three fundamental works (all by former students of Bultmann) are: Hans Conzelmann, *The Theology of St. Luke* (London: Faber & Faber, 1960); Willi Marxsen, *Mark the Evangelist* (Nashville: Abingdon, 1969); and Guenther Bornkamm, G. Barth, H.J. Held,*Tradition and Interpretation in Matthew* (London: SCM, 1963).

ment of exegetical insights into the Old Testament or through the theology of the Evangelists as developed by their particular communities. These are the actual phenomena that one finds in the sources and they force one to the conclusion that the burden of proof rests upon anyone who would claim historical authenticity. Jeremias works on the assumption of historicity unless proved otherwise, but in the light of Harvey's discussion on the morality of historical knowledge this would seem to be an unacceptable assumption. The biblical historian must be especially cautious in the claims he makes precisely because the sources he is using are so thoroughly oriented to an apologetic and confessional stance. This necessitates the use of oblique criteria, especially of unintentional data, in order to attain reasonable certainty. Perrin makes use of three which we will now consider.

The fundamental criterion is the *criterion of dissimilarity,* which he formulates as follows: "the earliest form of a saying we can reach may be regarded as authentic if it can be shown to be dissimilar to characteristic emphases both of ancient Judaism and of the early Church, and this will particularly be the case where Christian tradition oriented towards Judaism can be shown to have modified the saying away from its original emphasis."[49] This criterion is intentionally skeptical for the sake of method. It is obvious that Jesus was a man of his times and spoke and acted in the context of ancient Judaism. What this criterion proposes is a solid basis upon which to build. It seeks that which cannot be derived from elsewhere, that which is characteristic or distinctive of Jesus himself such that only he could be its source so far as reasonable historical judgment is concerned. Obvious examples are his unusual use of *Abbā* and *Amēn.* It should be noted in passing here, as Jeremias has pointed out, that we are not dealing with *ipsissima verba* (actual words of Jesus spoken on specific occasions) but with *ipsissima vox* (characteristic ways of speaking). Perrin writes most of his book on the basis of this criterion, but as a starting point it is of necessity limited in scope and needs to be supplemented by the other criteria.

The second criterion, which builds on the first, is the *criterion*

---

49. Perrin, *Rediscovering* 39.

of coherence: "material from the earliest strata of the tradition may be accepted as authentic if it can be shown to cohere with material established as authentic by means of the criterion of dissimilarity."[50] A good example of this, in my opinion, is the question of whether and in what sense Jesus made use of the late Jewish apocalyptic title "Son of Man." One can only establish such usage if it can be shown to harmonize with Jesus' proclamation of the Kingdom which will already have been more solidly established on the basis of the criterion of dissimilarity. The value of this criterion is that it allows us, with caution to be sure, to accept material that would be excluded on the basis of the first criterion and so allows us to expand our picture of Jesus.

The final criterion, which is even more supplemental in that its usefulness lies in arriving at general characteristics rather than at specific elements, is the *criterion of multiple attestation:* " . . . a motif which can be detected in a multiplicity of strands of tradition [Mark, Q, M, L, John, Paul, Thomas, etc.] and in various forms (pronouncement stories, parables, sayings, etc.) will have a high claim to authenticity, always provided that it is not characteristic of an activity, interest or emphasis of the earliest Church."[51] An example would be the saying about faith that moves mountains found in various strands (Mark, M, Paul, Thomas) and attached to various forms. On this basis, Perrin simply accepts the authenticity of Jesus' special concern for 'tax-collectors and sinners'. Actually, both examples could be established already on the basis of the criterion of dissimilarity. This criterion seems to function more by way of confirmation, although it is basic to the work of Jeremias and has been widely used in England (especially by T. W. Manson). For Perrin, however, its usefulness is limited and secondary.

These, then, are the criteria. On this basis, it is possible to reconstruct the five characteristics of the *ipsissima vox Jesu* (as Jeremias outlines them): (1) the parables; (2) the riddles; (3) the reign of God; (4) *Amēn;* (5) *Abbā* (including his reconstructed version of the Lord's prayer). But such reconstruction is not limited to Jesus' words; it includes such striking symbolic actions as healing the sick,

---

50. Ibid. 43.
51. Ibid. 46.

breaking the sabbath, driving the sellers out of the temple, and celebrating the presence of the Kingdom by eating and drinking with
tax-collectors and sinners. His words and deeds, as we shall see, also
tell us something about how he viewed his personal relation to his
Father, his own sense of his mission, and finally the possibility of
that mission ending in his own violent death. All of this is the subject-matter of the next chapter. That chapter will be more a summary of results than a detailed justification of each and every claim
made—that would require a whole book in itself!—but the reader is
forewarned that the whole chapter presupposes the methodology described in this chapter.

CHAPTER TWO

The Ministry of Jesus

If one were to seek the best historical category in which to place the earthly ministry of Jesus, it would be that of the prophetic. Yet, it should be emphasized at the outset that, insofar as salvation is already breaking through in his words and deeds, Jesus simply breaks the category of prophet and any other category as well. In what follows, we shall set Jesus' ministry in the context of the prophetic precisely in order to show how his ministry could raise questions intelligible to his contemporaries ('Are you he who is to come?') while he continually transcended their expectations ('Who do you say that I am?').

Correlative to this is the distinction that Jeremias makes between Jesus' exoteric and esoteric teaching, i.e., between his public proclamation and his private instruction to his disciples.[1] While this distinction could be made too rigid and artificial (and give solace to the gnostic desire for secret revelations!), it is valid at least in this sense that Jesus' words and deeds always carry with them a deeper dimension. Thus, in what follows, we will see that Jesus' proclamation of the Kingdom includes the deeper dimension of Jesus' personal relation to God as *Abbā*, that Jesus' healing ministry whereby he celebrates the presence of the Kingdom issues in a call to follow him and so help to bring the Kingdom to its full realization, and finally that Jesus' conflict with his opponents has its resolution in an absolute trust that his *Abbā* will vindicate him.

This chapter does not pretend to be an exhaustive account of everything that might be said about the earthly Jesus. A comparison

---

1. Jeremias, *Proclamation* 255–257.

of Perrin and Jeremias shows how one's methodological presuppositions determine how much one might be willing to say. The concern here is to focus upon certain emphases that are decisive for our image of Jesus as he is known to us in faith.

A. Mission:
Jesus as Eschatological Prophet

A prophet's career can be described as involving three dimensions: a prophet (1) teaches with authority (word); (2) performs signs and wonders (deed); and (3) suffers a martyr's death (fate).[2] It is interesting to note that this is precisely the pattern of Mark's Gospel: Jesus is presented as one who is mighty in word and work, yet who paradoxically suffers death on the cross. Although one cannot educe a biography of Jesus from Mark, this would indicate that Mark has a true historical reminiscence of the impact of Jesus' career as prophetic.

There can be no doubt that this was the popular estimate of Jesus. The crowds (Mark 6:14–15; 8:27–28) saw him as 'one of the prophets,' possibly even John the Baptist, whom they regarded as a prophet, or Elijah *redivivus* (the early Church tended to identify John the Baptist with Elijah). His ministry at least raised the question for the pharisees (Luke 7:39; Mark 8:11) and for the disciples (Luke 24:19), and it was the basis of John the Baptist's question: 'Are you he who is to come?' (Matthew 11:2–3 par). Finally, it is likely that the charge against Jesus at his trial before the Sanhedrin was that of being a false prophet which was punishable by strangulation (Mark 14:65 par: 'prophesy!').[3]

But, would Jesus have understood himself in these terms? He seems to have rejected any categorization of himself, including that

---

2. Ibid. 280. Jeremias maintains that it was a development of Late Judaism to see the prophets as martyrs, especially Isaiah, Jeremiah, Ezekiel, Amos, Micah, and Zechariah ben Jehoiada. He also maintains that the popular conception of such a death is that it had atoning power (287–288). However, this seems to be limited to the Maccabees and it is doubtful that it extends to prophets as such. Cp. Ferdinand Hahn, *The Titles of Jesus in Christology: Their History in Early Christianity* (New York: World, 1969) 361.

3. Jeremias, *Proclamation* 77–78.

of being called 'the Christ',[4] by his counter-question: 'Who do you say that I am?' (Mark 8:29). Yet, while it is most likely that Jesus made no direct claims about himself—he certainly raised a number of questions that could not be adequately answered in the categories of his day!—still the prophetic remains the best category for historical understanding. As Fuller puts it:

> It is the unexpressed, implicit figure of the eschatological prophet which gives a unity to all of Jesus' historical activity, his proclamation, his teaching with *exousia* ('authority'), his healings and exorcisms, his conduct in eating with the outcast, and finally his death in the fulfillment of his prophetic mission. Take the implied self-understanding of his role in terms of the eschatological prophet away, and the whole ministry falls into a series of unrelated, if not meaningless fragments.[5]

The evidence for Jesus' self-understanding as prophet can be briefly summarized.[6] Jesus spoke in proverbial terms of a prophet's rejection by his own (Mark 6:4; cp. Luke 4:24; John 4:44) and of a prophet's fate to die at Jerusalem (Luke 13:33). His own mission was

---

4. Fuller, *Foundations* 109, and Erich Dinkler, "Peter's Confession and the Satan Saying," in *The Future of Our Religous Past* (ed. James M. Robinson; New York: Harper & Row, 1971) 169–202, both reconstruct Mark 8:27–33 by excising the particular Marcan concerns so that the original version is a straight pronouncement story in which Jesus' rebuke of Peter is a rejection of the title 'Messiah'. Dinkler begins his article by quoting Martin Buber to the effect that anyone who would claim to be Messiah would be a false Messiah. The Messiah does not proclaim himself but the Kingdom of God. Jeremias, *Proclamation* 258 expresses something of a consensus when he says: "Son of Man is the only title used by Jesus of himself whose authenticity is to be taken seriously." The problem with even accepting the title offered by Peter is that in the popular mind of Jesus' day it would carry overtones of a nationalistic hope for a warrior-hero from the house of David, something that was antithetical to Jesus' mission.

5. Fuller, *Foundations* 130.

6. Ibid. 125–131. Fuller (139, n. 82) regards the classical treatment of Jesus as prophet to be that of C. H. Dodd in *Mysterium Christi* (ed. Bell & Deissmann; London: Longman, 1930) 56–66. See his other references, especially C. K. Barrett, *The Holy Spirit and the Gospel Tradition* (London: S.P.C.K. 1947) 94–99. See also Jeremias, *Proclamation* 76–80 and Raymond E. Brown, "Jesus and Elisha," *Perspective* 11–12 (1970–71) 85–104.

couched in the prophetic language of 'I have come' (to cast fire: Luke 12:49; to call sinners: Mark 2:17) and 'I was sent' (to the lost sheep: Matthew 15:24). These last two texts in particular manifest the special concern for the outcast which is characteristic of prophetic mission although Jesus himself transcends the merely prophetic as the eschatological prophet who brings on the scene the definitive salvific activity of God for his people. This final offer of salvation necessarily brings with it prophetic utterances of judgment pronounced over Israel (Matthew 23:29–39: v. 31, blood of the prophets; v. 36, righteous blood; v. 38, Jerusalem forsaken and desolate).

But, in all of this, *the* mark of prophecy for Jesus' contemporaries and so for Jesus himself was the possession of God's *Spirit*. Jesus acted as one having authority *(exousia)* which is certainly a prophetic trait. When asked by what authority he does what he is doing, he refers his opponents to the baptism of John (Mark 11:27–33 par). Fuller suggests that the historical core of the baptismal traditions is Jesus' awareness of his being called to mission in terms of Isaiah 61:1 (the Palestinian interpretation of it in terms of Isaiah 42:1 and the Hellenistic interpretation of it in terms of the Son of God-divine man concept being later). This is certainly Luke's interpretation of the beginning of Jesus' ministry in a quotation drawn from his special material (Luke 4:17–21) and it is in these terms that Jesus answers the questions of John the Baptist (Matthew 11:4–6 par, referring to Isaiah 61:1; 35:5). When his relatives think that he is out of his head (Mark 3:21) and his opponents think that he has an unclean spirit and so casts out devils by the power of the devil, he identifies his words and deeds as works of the Holy Spirit (taking Mark 3:29 as the original form of the saying about blasphemy). Matthew inserts into this context the Q saying about Jesus casting out demons by the Spirit of God (Matthew 12:28; Luke 11:20 has by the finger of God which is probably more original but both expressions carry the same basic idea of acting with the power or authority of God). Moreover, like Elijah, he was able to communicate his *exousia* to his disciples (Mark 6:7 par; cp. Matthew 10:8 but contrast John 7:39 where this giving of the Spirit before the glorification of Jesus was obviously a problem for the early Church). Finally, as Jeremias points out, even his characteristically poetic ways of speaking (parallelism, rhythm, word-plays, etc.), betray a strongly prophetic consciousness of mission which influenced his ministry.

> That Jesus was conscious of being a prophet and bearer of the spirit and was regarded as such does not, however, mean that he simply took his place as a link in the chain of the many Old Testament messengers of God. For this prophetic sequence had been broken off; it was the conviction of the synagogue that the spirit had been quenched. . . . This view took the following form: In the time of the patriarchs, all pious and upright men had the spirit of God. When Israel committed sin with the golden calf, God limited the spirit to chosen men, prophets, high priests and kings. With the death of the last writing prophets, Haggai, Zechariah and Malachi, *the spirit was quenched* because of the sin of Israel. After that time, it was believed, God still spoke only through the 'echo of his voice' (*bat qōl* = echo), a poor substitute.[7]

Jeremias admits that there are notable exceptions to this view, especially at Qumran, but he shows that this was the dominant view not only in Late Judaism but in the New Testament as well. The Spirit was expected to return only in the last days and the people longed for its coming. When Jesus came on the scene in the power of the Spirit he inevitably raised the question whether he might not be the one long awaited. If his ministry was truly charismatic, then he was not only a prophet but the eschatological prophet.

As we have seen, a prophet's career involves three dimensions: word, deed, and fate. The Spirit of God is revealed through the interplay of all three. In what follows, we will consider each of them in turn in order to discover what Jesus was about in his ministry, what he reveals to us of God and of himself. But, before that, insofar as we can already speak of Jesus' consciousness that he was anointed in the Spirit for a mission (Isaiah 61:1), we must raise for a moment

---

7. Jeremias, *Proclamation* 80–81.

the question of Jesus' prophetic knowledge.[8] Does the insight that Jesus' earthly career was prophetic allow us to draw out implications for his own awareness of his mission? In what way, particularly, is knowledge of the future intrinsic and necessary to any prophetic mission?[9]

First of all, it is helpful to contrast a thinker and a prophet. A thinker speaks for himself (autonomous), appeals to reason (assessment), and must allow his message to have a certain independence over against himself (sound judgment). The prophet, on the other hand, speaks for another (as one sent), calls for faith (simply claiming that his word is the word of the Lord), and most strikingly must identify himself with his message. As we shall see, Jesus did not simply proclaim the Kingdom of God and call for a response of faith but he laid his own life on the line for the truth of his message. It is this total commitment to one's message that gives prophetic utterance its true authority. It is on this level that we can profitably speak in historical terms of Jesus' own awareness of his mission.

Secondly, a prophet does not properly speaking predict the future. The classical prophet is much rather a conscience to Israel, calling the people to a deeper realization of their heritage and thereby opening up to them the possibilities of God's future. He characteristically speaks in terms of crisis/resolution. For example, in Jesus' ministry, the crisis of the people's suffering has its resolution in the image (and, as symbolic action, in his table-fellowship) of banqueting at God's table; of the temple's destruction in the symbol of a new

---

8. Traditionally, three types of knowledge have been attributed to Jesus' human consciousness in the light of the incarnation: infused divine knowledge, inspired prophetic knowledge, and normal human experimental knowledge. The first often gives rise to the question: did Jesus know he was God? From an historical point of view that would be critical of an *a priori* dogmatic point of view, this is a badly posed question for it asks a psychological question (about Jesus' interior states of mind) with a theological predicate (divinity was attributed to Jesus in the light of the resurrection and as a result of a long theological development). The third type of knowledge can simply be assumed on the basis of Jesus' humanness and is demonstrated by texts which portray Jesus in weakness and ignorance. The second is the further question that can be legitimately raised at this point in the light of our methodological presuppositions insofar as it is historically established that Jesus' career was prophetic.

9. For the general remarks on the nature of prophetic knowledge, I am particularly indebted to Ben F. Meyer, *The Man For Others* (New York: Bruce, 1970) 55–70.

temple; of his own imminent and seemingly unavoidable violent death in the image of 'the day of the Son of Man'. It is thus characteristic of prophetic knowledge that future events are held in the vision of a schematic, symbolic whole. The prophet speaks for God in completely symbolic language and he does not necessarily have determinate knowledge of the course of events intended by God. There is no point by point correlation between prophetic word and historical events. This implies a certain ambiguity between prophecy and fulfillment that demonstrates the inadequacy of fundamentalism and the irrelevance of rationalism. For example, the reconstructed saying of Jesus, 'The temple will be destroyed and in three days rebuilt', can only be understood if the temple is seen as a symbol of the whole identity of Israel, the new temple as a symbol of the new identity of Israel as the eschatological people of God, and the three days as a symbol for a limited time in which it is God who sets the limits.

As we shall see, Jesus in his proclamation of the Kingdom intended imminence without reserve. There was no clear differentiation into a neatly demarcated sequence of events, such as we find in Luke-Acts, but rather a strong sense of urgency and immediacy, of the crucial and vital importance of the here and now for those who listened to him. History deciphers the symbols, translating image into event and symbolic time into real time. Thus, the temple becomes Jesus' body which was raised on the third day (John 2:18–22). Like the classical prophets, Jesus' word was retained, repeated, and interpreted by subsequent events. Primitive Christianity, stimulated by the intensity of his eschatological consciousness and by the apocalyptic event of resurrection, developed apocalyptic as a hermeneutic of the changing times.[10]

Given the nature of Jesus' mission as prophetic yet eschatologi-

---

10. For an interesting discussion of the relationships, see Robert W. Funk (ed.), *Apocalypticism* (*Journal for Theology and the Church* 6; New York: Herder & Herder, 1969), especially the contributions of Ernst Kaesemann. On Jesus' sense of urgency and immediacy that would preclude any sort of apocalypticism in his message, see especially Hans Conzelmann, "Present and Future in the Synoptic Tradition," in *God and Christ: Existence and Province.* (JThC 5; 1968) 26–44. Also, Guenther Bornkamm, *Jesus of Nazareth* (London: Hodder & Stoughton, 1960) 178.

cal, we must now examine in greater detail how he revealed the Spirit of God (and hence his own personal relation to God) in what he said, what he did, and what happened to him. What emerges is an interesting correlation in Jesus' earthly ministry between proclamation (word) and healing (deed). On the one hand, 'Kingdom of God' is his comprehensive term for the blessings of salvation insofar as it denotes the divine activity at the center of all human life and, on the other, 'faith' is his human, experiential term for salvation itself insofar as it denotes the human response, universally valid, of openness, acceptance, and commitment. These two dimensions must be seen as inseparable. They frame what follows.

B. WORD

(1) *Proclamation of the Kingdom: the challenge of being human.* It is generally agreed today that the phrase 'Kingdom of God', as used by Jesus, is not a static concept that would point literally to a specific place or time but is a dynamic symbol intended to evoke the concrete activity of God among his people.[11] There are three fundamental emphases that characterize the teaching of Jesus. First, the Kingdom is eschatological, i.e., it is a symbol for the final and definitive activity of God on behalf of his people. Insofar as Jesus' usage focuses upon the concrete activity of God in the particular here and now situation of the people he addresses, I would characterize his use of the symbol as prophetic rather than as apocalyptic. As we have seen, he is, like the prophets of old, a conscience to Israel, calling the people to a deeper realization of their heritage and thereby opening up to them the possibilities of God's future. This means that God's activity for his people in the future can only be correctly discerned by embracing in new and unforeseen ways the deepest level of what God has done for his people in the past. In a word, God's future comes through the past into the present.[12]

This is to be distinguished from apocalyptic insofar as the lat-

---

11. Perrin, *Language* 32–40. For the three fundamental emphases, see his *Rediscovering* 54–63.

12. This is fundamental to Hodgson's *(Jesus)* description of Word as the medium of presence.

ter's dualistic emphasis upon a 'break' between this present evil age and the age to come leads to an emphasis upon God acting at the end and from outside to destroy the present and to create a completely new future. This pessimism and despair about history and about the present carries with it a correspondingly urgent desire to know exactly when, where, and how this coming moment will take place. The conviction is that it is possible to recognize the signs of that moment; God uncovers his plan in dreams or visions to a 'seer' who reduces the symbols of the past (involving extensive quotation of previous texts considered to be sacred and so revelatory) to literal signs of the future. In this way (and as a consequence of the Spirit being quenched), apocalyptic replaced prophecy as one way (along with the Law) of discerning God's will for his people. Jesus, as the eschatological prophet whose ministry was characterized by the return of the quenched Spirit, employed apocalyptic imagery not in the manner of a 'seer' who seeks a one-to-one correspondence but, as we have seen, in the manner of a prophet who speaks for God in completely symbolic language that is evocative of the divine activity but that does not pretend to have determinate knowledge of the course of events intended by God.

The second emphasis in the teaching of Jesus is that 'Kingdom of God' is Jesus' own comprehensive term for the blessings of salvation. Insofar as he understood the Kingdom as already beginning to take place in his ministry, he was making the extraordinary claim that salvation was breaking through in his words and deeds. This brings us to the third emphasis, viz. that the Kingdom is spoken of as 'coming' rather than as 'established.' This means that there is a tension between the present realization of the Kingdom and its future consummation. In Fuller's terms: ". . . the message of Jesus proclaims the *proleptic presence* of the future Kingdom of God . . . Jesus does not offer teaching about the future, but enforces the decisiveness of the present for the future."[13] Yet, the remarkable, and indeed startling, thing about Jesus' message is not whether the Kingdom is present or future but where one is directed to look if the symbol is to be understood at all. It is not a matter of apocalyptic signs or of messianic pretenders. "The Kingdom of God is in your midst!"

---

13. Fuller, *Foundations* 104.

(Luke 17:20–21). Do not look away from your human life to discover the activity of God. God is acting at the very center of human life and human experience. When an individual, concretely and personally, experiences liberation from the power of evil that holds him in thrall, "then the Kingdom of God has come upon you" (Luke 11:20 par). And it comes in a surprising way, for it demands an openness to the gift that those who consider themselves justified by their own efforts cannot understand. It is the tax-collectors and the prostitutes, those outcasts whom the self-righteous can only castigate as 'violent intruders' *(hoi biastai),* who are 'grasping' the Kingdom (Matthew 11:21; cp. Matthew 21:31b).[14]

Jesus challenged his hearers at the deepest level of their heritage to a radical reversal of their expectations and their values. He did this through symbolic actions, as we shall see, and through a number of proverbial sayings, but his favorite way of expressing what he meant by the Kingdom of God was in telling stories.[15] According to C. H. Dodd: "At its simplest the parable is a metaphor or simile drawn from nature or common life, arresting the hearer by its vividness or strangeness, and leaving the mind in sufficient doubt about its precise application to tease it into active thought."[16] Jesus talked about things that were familiar to his listeners, the ordinary, everyday human experiences that made up his own life and the lives of his contemporaries. In this way he drew the listeners into the story

14. For the exegesis, see Perrin, *Rediscovering* 63–77 and compare his new emphasis upon symbol in *Language* 42–46. For the interpretation of *hoi biastai,* see Jeremias, *Proclamation* 111–112.

15. On proverbial sayings, see Perrin, *Language* 48–54. On parables, see Perrin, *Rediscovering* 82ff and, for an excellent summary of current developments, Perrin, *Language* 55–56, 89–193. Two recent authors who have greatly influenced me are Robert W. Funk, *Language, Hermeneutic, and Word of God* (New York: Harper & Row, 1966) and John Dominic Crossan, *In Parables. The Challenge of the Historical Jesus* (New York: Harper & Row, 1973). The latter offers an interesting attempt to unify the parabolic teaching of Jesus as a whole around the main verbs (finds-sells-buys) of what he calls the 'key' parables: the treasure (Matthew 13:44), the pearl (Matthew 13:45), and the great fish (Thomas 81:28–82:3). Thus, he structures his book around parables of *advent* (which opens up a new world and unforeseen possibilities), of *reversal* (of one's entire past), and of *action* (which brings this new world and these new possibilities to concrete expression). See Crossan, *Parables* 32–36.

16. C. H. Dodd, *The Parables of the Kingdom* (London: Nisbet & Co. 1936) 16. See Funk's excellent analysis of the implications of Dodd's description in Funk, *Language* 133–162.

so that they would begin to identify with the various experiences or characters. But then, frequently, the story would take an unexpected turn, the ground would shift, the familiar become unfamiliar and strange, and the listeners would find themselves confronted quite simply with themselves, with their own presuppositions and prejudices. For example, in the parable of the Good Samaritan, one can imagine the listeners, identifying with the man in the ditch, watching the priest and the Levite pass by as one would expect and thinking that now a good layman, perhaps a Pharisee, will come by and help the man. And when Jesus said: "But a certain Samaritan came by . . ." and then went on to elaborate his actions in terms of unheard-of generosity, suddenly the whole focus of the story shifted from the man in the ditch to the question of whether one could conceive of a Samaritan acting in this manner. A whole set of presuppositions and prejudices in regard to Samaritans was being called into question. It is important to note here that, in Jesus' parables, the application was generally left open. It was up to the listeners to hear the parable and to respond to it freely in the concrete conditions of their own lives. The later allegorizing (characteristic of Matthew) and moralizing (characteristic of Luke) were legitimate attempts to apply the parables in specifically Christian ways in the early Church, but it was precisely the openness that the parables had to diverse concrete situations that made such later interpretations possible.

It cannot be emphasized enough at this point that the *focus* of Jesus' parables is not upon himself or even upon God but upon the world of his listeners, a world indeed to which he belongs. In saying this, I am not denying the centrality of the Father for Jesus and the importance of Jesus himself for his listeners. But this makes it all the more remarkable that the medium chosen by Jesus to communicate the activity of God is to tell stories about the ordinary, everyday experiences of God's people. The point is that the listeners must enter into *this experience*—the experience of the parabolic world where the creative power lies not in information but in participation—in order to discover the activity of God, an activity indeed *in the midst* of his people. Hence, the parable of the Prodigal Son is not an allegory about God the Father, although it can be used in this way. It is fundamentally a story about how fathers treat sons and sons treat fathers, yet it is not simply a good story. Jesus is saying, in effect, that if you would know what it means to call God Father, then you must enter more deeply into the human relationship of father-child. God is not to be experienced at a distant remove from that relationship but rather at the very center of such relationships. It is like the central petition of the Lord's prayer, with its unusual simultaneity of divine-human action: "Forgive us our offenses as we *herewith* forgive those who offend us." One could say theologically that in the order of causality God's forgiveness is primary and it is God's prior forgiveness of us that makes it possible for us to forgive one another, but in the order of discovery it is only in our actual forgiving of one another that we can experience and hence know what it means to say that God forgives us.[17] To repeat a point made earlier: the divine is not in competition with the human, somehow alienating us from our own humanness; rather it is union with the divine that makes our humanness possible at all. Hence, it is only in and through that humanness, the gift of life that God has given to each one of us, that we can discover the divine. This is the whole point of our Christian belief in incarnation, as it was of the message of Jesus himself. Norman Perrin, in his summary conclusions, puts it this way: "The challenge of the message of Jesus was to recognize the reality of the activity of God in the historicality of the hearer's existence in the world, and especially in the experience of a 'clash of worlds' as the hearer came to grips with the reality of everyday human existence."[18]

If the focus of the parables is upon the world of the listeners, then in Robert Funk's terms: "Strictly speaking, Jesus belongs to the penumbral field (the zone of partial illumination, that which is caught out of the corner of the eye), while God and Christ belong to the umbral field (the zone of perfect shadow)."[19] Early Christian-

---

17. For the translation and interpretation of this petition, see Perrin's fine analysis in *Rediscovering* 151–153. He summarizes it well on p. 153: "In the context of God's forgiveness men learn to forgive, and in the exercise of forgiveness toward their fellow man they enter ever more deeply into an experience of the divine forgiveness." See also Jeremias, *Proclamation* 201.

18. Perrin, *Language* 196.

19. Funk, *Language* 246, n. 64. See below for the application of this photographic analogy to Jesus' notion of faith. Funk, like Perrin, is influenced in his terminology, especially here the contrast between sharp and soft focus, by Philip Wheelwright, *The Burning Fountain* (Bloomington: Indiana U. Press, 1968). Funk's concern at this point in his book is to demonstrate that while Paul brings the umbral

ity, especially Paul, brought the umbral field into the visible field. That is a legitimate development to be discussed later. Jesus, as belonging to the penumbral field, stands in a more immediate relationship to the parabolic world, and that in a twofold way. First, as the 'witness to the Kingdom' he himself belongs on the side of the hearers. He belongs to the same ordinary, everyday world and he must hear the claims the parables make as standing over against himself and outside of his control. This is the force of his use of *Amēn* (he first hears what he proclaims) and of his identifying himself with what he says not only by speaking in the first person ('Amen, I say to you . . .') but also by laying his life on the line through such striking symbolic actions as breaking the sabbath, driving the sellers out of the temple, and celebrating the presence of the Kingdom by eating and drinking with tax collectors and sinners. Second, as the 'language-event of the Kingdom' he is the one who uniquely brings it to expression through the above-mentioned words and deeds and so makes it happen.

Jesus is the *Amēn* to God (2 Cor. 1:19–20; Rev. 3:14), a word that has been said to contain the whole of christology *in nuce.*[20] As such, it can tell us a great deal about Jesus' own sense of personal identity in the mission that the Father had given him. The deepest dimension of that mission, however, is to be found in his personal relation to God as *Abbā,* a dimension that he communicated to those whom he called to follow him as his disciples. It is to these two aspects of his proclamation that we now turn.

(2) *Amēn to Abbā: the deeper dimension.* The fact that Jesus uses the word *Amēn* not as a response to someone else's statement, which is always religious in meaning, but as a way of beginning his own statements which are frequently 'non-religious', i.e., drawn from

---

field of the parables into view, he does not submit to the danger of fragmenting the totality of significations of the parabolic world into objects, thereby losing that world, but that he successfully preserves the intentionality of that foundational language by bringing it into the world of his listeners through that most radical 'clash of worlds' represented by the cross. That is, Paul does in his situation what Jesus did in his and thereby remains true to Jesus. See his whole discussion of the phenomenology of parable and letter, 224–249. This viewpoint should be kept in mind when we consider the question of the continuity between the Jesus of history and the Christ of faith.

20. Heinrich Schlier, *"Amēn,"* TWNT I 339–342, cited in Ebeling, "Jesus" 236–238. See Ebeling's whole discussion there and also Jeremias, *Proclamation* 35–36.

the midst of ordinary, everyday life, marks the usage as characteristic of his own way of speaking. The implications of this unusual
and unique usage are striking. I will consider them summarily in
terms of Jesus' certainty, authority, and power.

Jesus' certainty is not grounded in himself but in his Father
whose Kingdom he proclaimed as coming. Like the prophets of old
who used the messenger-formula, 'Thus says the Lord . . .', to show
that their message was not their own but that of the One who sent
them, Jesus speaks what he hears, viz. the truth and reality of God.
Thus, his use of *Amēn* is in response to another, to the Father who
sent him, and everything he says is in the context of that mission.

But, more than the prophets of old, Jesus speaks in the first person, 'Amen, I say to you . . .', and this implies a truly amazing claim.
He identifies himself entirely with what he says and this, most strikingly, in his willingness to lay his life on the line in obedience even
unto death. This is what gives authority to his message, not extrinsic
coercion but the personal involvement of one's very self in the message. But, this can be said of all true authority. Certainly, the prophets were identified with the message given them. The extraordinary
claim being made here is that the very identity of God is at stake.
Jesus, to be sure, is more than a prophet (Matthew 11:9 par. said of
the Baptist), more than Jonah (Matthew 12:41 par), more than the
Baptist (Matthew 11:11 par). But, the amazement that his teaching
provoked among his contemporaries was the claim implicit particularly in the great antitheses (Matthew 5:21–48) that he was even
more than Moses! There is an unparalleled claim to authority in
those antitheses which not only sharpen the *Torah* but actually transcend it. "The one who utters the *egō de lēgō humin* in the antitheses
not only claims to be the legitimate interpreter of the *Torah,* like the
Teacher of Righteousness, but also has the unparalleled and revolutionary boldness to set himself up in opposition to the *Torah.*"[21]
When Jesus combines this *egō* with *Amēn,* he is claiming to speak

---

21. Jeremias, *Proclamation* 253. See his whole discussion of the emphatic *egō*,
250–255. Jeremias would also attribute Matthew 5:17 to Jesus (82–85) but this is historically difficult to establish given the way in which the saying is structured into Matthew's particular theological concern to establish the abiding validity of the Law and

with divine authority. His identity was inextricably intertwined with that of the Father who sent him.

This brings us to the third dimension of Jesus' use of *Amēn,* his power, the impact that he had on those around him. It was precisely his complete and total response to the Father in obedience (what I would call his radical single-mindedness) that awakened the possibility of just such a response for each person in his or her own concrete situation. We will return to this impact he had when we treat faith and discipleship. But first we must consider what makes such power possible: the fact that Jesus' whole life, at its deepest center, was concentrated upon the will of his *Abbā.* It was surely the intensity of that concentratedness that eventually led his followers to see him as 'the Son' in a way that was unique to him.

Abbā was a child's word (in Aramaic), used in the ordinary, everyday language of the people as an expression of courtesy and familiarity. However, it was not limited to children; adults also used the word, just as in our culture a son or daughter might continue to refer to his or her father as 'poppa' or 'daddy' throughout adult life. Used in this way, it should not be understood as childish; such a word evokes in a mature adult the most profound depths at the very center of one's existence. It can evoke all the intimacy and familiarity and tenderness that one has experienced with one's father from the first moment of one's existence and which continues, through all the transformations of life, even to the moment of death. It was unheard of in Jesus' day that anyone would address God with this child's word and there is a clear tendency in the early Church to return to the more formal way of addressing God as Father in the

---

Jesus as its correct interpreter. Matthew does not, however, resolve all the tensions in this position. It is interesting to note that, despite the Mosaic typology applied to Jesus especially in the infancy narratives, Matthew 5:1–2 represents the disciples in Mosaic terms and Jesus as the divine lawgiver on the mountain. It is the disciples who receive the new law and who in turn are to communicate it to the people (Matthew 10; 28:16–20). That there is a tension is clear from the fact that in the fourth antithesis (Matthew 5:33–34) and in the fifth (Matthew 5:38–39a) Jesus not only deepens the Law but abrogates it. This may explain why in the third antithesis on divorce (Matthew 5:31–32) Matthew reintroduces the Deuteronomic exception which is not present in the Marcan and Lucan parallels (Mark 10:10–12 par). On the antitheses, see Jeremias, *Proclamation* 251–253.

tradition of Judaism (cp. Matthew 6:9 with Luke 11:2). Yet, Jesus always addressed God in this way in his prayers and he taught his disciples to do the same.[22]

If there is anything that expresses the profound depths of Jesus' personal relationship to God, it is this word *Abbā*. He proclaimed a God who is a loving and forgiving *Abbā* who has special care and concern for the seemingly most insignificant details of our personal lives, even for the hairs on our heads. His own reverential obedience was grounded in the childlike simplicity of absolute trust. Without such trust, which goes beyond the level of asking in prayer for this thing or that because it is grounded in the depth of a personal relationship, Jesus could not have endured. That personal relationship, and hence the whole basis and justification of his mission, is expressed in that little parabolic statement hidden in Matthew 11:27 par (cp. John 5:19–20) that only a father and son really know each other. "What Jesus wants to convey in the guise of an everyday simile is this: Just as a father talks to his son, just as he teaches him the letters of the Torah, just as he initiates him into the well-prepared secrets of his craft, just as he hides nothing from him and opens his heart to him as to no-one else, so God has granted me knowledge of himself."[23] It is that knowledge that Jesus is called to reveal, the knowledge of a gracious and loving *Abbā*.

All the prayers of Jesus, as they are given to us in the gospels, are certainly historical in this: that they express his absolute trust in the faithfulness of his *Abbā*, particularly in the face of what would appear to contradict such trust. He thanks the Father for his wisdom in the face of the conflict and failure he was experiencing in his ministry (Matthew 11:25 par). He affirms the priority of his Father's will to his own in the midst of his agony (Mark 14:35 par). He invokes Psalm 22, a psalm of trust, in his final death-throes when the Father seems to have abandoned him (Mark 15:34 par; Luke 23:34, 46, replaces this with a prayer for forgiveness and a prayer of trust direct-

---

22. Jeremias has done the decisive historical work on the uniqueness of Jesus' use of *Abbā* as an address to God. See *The Prayers of Jesus* (London: SCM, 1967) 11–65. This work is summarized in *The Central Message of the New Testament* (London: SCM, 1965) 9–30 and in *Proclamation* 36–37, 61–68, 178–184. See also Perrin, *Rediscovering* 40–41.

23. Jeremias, *Proclamation* 60.

ed to *Abbā*). Finally, however unhistorical the Gospel of John may be, it certainly captures what is central and decisive in the ministry of Jesus: his personal relation to the Father. Here, too, his prayer is one of trust in the face of his 'hour' (John 11:41; 12:27ff; 17:1, 5, 11, 21, 24ff).

Jesus invited his disciples not only to hear this deeper dimension of his message but to enter themselves into his own unique and personal relation to his loving Father by praying: *"Abbā,* may your name be held holy . . ." (Luke 11:1–4). Paul gives expression to this when he says, in effect, that if one wants a sign that one is truly a child of God, that one truly has the Spirit of Jesus, it is the ability to pray, from the very depths of one's heart, *Abbā!* (Gal. 4:6; Rom. 8:15).

The Spirit of God is revealed in Jesus' proclamation of the Kingdom, a challenge to humanness which recognizes that in the final analysis no human activity can be truly human if it is divorced from the divine activity at the center of each and every being. That divine activity is characterized by Jesus in such a way that reality is seen to be ultimately gracious, for at the very center of all reality is a loving and gracious Father who has care and concern for the very least, the little ones, the despised, the outcast, the rejected. Jesus not only proclaimed this message; he lived it, and it is that which gave such powerful impact to his words. It is, then, to his deeds that we must now turn.

C. Deed

(1) *Healing ministry: a call to faith and discipleship.* As noted earlier, there is an interesting correlation between Jesus' proclamation of the Kingdom and his use of the word 'faith' in his healing ministry. In one of his finest essays,[24] Gerhard Ebeling seeks to establish the "peculiar structure" of Jesus' view of faith. He sees the central importance of faith in its religious sense as peculiar to the Judaeo-Christian heritage but, in tracing the history of the concept from the Old Testament through Late Judaism into the New Testament, he is seeking that creative linguistic event which might help

---

24. Ebeling, "Jesus" 201–246. Both Perrin, *Rediscovering* 130–142 and Marxsen, *Beginnings* 44–57 have high praise for this article and make extensive use of it.

us to grasp the decisive difference between Judaism and Christianity. He finds it in Jesus' own distinctive use of the word both in the logion about faith that moves mountains and in those healing stories that focus upon faith as the central and decisive factor. These data make it "very probable that Jesus affirmed a connection between faith and the event of healing—and that, too, in a thoroughly unusual way—and that this became an element in the form of the healing stories in the synoptic tradition. It has thus nothing to do with a particular wording, but only with the peculiar structure of this concept of faith."[25] In expounding this peculiar structure, his treatment is remarkably similar to Funk's view of the relationship of God and Jesus to the parables as they focus upon the listener. I will discuss these three elements in the order in which Ebeling treats them.

God (and, I would add, the Christ understood as properly revealed in the act of raising Jesus from the dead) belongs to the umbral field here as well. It is true that God is the context, the ultimate ground, for everything that Jesus said or did, but then it is even more astonishing that faith is used here absolutely and in such a completely non-religious way.

> Jesus does not speak in this context of God. He does not
> exhort to faith in God, nor does he ask what sort of views
> of faith and what sort of ideas of God the people have with
> whom he has to do in these encounters. He imputes faith
> to the Samaritan, the Syro-phoenician woman, the Gentile
> nobleman irrespective of any confession of faith—and such

---

25. Ebeling, "Jesus" 231. The logion about faith moving mountains is found in Matthew 17:20 with an independently parallel saying that makes the same point about the improbable power of faith in Luke 17:6. The healing stories where faith is central include the paralytic (Mark 2:1–12 par), the woman with the issue (Mark 5:25–34 par), blind Bartimaeus (Mark 10:46–52 par), the two blind men (Matthew 9:27–31), Jairus' daughter (Mark 5:21–24, 35–43 par), the epileptic (Mark 9:14–29 par), the nobleman of Capernaum (Matthew 8:5–13 par), the Syro-phoenician woman (Matthew 15:21–28), the ten lepers (Luke 17:11–19), plus the similar story of the woman's forgiveness (Luke 7:50). One could add the explicit connection between faith and healing made by Matthew 13:58. It should be noted that, for his purposes, Ebeling is not concerned with discussing the historicity of miracle stories as such, but only the historicity of Jesus' use of faith in those stories where it is central. For a fine discussion of the historicity of miracle stories, see Jeremias, *Proclamation* 86–92.

faith, too, as he has not found in Israel. If the faith in question here is really faith towards God, then it is manifestly directed concretely towards God in concrete encounter with him.[26]

Jesus, likewise, belongs to the penumbral field in the twofold manner mentioned above. As the 'witness to faith', as the one who brings it on the scene and awakens it in others, he must have that which he offers and bring it into play even though he never speaks directly of his own faith. On the other hand, it is remarkable that the Synoptic gospels, unlike John, never have Jesus speak of himself as the object of faith. Jesus is presented as the one who has power to awaken faith in others.

> The whole point of all these healing stories is surely that Jesus in a peculiar way awakened confidence, hope, courage in the people concerned, that something went out from him which drew them to him. Add to that that he did not merely awaken faith, but also ascribed this faith to those who had no idea what was really happening to them, told them as it were to their face: You just do not know what has really happened—*hē pistis sou sesōken sē!* Such a concrete imputation of faith is without parallel.[27]

It is true that the situation of the people involved is conditioned by the physical presence of Jesus but, as we shall see, this does not necessarily imply a call to discipleship.

Like the parables, the focus of Jesus' use of faith is upon the concrete existence of the believer. The remarkable thing is that the people involved in these stories do not necessarily belong to a tradition of faith nor are they asked to recite a creed. Faith is used here in a much more fundamental sense, one that I would characterize as constitutive of what it is simply to be human. Ebeling speaks of the concentratedness of human existence, of the fact that it is one's own personal existence, one's own faith—"It is *your* (sing.) faith that has

---

26. Ebeling, "Jesus" 233–234.
27. Ibid. 235.

saved *you* (sing.)"—that is involved and that not in a partial but in a total way.

> . . . the blind man who cries out to Jesus, the Syro-phoeni-
> cian who does not give up praying for her daughter—all
> these figures are outstanding in this: that they are totally
> involved, totally concerned, not merely half-heartedly in-
> terested in what now happens or fails to happen, but rather,
> just like the dog watching tensely for the morsel that falls
> from the table, they are concentrated on one single point
> with every nerve of their being tense with attention and ex-
> pectation.[28]

Ebeling then elaborates upon six structural aspects of this view of faith, viz. "existence in certainty," "bringing about the future," "par-ticipation in the omnipotence of God," "encounter with the man Je-sus," "being related to a concrete situation," and "salvation itself." While drawing upon his analysis, I prefer to discuss what is involved in terms of openness, acceptance, and commitment.

The most fundamental condition that makes faith of any kind possible is openness to the gift. The people whom Jesus could not touch in his ministry were precisely those who were self-righteous, those who figured that God owed them something because of their accomplishments. The paradox is that they were in the greatest need precisely because they refused to recognize their need. The people whom Jesus did touch in his healing ministry were those who, in very concrete and personal ways, were being overwhelmed by the massive realities of sickness and death. They were experiencing their own helplessness and powerlessness; they seemingly had ground only for despair but, as a paradoxical consequence, they could be open to the free gift because they had nothing to cling to. Faith finds its ground here not in despair but in the ability, in the face of the abyss, to hope against hope.

Such faith involves as inextricably intertwined not only the rec-ognition of one's need but the acceptance of one's neediness, of one's dependence upon another. To accept the truth about oneself is to ac-

---

28. Ibid. 239–240.

cept the gift of life in all of its relationships. Such acceptance enables one to reach out beyond oneself, to transcend the enclosed world of oneself and to rejoice in the gift that others can be and are to that self. In the healing stories such faith always depends on the encounter with Jesus, but it is worth noting again that Jesus always places the emphasis upon the personal faith of the individual involved. "It is *your faith* that has saved you." Believing itself, understood simply as the ability to reach out beyond oneself in the face of one's need, has power. Thus, acceptance should not be understood as submission or resignation but rather as power, as the ability to embrace the gift of life as it is given to one, in all its concreteness and particularity, and to affirm it in such wise that it opens up new possibilities for the future, indeed is creative of the future. Such faith is "participation in the omnipotence of God" or, more strikingly put, "the essence of faith is participation in the essence of God."[29] As human beings, we exist only in participation in another. From the Christian perspective, this willingness to reach out beyond oneself and to trust another is only possible because of the divine activity at the center of all human life. Such faith is "salvation itself" as Jesus makes clear by the association of *pistis* and *sōtēria* in the phrase *hē pistis sou sesōken se* ("It is your faith that has saved you"). Faith itself is the power that saves. "For where there is faith, there by definition, one way or another, existence becomes whole, is healed."[30] In the healing stories, faith itself is the miracle. But, is this adequate? We must still ask the question: to what, or better, to whom does faith commit us?

---

29. Ibid. 242. Ebeling argues as follows: if the essence of faith is participation in the omnipotence of God, then the essence of faith is participation in the essence of God, for "the thing in which faith participates belongs inseparably to faith itself." Ibid. The power of God is known in our experience of absolute powerlessness, manifest above all in the cross (1 Cor. 1:18, 25). The cross is the supreme manifestation of the essence of God as love, a point which Ebeling develops further in *The Nature of Faith* (London: Collins, 1961), especially chapter XI, "The Power of Faith," 128–137. Only faith ascribes to God such power. The conclusion that I draw from this is that faith does not give us information about God but gives us God himself in his very essence, for it is finally as Ebeling says the experience of being loved. The power of faith gives us a different relation to God, the world, and oneself. "In what way different? One could simply say, in that he knows that he is loved. For faith comes from and goes to being loved" Ibid. 137.

30. Ibid. 245.

I have placed a great deal of emphasis upon what I consider to be the key to Eberling's treatment, viz. the importance of the concrete situation. In my own terms, I would say that faith analyzed here as Jesus' own distinctive usage commits us—at the most fundamental level of human existence—to embrace the gift of life as it is given to each one of us, in our own concreteness and particularity, and to live that gift to the full. Not all are given the same gift. Each one is called to live his or her own gift, not someone else's. There is a natural tendency to interpret Jesus' use of faith immediately as a call to discipleship.[31] There is no question that Jesus called certain individuals to follow him and that others, like Bartimaeus, spontaneously "followed him on the way" (Mark 10:42). But, in most of the healing narratives, there is no indication that those who were healed became his disciples. Nor, I submit, is there any necessity to think that they did. Have we not always understood Christian faith as the free gift of God's grace that calls a particular individual into a communal relationship called Church? The mystery has always been why he calls this one and not that one (predestination) and the difficulty has been to reconcile the particularity of God's call in sovereign freedom with the universality of God's love. What I am suggesting is that God, in his creative love, gives to each and every person throughout the whole of human history a very particular gift: his or her own identity. In a word, God gives us ourselves and calls us to be ourselves, a self we cannot be except in personal response to the divine initiative. As human history shows, this call is shaped in myriad forms because each one is given that call within the concreteness and particularity of one's own situation.

What, then, is the point of discipleship? We have seen that 'Kingdom of God' is Jesus' comprehensive term for the blessings of salvation insofar as it denotes the divine activity at the center of all

---

31. Perrin does this in his interpretation of Ebeling's data in *Rediscovering* 139–145. He describes Jesus' challenge to faith in terms of recognition and response: recognition that God is active in Jesus' ministry and response in terms of absolute trust and complete obedience. This could all be interpreted in the more generic way that I am proposing, but Perrin characterizes it as the "challenge of discipleship." I am limiting the term discipleship to those who are called specifically for the purpose of continuing the mission of Jesus in their own preaching, teaching, and healing (cp. Matthew 10).

human life and that 'faith' is his human, experiential term for salvation itself insofar as it denotes the human response, universally valid, of openness, acceptance, and commitment. Why, then be a disciple? The answer, it seems to me, lies in the notion of mission. Jesus calls certain individuals into a closer relationship with himself in order to give them a mission just as he was given a mission from the Father. The mission is fundamentally the same: to help bring the Kingdom to its full realization, i.e., to enable each and every person in the concreteness of one's own situation to embody that most fundamental human value which Jesus embodied and without which humanness is impossible: union with the divine. The primary value is the Kingdom which Jesus proclaimed and the Church (the community of Jesus' disciples) functions in service to a world in which that Kingdom is in process of being realized.[32] The saying at Mark 4:11 ("To you has been given the secret of the Kingdom of God") cannot refer, in the context of Jesus' ministry, to any kind of exclusivism[33] but only to the fact that the disciples have been called into a very special relationship with Jesus so that, knowing experientially the deeper dimensions of his message and especially his personal relation to his *Abbā*, they might in turn become an extension of himself (a 'body') in the world.

Hence, Jesus demanded of his disciples what he demanded of himself: he challenged them to a radical single-mindedness. They must embody in their personal lives what Jesus did in his if they are to be effective and this means that they must have the same kind of dedication to the task: they must know that they will have nowhere to lay their heads, that they must transcend even the most sacred of human responsibilities such as burying the dead, and that they must never look back (Luke 9:57–62 par). Like Jesus, their lives must be centered on the one thing necessary: the Father's Kingdom. Everything else in human life takes on meaning only in relation to this. Such an attitude of radical single-mindedness is not a denial of the

---

32. See Richard P. McBrien, *Church: The Continuing Quest* (New York: Newman, 1970) 73–85. Also, the interesting discussion in *Theological Studies* 37 (1976) entitled "Why the Church?" especially the debate between Roger D. Haight and Robert T. Sears.

33. Jeremias, *Proclamation* 120,156.

beauty and the pleasure and the joy of human life but the recognition, once again, that true humanness is only possible in union with the divine. Hence, Jesus not only proclaimed the Kingdom of God; he celebrated it.

(2) *Table-fellowship: a celebration of the Kingdom.* "Can the wedding guests fast while the wedding is going on?" (Mark 2:19 par).[34] The image of the wedding indicates that Jesus regarded his ministry as a time of release from normal religious obligations—it is striking that he and his disciples did not fast—and as a time of great joy because the wedding is a symbol of the day of salvation, of the decisive activity of God in the midst of his people. The *Sitz im Leben Jesu* for this image, and to be sure for a great deal of Jesus' teaching, was a joyous table-fellowship that excluded no one, not even tax-collectors and sinners.

Jesus shocked his contemporaries by reclining at table with tax-collectors and sinners at festive meals (Mark 2:15–17 par; cp. Luke 15:1–2). Their distaste is caught well in the taunt that they throw at him: "Behold, a glutton and a drunkard, a friend of tax-collectors and sinners!" (Matthew 11:19b par). Generically, there were three kinds of sinners in Jesus' day.[35] There were Jews who transgressed the Law but who could hope for divine forgiveness, especially if they performed the appropriate sacrificial action. There were Gentiles who were sinners by definition because they stood outside the Law. It was disputed whether they could hope for forgiveness in the 'age to come.' Finally, the worst group of all, there were Jews who in effect had made themselves to be as Gentiles, usually by reason of their occupation which was thought to lead to immorality, especially to dishonesty. Such proscribed trades included dice players, usurers, herdsmen (shepherds, swineherds, etc.), prostitutes, but the most hated of all were the tax-collectors and toll-collectors (publicans). Not only was this latter group considered to be dishonest, but they were open to the possibility of ritual defilement and, worst of all,

---

34. For the historical reconstruction of this saying, see Perrin, *Rediscovering* 79–80. He refers to Joachim Jeremias, *The Parables of Jesus* (London: SCM, 1963) 52, n. 14.

35. For greater detail, see Perrin, *Rediscovering* 90–94 and Jeremias, *Proclamation* 108–113.

were traitors to their own people because they were collecting taxes for the hated Romans. For this group, forgiveness, if not utterly impossible, was practically so. They had betrayed their very heritage as God's people.

Jesus not only proclaimed forgiveness to such as these (the shocking reversal in the parable of the Prodigal Son lies in the fact that the younger son had sunk so low as to become a swineherd and yet was treated with such an extraordinarily forgiving and generous love by his father when he returns), but he celebrated that forgiveness by dining with them. It is important to realize that in Jesus' day sharing a meal was no mere casual act; it had profound significance in terms of human friendship.

> To understand what Jesus was doing in eating with 'sinners', it is important to realize that in the east, even today, to invite a man to a meal was an honor. It was an offer of peace, trust, brotherhood and forgiveness; in short, sharing a table meant sharing life. . . . In Judaism in particular, table-fellowship means fellowship before God, for the eating of a piece of broken bread by everyone who shares in the meal brings out the fact that they all have a share in the blessing which the master of the house had spoken over the unbroken bread.[36]

By his table-fellowship, Jesus was concretely living out the content of his proclamation: "Blessed are you poor, for yours is the Kingdom of God" (Luke 6:20). He was saying with as strong a symbolic action as was possible in his day that those whom his opponents termed 'violent intruders' *(hoi biastai)* were the ones who were truly 'grasping' the Kingdom (Matthew 11:12), even to the point of displacing the self-righteous (Matthew 21:31), because they—and they alone— were open to the free gift of a gracious God: "I have not come to call the righteous [a self-designation of the Pharisees?] but sinners" (Mark 2:17 par). These meals, then, express symbolically the whole mission and message of Jesus as they anticipate the final consumma-

---

36. Jeremias, *Proclamation* 115.

tion of the Kingdom that is coming: "I tell you, many will come from east and west and sit at table with Abraham, Isaac, and Jacob in the Kingdom of heaven" (Matthew 8:11 par). Perrin sees this table-fellowship

> as the central feature of the ministry of Jesus; an anticipatory sitting at table in the Kingdom of God and a very real celebration of present joy and challenge. Here a great deal of the private teaching of Jesus to his disciples must have had its *Sitz im Leben*—especially the Lord's Prayer must belong here—and here the disciples must have come to know the special way that Jesus had of 'breaking bread' which gave rise to the legend of the Emmaus road (Luke 24.35).[37]

(3) *Disciples' prayer: 'may your Kingdom come'.* The prayer that Jesus taught his disciples was not intended to be an esoteric formula known only to the initiates so that it would separate the disciples from the rest of the people. Rather, the prayer functions as a sort of résumé that encapsulates in a brief and simple way everything that Jesus stood for in his ministry. In giving the prayer to his disciples, he was calling them once again to the same mission that he himself had received from the Father.

Coming from a heritage of liturgical prayer that tended to be fixed and formalized, Jesus' own prayer[38] is distinctive in that he would spend hours, even whole nights, in solitary prayer (Mark 1:35; 6:46 par; Luke 6:12), in that he prayed in the language of the people (Aramaic) which had the effect of removing his prayer from the liturgical sphere of the sacral and putting it in the center of ordinary, everyday life, and in that he prayed simply and directly with the supreme and unshakeable confidence of a child who can say *Abbā*. Thus the instructions on prayer, the catecheses of Matthew and Luke in which they set the transmission of the Lord's Prayer, emphasize that one must pray unceasingly with a kind of beggar's wis-

---

37. Perrin, *Rediscovering* 107–108.
38. For a fuller analysis of Jesus' way of praying, see Jeremias, *Proclamation* 184–203 and *Prayers* 66–107.

dom that knows one will be heard (Luke 11:5–13) and that one must take with the utmost seriousness the primacy of one's relationship to the Father by praying in secret and with few words (Matthew 6:5–8).

Following Jeremias' reconstruction of the Lord's Prayer into the original Aramaic, using the shorter length of Luke 11:2–4 but the more difficult wording of Matthew 6:9–13, I would offer the following version in English:

> *Abbā,*
> > may your Name be held holy,
> > may your Kingdom come.
> > Bread for tomorrow give us today,
> > and forgive us our offenses as we herewith forgive
> > > those who offend us.
> > And do not let us fail at the time of the trial!

In these few, tight-knit words, Jesus has given us a prayer that goes to the very heart of his ministry and therefore of ours as well. His special word for God was *Abbā*. He invites us to use that word as well and so enter into the very center of his personal mystery. Everything, really, is contained in this one word. The rest of the prayer simply makes explicit in the context of his public ministry some of the essential dimensions of what it means to call God *Abbā*.

The two 'thou' petitions would have been immediately familiar to the disciples as they are an abbreviated and modified form of the Kaddish prayer, one of the few prayers in the language of the people (Aramaic) which was prayed in the synagogue liturgy after the sermon. This prayer is much longer and more formalized in language. Jesus has picked out two essential elements, the Name and the Kingdom, and personalized the prayer by using the second person following the address of *Abbā*. By praying first for the Name and the Kingdom, Jesus exercises once again his prophetic role of calling the people of Israel to a realization of what is deepest in their own heritage. His mission was always first and foremost to the lost sheep of the house of Israel (Matthew 15:24). He opened up to them the possibilities of God's future by calling them to embrace in new and unforeseen ways the deepest level of their past. What is new here is that the proper name of Yahweh is *Abbā,* with all that that implies about the character of God, and that his Kingdom is already being realized in the midst of their ordinary, everyday lives. The prayer for its 'coming' (rather than its being 'established' as in the Kaddish prayer), while still looking for a future consummation, recognizes the decisiveness of the present for the shape of that future. These first two petitions, then, focus upon *Abbā* but already imply the importance of human response, something the next three petitions make even clearer.

The two 'we' petitions, for bread and for forgiveness, belong closely together both in form and in content because they reflect that central and distinctive feature of Jesus' ministry, his table-fellowship with tax-collectors and sinners. Jeremias interprets 'bread for tomorrow' as symbolic of God's future, the time of salvation. Hence, it could also be called the 'bread of life'. But this bread should not be understood in purely spiritual terms, for the prayer is that this bread be given *today,* i.e., in the concrete, here and now situation in which we break and share earthly bread. Once again, the divine action takes place in the midst of human action, and not apart from it. Correlative to this is the prayer for forgiveness which, interpreted from the Aramaic, emphasizes the simultaneity *(herewith)* of divine-human action. This is the only petition that explicitly mentions our human response but it is implied throughout the prayer. God's action makes possible our response but it is only in actually responding to the divine initiative that we can 'know' in the experiential sense the divine activity at the very center of our being. For Jesus in his ministry, the actual breaking and sharing of earthly bread embodied the divine forgiveness and so was a celebration of the presence of the Kingdom in the midst of human life.

The final petition is intentionally abrupt and harsh. It looks to the final trial *(peirasmos)* and so throws us back upon the one to whom the prayer is directed. The prayer is not to have the trial removed but to be faithful to *Abbā* as he is to us. The very abruptness of the ending emphasizes that we stand in the midst of life completely dependent upon this *Abbā.* The future is his! No one was more aware of this than Jesus. This final petition takes on a special poignancy in the context of Jesus' ministry as he experienced an ever-greater opposition that must have forced him to consider the very real possibility of his own violent death.

D. FATE

(1) *Jesus' awareness of his death.* Jesus knew that the prophetic vocation frequently ended in martyrdom (Luke 13:33b; cp. Luke 13:34 par; Matthew 23:35 par). He had the example of John the Baptist before him and so had to take seriously the warning 'Herod wants to kill you' (Luke 13:31). Moreover, his most significant actions incurred the likelihood of a violent death (normally by stoning except for being a false prophet which was punishable by strangulation). He was accused of being a blasphemer in proclaiming God's forgiveness as present in his own healing ministry (Mark 2:7 par), of casting out demons by the power of Beelzebub (Mark 3:22 par), and finally of being a false prophet (Mark 14:65 par). Among his most offensive actions were his challenges to the legalistic mentality of his day by breaking the sabbath (Mark 2:23–3:6 par; Luke 13:10–17; 14:1–6; John 5:1–18; 9:1–41), his blow at the very heart of self-righteousness in Judaism by symbolically cleansing the temple (Mark 11:15–19 par), but perhaps none of his actions was so offensive as his eating with tax-collectors and sinners. It undermined the whole structure of Jewish society. It offended the sense of ritual purity and moral uprightness, but even worse it undermined the religio-political hope that the Kingdom of God would be established by overthrowing the hated Romans. Jesus challenged the fundamental assumption that held the whole society together, viz. that God was on their side and that he would eventually give them—or at least the purified remnant among them—the final triumph over their enemies. Jesus indeed laid his own life on the line by such actions![39]

---

39. Jeremias, *Proclamation* 278–280; Fuller, *Foundations* 106–108; Perrin, *Rediscovering* 102–103. Jeremias sees the cleansing of the temple as the occasion for the definitive official action against Jesus. Also, he considers (111) the primary offense of Jesus' table-fellowship with tax-collectors and sinners to be exclusively moral. I would tend to agree with Perrin that the offense was more political, although it certainly included the moral offense. It must be remembered, as Perrin emphasizes, that tax-collectors particularly were considered to be traitors.

Only intense conviction can explain such actions on the part of Jesus. Such conviction led him finally to set his face toward Jerusalem (Luke 13:33; cp. 9:51). He went up to Jerusalem, not in order to die, but in order to remain faithful to his mission. The cry of the crowds: "Blessed is the kingdom of our father David that is coming!" (Mark 11:10) almost demanded a symbolic cleansing of the temple. The Kingdom that Jesus proclaimed is not what the people were looking for. Their hardness of heart could mean his death. To be sure, Jesus must have reflected on that possibility and on what his death might mean for his mission as a whole. The only problem, methodologically, is that Jesus' death is the crucial event that demanded interpretation in the early Church. Hence, the early Church developed a passion apologetic out of the scriptures to demonstrate the divine intention in the crucifixion. The earliest text used was probably Psalm 118:22, which emphasizes Jesus' rejection reversed by the divine vindication. This lies closest to Jesus' own understanding. Following closely upon this was the early Palestinian community's interpretation of Jesus' death in explicit soteriological terms using Isaiah 53.[40] But, granted that the fulfillment of scripture is an apologetic motif of the early Church, is there any indication in our sources of how Jesus himself interpreted the very real possibility of his own death? There seem to be at least two possibilities.

The first is a saying that occurs in the Last Supper scene. In the context of his ministry of table-fellowship and of the very real possibility of his own violent death that that ministry entailed, there is no reason not to accept the tradition that Jesus shared a final meal with his disciples. The bread and cup words have obviously been de-

---

40. Jeremias, *Proclamation* 286–299, seeks to demonstrate that Jesus himself understood his death in terms of the atoning suffering of Isaiah 53. What he does demonstrate is that the texts involve an Aramaic substrate, but the weakness in his argument is the assumption that getting back to the Aramaic is the same as getting back to Jesus. Fuller, *Foundations* 118–119, 136–137, n. 63, following H. E. Toedt, *The Son of Man in the Synoptic Tradition* (Philadelphia: Westminster, 1965), agrees that the passion predictions belong to the Palestinian rather than the Hellenistic stratum but disagrees with Jeremias that Jesus ever understood himself as the servant of the Lord, much less the suffering atoning servant of Isaiah 53. He goes on to say: "The soteriological interpretation, far from being an arbitrary imposition on the history of Jesus, unfolds the implications of the authentic eschatological prediction of Mark 14:25" (119).

veloped theologically in the light of the crucifixion, but there is one independent saying in the pericope which tended to suffer progressive atrophy in the liturgical tradition: "Amen, I say to you, I shall not drink again of the fruit of the vine until that day when I drink it new in the kingdom of God" (Mark 14:25 par). This corresponds to his expectation of the consummation of the Kingdom in the image of banqueting at God's table (Matthew 8:11 par). What is new here, granted the authenticity of the saying, is that Jesus now sees his own impending death, almost certain given the growing hostility and opposition he experienced at Jerusalem, as somehow directly operative in the final and decisive (eschatological) action of God in bringing that Kingdom to its consummation. Exactly how remains, of course, hidden in the Father's will and, from our perspective, was only revealed in the decisive event of Jesus' death-resurrection.[41]

The second possibility follows from the first. If Jesus could have predicted his death using the image of the meal, he could have done it in other ways as well. However, this possibility involves the intriguing question of whether Jesus used the enigmatic phrase *bar 'enāšā*. Jeremias sees, underlying the three passion predictions at Mark 8:31 par; 9:31 par; 10:33ff par, an original *māšāl* (riddle) in Aramaic reconstructed from Mark 9:31a (cp. 14:21, 41): *mitmᵉsar bar 'enāšā līdē bᵉnē 'enāšā*, which he translates (changing the divine passive into an active subject) "God will (soon) deliver up the man to men." This saying is a riddle because it involves a word play on *bar 'enāšā* which could be understood either as a title or generically.[42] The phrase *ho huios tou anthrōpou* in the Greek text of the gospels is always a title, but the Aramaic can have the generic sense of 'the man', 'a man', 'someone', or when it includes the speaker

---

41. For this interpretation of Mark 14:25, see Fuller, *Foundations* 107–108. Jeremias, *Proclamation* 298, interprets the saying as a solemn avowal of abstinence in order to make intercession for the guilty and so relates it to Isaiah 53:12. However, this seems to be reading too much into the saying, especially if one treats it as an independent saying. Also, it is interesting to note that Luke 22:16, 18 makes this saying the major motif of his Last Supper scene in order to emphasize his view that the passion is a transitory exodus into glory (the saying is fulfilled for Luke in the resurrection narratives of chapter 24 where Jesus eats and drinks with his disciples) and so to omit any soteriological meaning for the passion itself (Luke 22:19b–20 being a later addition). Cp. Conzelmann, *Luke,* 201.

42. Jeremias, *Proclamation* 281–282. See 260–262 also.

(though not a simple paraphrase for 'I') 'a man like myself'. On the historical level, this is the best explanation of the original import of the so-called 'present' sayings at Mark 2:10 par; 2:28 par; 3:28 par; Matthew 8:20 par; 11:19 par. But, if Jesus did speak about his impending death, then there is no reason to think that he did not use the phrase similarly in a 'suffering' saying. What would be expressed by such a statement is not so much a prediction of the future as a recognition of the present crisis. He is experiencing a 'being handed over' into the hands of 'the men' who reject him. (We will treat this more fully in the next chapter.)

The real difficulty is not whether Jesus might have used *bar 'eṇāśa* in this generic sense, but whether he might not have intended more by the phrase. As Fuller puts it: "The real difficulty about them is that it is impossible to account for these sayings within the framework of Jewish apocalyptic, where the Son of Man is a transcendent figure coming on the clouds of heaven."[43] The enigma is caught well in the question: "Who is this Son of Man?" (John 12:34).

(2) *The day of the Son of Man.* Our concern now is with the use of Son of Man as a title deriving from Late Jewish apocalyptic, particularly from Daniel 7 (ca. 164 B.C.), I Enoch 37–71 (the Similitudes: ca. 40 B.C.), and IV Ezra 13 (ca. 94 A.D.). The title was also used sparingly in the later talmudic and midrashic tradition in connection with the Messiah. It is worth noting that in this later tradition for the first time the 'clouds' phrase is understood as a description of the figure's movement not only in the sense of coming to God but in the sense of coming from heaven to earth.[44] Perrin makes the point, contrary to the widespread assumption of the existence of a unified and consistent conception of the Son of Man as transcendent bringer of salvation, that there is rather varied use of 'Son of Man imagery' derived from Daniel 7:13. The interpretation of Daniel 7 as a cryptic image of divine vindication for the suffering of the Maccabean martyrs comes closest to Jesus' own usage. The interpretation of I Enoch that Enoch becomes the Son of Man by rea-

---

43. Fuller, *Foundations* 124.
44. Perrin, *Rediscovering* 171–172. For a full account of the Son of Man in Late Judaism, see 164–173. Also, Toedt, *Son of Man* 22–31; Fuller, *Foundations* 34–43; Jeremias, *Proclamation* 268–272.

son of his translation to heaven obviously parallels the early Church's identification of Jesus with the Son of Man by reason of his resurrection.

While the prevailing and popular expectation in Jesus' day was for a warrior hero from the house of David who would usher in the Kingdom of God, God's final and definitive activity to redeem his people, understood in nationalistic terms, there were also more esoteric and supra-national expectations usually couched in apocalyptic terms. The apocalyptic expectation was for a 'break' between this present evil age and the age to come and the figure of the Son of Man, however diversely interpreted, represented the hope for a transcendent bringer of salvation. The point is that both images, 'Kingdom of God' and 'Son of Man', are ciphers that had to be filled with concrete content. We have seen how Jesus gave his own meaning to the phrase 'Kingdom of God'. This is his basic proclamation. If he used the image of 'Son of Man' at all, his usage must basically cohere with his more fundamental message. Jesus proclaimed the Kingdom of God as 'coming' by directing attention to those dimensions within his own ministry where it was presently being realized. The early Church proclaimed Jesus as the Son of Man who is coming at the end of the age for judgment. Hence, any texts in our sources that speak of Jesus' return would have to be ascribed to the early Church's interpretation in the light of the resurrection. The possibility of ascribing any usage to Jesus seems to me to lie in a careful distinction between talk about the 'coming' (parousia) of the Son of Man and talk about the 'day' of the Son of Man.

There is a strong argument in favor of authenticity, i.e., of saying that Jesus used the phrase in some form, viz. the remarkable phenomenon that in all four gospels the phrase occurs exclusively on the lips of Jesus.

How did it come about that at a very early stage the community avoided the title *ho huios tou anthrōpou* because it was liable to be misunderstood, did not use it in a single confession, yet at the same time handed it down in the sayings of Jesus, in the synoptic gospels virtually as the only title used by Jesus of himself? How is it that the instances of it increase, but the usage is still strictly limited

to the sayings of Jesus? There can be only one answer; the
title was rooted in the tradition of the sayings of Jesus right
from the beginning; as a result, it was sacrosanct, and no
one dared to eliminate it.[45]

This does not mean, of course, that all the instances go back to
Jesus, but rather that the development of the title is grounded in Jesus' own usage. In fact, as we shall see in chapter four, it forms the
earliest christological link of continuity between Jesus and the early
Church. Jeremias, in his analysis, points out that there are fifty-one
distinct uses in the gospels. If one eliminates, on philological
grounds, those sayings which probably go back to a misunderstanding of a generic use and, on traditio-historical grounds, those sayings
which have a competing tradition in the parallels (usually an 'I' or
'me') because the tendency of the tradition would be for the title to
supplant the pronoun, then one is left with eleven sayings in which
the apocalyptic title is clearly intended (no mistranslation) and in
which there is only one version (no competitors), viz. Mark 13:26
par; 14:62 par; Luke 17:24 par; 17:26 par; Matthew 10:23; 25:31;
Luke 17:22; 17:30; 18:8; 21:36; John 1:51. In what follows, we will
also give consideration to Luke 12:8–9 par because of its strong
claims to historicity.

Perrin argues that Mark 13:26 and 14:62 are the end-products
of early Christian exegetical traditions, that "there are three Christian exegetical traditions using Daniel 7.13: a parousia tradition
(Mark 13.26); an ascension tradition developing from an interpretation of the resurrection in terms of Psalm 110.1 (Mark 14.62a and
Acts 7.56); and a passion apologetic tradition using Zechariah
12.10ff. (John 19.37; Rev. 1.7; Matthew 24.30)."[46] Perrin does a brilliant analysis of the latter, which appears in these texts in the phrase
'they will see' and 'you will see', showing that this could only have
developed on the basis of the Greek text (LXX). I would argue, contra Perrin, Jeremias, and Fuller, that this is also true of the use of
Psalm 110:1. It will be argued later that the transition from a focus
upon the coming Son of Man to a focus upon the exalted Lord first

---

45. Jeremias, *Proclamation* 266.
46. Perrin, *Rediscovering* 183. Cp. Jeremias, *Proclamation* 272–276.

occurred when the title *Kyrios* was applied to Jesus using Psalm 110:1, something that could only happen on the basis of the LXX text.[47] It seems to me more natural sequentially to assume that this text was first applied to Jesus *in toto*, i.e., with the *Kyrios* title, and that only subsequently was it modified when the parousia and exaltation themes were combined (Mark 14:62). This means that Luke 22:69 (cp. Acts 7:56) is not, as Jeremias argues, the preservation of a more primitive tradition. Jeremias bases his argument upon the fact that an assumption to God (a movement from below upwards) corresponds to the Jewish apocalyptic expectations while the parousia in the gospels is thought of as a movement from above downwards. Apart from the question of whether there is any notion of movement prior to IV Ezra, the real question is what use Jesus and the early Church made of the Danielic image of the Son of Man, i.e., what best explains the development of the image in our sources. I would maintain that the earliest tradition in these two texts is the 'coming in clouds' in which, as Perrin holds, the close connection of the clouds with the coming suggests the clouds as the medium for a movement from heaven to earth. This is an interpretation only possible in the light of Jesus' resurrection. Subsequently, this more primitive interpretation is combined with a more developed exaltation christology. Thus, those texts which reflect either 'coming' or 'exaltation' must be assigned to the developing tradition of the early com-

---

47. Fuller, *Foundations* 184–186. Fuller remarks (185): "As we have seen from Mark 14:62, the motif of the session at the right hand had already been taken up from Psalm 110:1 in the earliest community. But there are difficulties in the way of inferring from this that the earliest Palestinian church applied Psalm 110:1 *in toto* to Jesus' exaltation, as in Acts 2:36." The difficulty is that the title *Kyrios* could only have been applied to Jesus on the basis of the LXX text. Similarly, Wm. O. Walker, Jr., "The Origin of the Son of Man Concept as Applied to Jesus," JBL 91 (1972) 482–490, has shown that the *verbal link* between Psalm 110:1 and Daniel 7:13 is only possible on the basis of the LXX texts. This would tend to confirm my contention that the earlier coming Son of Man was combined with the exalted notion only after Psalm 110:1 had been used to proclaim Jesus as *Kyrios*. This view is also confirmed by Toedt, *Son of Man*, 291: "Our conclusion is as follows. The concept of exaltation does not belong to the sayings about the coming Son of Man as a christological element specific to them. It is mostly absent from these sayings. Where its influence can be seen in the Son of Man sayings—Luke 22.69—the concept of exaltation has been adopted from a sphere of christological cognition which is not immediately connected with the Son of Man concept. The title of *Kyrios* is in the main coordinated with that other sphere of christological cognition. . . ."

munity. This would include, besides Mark 13:26 par; 14:62 par, also Matthew 10:23; 25:31; Luke 18:8; 21:36; John 1:51.

This leaves from Jeremias' original list only Luke 17:22, 24, 26, 30. Note that Matthew in the parallels (Matthew 24:27, 37b, 39b) uses the technical term for Jesus' expected return, viz. *parousia,* while Luke has the *day* of the Son of Man (the plural probably represents Luke's tendency to periodize salvation history as Fuller maintains). It is worth noting that this special Lucan apocalypse, unlike the Marcan apocalypse (Mark 13:1–37 par) with its emphasis upon preliminary signs, emphasizes the suddenness and unexpectedness of that day. The saying that has the greatest claim to authenticity is at 17:24: "For as the lightning flashes and lights up the sky from one side to the other, so will the Son of Man be in his day." Perrin, although he acknowledges that even Bultmann accepts this saying, too easily dismisses it as a piece of commonplace apocalyptic terminology. He remarks that when Jesus used Kingdom of God, which is also an apocalyptic concept, he used it in an unusual and distinctive way. My contention is that Jesus did the same with the day of the Son of Man. He uses it as a prophetic symbol of the divine vindication of his ministry in the face of the present crisis. Perrin's concern is to show that Jesus was not an apocalypticist, that he was not interested in predicting exactly when, where, and how the end would take place, and with this I agree. In fact, Perrin admits that Jesus could have used the imagery of Daniel 7:13 in exactly the way I have described. I think it necessary to affirm that he did in order to explain the indubitably strong evidence of our sources that the use of the title in some form originated with Jesus.

In form Son of Man is always in the third person in the gospels. In the 'present' and 'suffering' sayings the Greek text is clearly identifying the title with Jesus. Yet, in the apocalyptic sayings, there are some texts in which Jesus seems to be making a clear distinction between himself and the Son of Man, such that he himself appears as the forerunner and prophet for a savior figure still to come. Appeal is made above all to Luke 12:8 par (Mark 8:38 par being clearly a later development): "And I tell you, everyone who acknowledges me before men, the Son of Man will also acknowledge before the angels of God." For Jeremias, this saying falls out because there is a competing tradition in the parallels. For Perrin, the original saying probably used the divine passive but even if the Son of Man reference is original it is only, once again, a symbol for vindication. The important point here is that it would not be used in an apocalyptic way to signify quite literaly another savior figure distinct from Jesus but rather in a prophetic way. (As will be seen in chapter 4, I reject this saying as coming from Jesus because it is already a too personalized use of the imagery.) The 'day' of the Son of Man (and any other use of the image by Jesus) is intended to evoke the universal dominion of God, the final consummation of the Kingdom. The distinction is thus not between Jesus and another figure known as the Son of Man, but between the present crisis of suffering (both Jesus' and his disciples') and the future resolution of that crisis in the divine activity of vindication. The day of the Son of Man is the day of the Lord. Thus, the basis for accepting those sayings as authentic which make a distinction between Jesus and the Son of Man (because the early Church identified the two) falls out once it is recognized that Jesus' use of this enigmatic title is not concerned with the literal identity of a savior figure (himself or someone else) but with the salvific activity of God who will vindicate his own proclamation of the Kingdom. The day of the Son of Man is internally consistent with the Kingdom of God which from the days of John the Baptist until the final meal of Jesus has suffered violence (Matthew 11:12 par).[48]

Paul sums up the fate of Jesus when, speaking of Jesus' final meal, he tells the Corinthians: ". . . as often as you eat this bread and drink the cup, you proclaim the death of the Lord until he comes" (1 Cor 11:26). The earliest understanding of Jesus' eating and drink-

---

48. Fuller, *Foundations* 121–124, follows Bultmann in insisting that those sayings which make a distinction between Jesus and the Son of Man must be accepted as authentic. But, he follows Toedt in interpreting Luke 12:8 in a non-apocalyptic way. The saying is concerned with *soteriological* continuity, though it implies a christology. It is the early Church which, once it has identified Jesus with the Son of Man, elaborates the apocalyptic dimensions on the basis of this christological judgment. Thus, the apocalyptic understanding comes from the early Church in the light of the resurrection (an apocalyptic event) and not from Jesus. Moreover, contra Fuller, I would maintain that once the early Church had made the identification, then there is no problem in understanding how it could replace 'I' sayings with the Son of Man title even though this would appear to make a distinction between Jesus and the Son of Man. Thus, it is not necessary to accept Matthew 19:28 as historical, which Fuller thinks we must do.

ing was that, in so doing, he was laying down his life for his friends
(John 15:13). At the same time, he trusted in the divine vindication
which, for the early Church, took place in the apocalyptic event of
his resurrection, an event that would be consummated when he
comes again. For Jesus, that event was his final trial. He taught his
disciples to pray: "*Abbā*, do not let us fail at the time of the trial!"
That prayer takes on particular poignancy for Jesus in the light of
his crucifixion. Was he right about God, the God whom he knew and
loved and prayed to as *Abbā*, a God of wonderful intimacy and familiarity, a loving, caring, forgiving Father who calls us into a profound communion of simple, child-like trust rooted so deep in our
consciousness that nothing in all creation can ever separate us from
such love (cp. Rom. 8:38–39)? His crucifixion put a question-mark
before all that he stood for. We must now take a look at that event
which Christians have always seen to be decisive for the salvation of
the world.

CHAPTER THREE

The Decisive (Eschatological) Event

The Kingdom that Jesus proclaimed did not fulfill many of the expectations of his day. He offered no political revolution to restore Israel, no cataclysm to destroy this evil age. Indeed, the God who reveals himself in Jesus offers us nothing, i.e., no thing. His offer is much more radical and, for that reason, much more threatening. In his appeal to the heart of each one of us in the concreteness of our own lives, he is offering us himself and asking for nothing less than ourselves in return. He does this indirectly by unveiling to us in new ways the world that we thought we knew and by directing us to take a fresh look. If we penetrate deeply enough into our world, we will discover at its very center the God whom Jesus knew and loved and prayed to as *Abbā*. Jesus' whole life was concentrated upon the will of his *Abbā* and it was surely the intensity of that concentratedness that eventually led his followers to see him as 'the Son' in a way that was unique to him. Yet, Jesus is known to us not simply in his earthly ministry, his words and deeds, but primarily in his fate, as Paul's writings make clear. Christians have always known that the definitive act of God, the eschatological event, was Jesus' death and resurrection.

In order to interpret this event properly, it is necessary first of all to understand that it is not an isolated event but one that can only be understood in the light of the earthly ministry of Jesus that precedes and of the kerygmatic ministry of the early Church that follows. Furthermore, the cross-resurrection is a single event such that one cannot properly speak of the one without the other. If the resurrection is Jesus' vindication and so gives meaning to the absurdity of the cross, it is at a more fundamental level his death on the cross

73

that alone can give us the properly critical understanding of what *this* resurrection means. It is far easier to believe in the resurrection than in the cross, as Luke's concern to present Jesus' suffering as an exodus into glory shows (Luke 24:26). Yet, I think Mark has the deeper insight when the centurion, seeing how Jesus died, exclaims: "Truly, this man was son of God!" (Mark 15:39 par).

A. THE FINAL TRIAL: CRUCIFIXION

For Christians, the only and true God is the God revealed to us in the personal life and destiny of Jesus. Juergen Moltmann radicalizes this understanding with his focus upon the cross as the critical factor: for a Christian, 'God' is what takes place between Jesus and the Father on the cross.[1] What follows will draw somewhat on his analysis but in my own terms. In the light of what has been said in the preceding chapter on Jesus' awareness of his death, I will simply presuppose as having the greatest historical likelihood Moltmann's analysis that Jesus was condemned as a blasphemer by the Jews and executed as a rebel by the Romans (the title 'King of the Jews' at Mark 15:26 being the most striking bit of evidence for the latter). What is crucial to understanding Jesus' death is not primarily his relation to the world in which he lived but to the God whom he proclaimed. Whether he actually uttered it or not—although it is difficult to understand why the early Church would create it—the deepest understanding of Jesus' way to the cross is expressed in the cry: "My God, my God, why have you forsaken me?" (Mark 15:34 par). This can be understood on two levels.

The first level is that of our common human experience in the face of death. In my opinion, it is not so much death as the fear of death that is the real evil here, for such fear can destroy trust and lead to despair. This sense of ambiguity before suffering and death and its corresponding temptation would be as true of the author of Psalm 22 as of Jesus. One could coin a divine answer to this question in the form of another question: 'My children, why have you forsaken me?' The key here is not God's abandonment of us but our abandonment of God. The Father did not send the Son into the world

---

1. Moltmann, *Crucified* 204–207.

in order to die on the cross. Jesus' mission was to proclaim the depth of the Father's love in the midst of human life. It was not the Father but human sinfulness in its rejection of such love that created the cross. The only 'necessity' for the cross is to be found in that freely chosen rejection. Here I differ from Moltmann's notion that the Father, in sending the Son, handed him over to the cross and so abandoned him that it must be said that God is not only crucified but crucifying. On the contrary, the cross is first and foremost, in all its nakedness and ugliness, the ultimate symbol of mankind's rejection of divine love and only so can it become the symbol of the divine love itself.

The second level is that of Jesus' unique experience. Moltmann cleverly rephrases the question to read: "My God, my God, why have you forsaken *yourself?*" Historically, Jesus' death was not the noble death of a hero, like Socrates. Such a hero dies knowing his cause is inviolable, but Jesus' death called the very thing he stood for into question. He died with a loud cry, with the signs and expressions of a profound abandonment by the God whom he called *Abbā*. Condemned as a blasphemer and crucified as a rebel, it was possible for Jews and Romans to misunderstand but there can be no misunderstanding here. The agony of Jesus did not lie simply in his being rejected by the leaders of his people (Mark 3:6) or by the people whom he had known and loved from his earliest childhood (Mark 6:1–6a) or even by those whom he had called to follow him more closely (Mark 8:14–21), especially Peter (Mark 8:32–33; 14:29–31, 66–72) and Judas (Mark 14:10–11, 17–21, 43–50), but in the fact that such rejection, alienation, and utter aloneness—the overwhelming experience of human sinfulness—led him to experience even his *Abbā,* the loving and caring Father on whom he had staked his whole life, as distant and removed. This is the profound insight of Mark's whole gospel, culminating in Jesus' cry of abandonment at the moment of his death.

Moltmann goes so far as to say that Jesus is rejected by his Father, that the cross divides God from God—creates a *stasis* within God so that the very deity of God is at stake. While there is an advantage to this way of putting it in that it does not allow us to domesticate the naked awesomeness of Jesus' experience of death, I would say that its truth lies not in a division within God but in the fact that on the cross God takes human divisiveness—death being the ultimate symbol of every human conflict—into his own life. The truth of the quotation from Goethe, viz. *Nemo contra Deum nisi Deus ipse,* is not that God *qua* God is divided against himself but that God *qua* Creator has freely chosen to create a world in which he risks his personal identity as Creator in the free response of his creatures. It is God's profound respect for the dignity and integrity of his creatures that creates the possibility of a *stasis* and it is his fidelity in creative love that finds a way to transform even that into the good of his beloved creatures.[2]

God embraces the world as it is. Just as it makes better sense to say that the world is in God rather than that God is in the world, so we can properly speak not of the death *of* God but of death *in* God. The divine answer to Jesus' question on the cross is contained in the early Christian proclamation: 'God raised Jesus'—the Father embraced the Son at the moment of his death and, in so doing, he embraced all of us as well. For me, the most moving image of resurrection is not in any of the Easter narratives, as beautiful as they are, but in the parable of the Prodigal Son. The son had become a

---

2. One of my students, Gary M. Scharff, has proposed what he calls a third option between Moltmann's notion of a division within God and my attempt to locate the act of separation in human sinfulness rather than in divine abandonment. He desires to take Jesus' cry of abandonment quite literally. He correctly notes: "Even in his anguish, Jesus knew the Father and his presence, and the power and effects of sin, too well to confuse the effects of sin with the absence of God." The heart of Scharff's argument, as I see it, is that the Creator, in order to remain faithful to his essence as love (which has taken the form of covenantal relationship in human history), must turn away from human sinfulness and hence abandon the human sinner to his or her own freely made choice. Sin has both a moral and an ontological power as it is factually constitutive of the human condition. Hence, it is not God but sin that brings about the death of creation. Jesus freely chose (this is a theological argument based on the cross and resurrection, not a psychologizing of Jesus) to identify himself with sinful humanity and so experienced the consequence of that choice in the Father's abandonment. As Scharff puts it: "The profound mystery of the crucifixion is that Jesus chose to love man in the fullest sense of identification—becoming fully us not *for* sin, but *in* and *despite* sin. He descended to the depths of a hell far crueler in its impact and more severe in its nothingness, than the chaos which preceded creation. He descended into the depths of sinfulness where even the Father, whose creative involvement in man is intrinsically and absolutely good, could not follow. If it were possible for the Father to experience these depths, the incarnation would not have been necessary for salvation. Jesus' crucifixion, as his last living act, culminated God's creation by plunging the full image of God beyond the nothingness of the chaos from which

swineherd, symbolic of the deepest degradation imaginable, but when the father sees him coming from a far way off he does not stand on his prerogatives and insist upon his rights but in a surprisingly undignified manner he runs down the path, embraces his son, and kisses him. The poignancy of the story lies in the completely unexpected and overwhelming generosity of the father's love. He sets no conditions to that love. He embraces the son completely and totally—even in his negativity. As Moltmann points out, the scandal of the cross is that the one who was raised was this man who had been condemned as a blasphemer, executed as a rebel, and had died as one cursed by God (Gal. 3:13). It is in this way that the cross interprets the resurrection, for God "became the kind of man we do not want to be: an outcast, accursed, crucified."[3]

The issue, as much for Paul in his proclamation of the cross as for Jesus in his proclamation of the Kingdom is the righteousness of God in history: the actuality of unconditional grace. In this fundamental insight, the proclamation of Jesus and Paul is identical, however much they may differ in the expression of it. What is crucial for Moltmann's approach is the conviction that for the Christian 'God' is what takes place between Jesus and the Father on the cross. To

---

Adam was called forth, into the uglier chaos of *sin,* from which Jesus was called forth in the resurrection. The creativity of God in Adam, as an affirmation of the goodness of human existence in his image called forth from nothingness, was deepened into an affirmation of the goodness of human existence in his image of Jesus, whom God called forth from the sinful human defiance of God. Thus the fidelity of Jesus to God and mankind in the crucifixion represents an absolute *gift* from the Son to the Father for the sake of mankind; the fidelity of God to Jesus and mankind in the resurrection represents an absolute *gift* from the Father to the Son for the sake of mankind." And further: "Jesus' death endured the abandonment of God by man as man absorbed himself into sin, and the abandonment of himself by God as Jesus drew man into himself, eliciting the Father's turning away from sin. God's experience of death was the abandonment of his own image by man in the rejection of Jesus, and his own abandonment of his Son as Jesus absorbed the broken image of man into himself for the sake of love." (Quotations from a paper turned in as a class assignment.) I would accept this qualification of my position as it focuses upon the human freedom of Jesus as the locus of God's creative-salvific love. In Chapter 5, I will attempt to demonstrate that it is precisely Jesus' human freedom that *constitutes* our salvation.

3. Moltmann, *Crucified* 205. On God's acceptance of us even in our negativity, Walter Kasper, *Jesus the Christ* (New York: Paulist Press, 1976) 58, remarks: "The compelling and convincing aspect of Jesus Christ is that in him both the greatness and the inadequacy of mankind are accepted, and accepted infinitely. In *that* sense, Jesus Christ is the fulfillment of history."

say "God is love" is to say that "God did not spare his own Son, but handed him over" (Rom. 8:32). This means, in Moltmann's terms, that God did not spare himself: the Father suffers the death of his Son in the infinite grief of love and the Son suffers dying because of his total response to that same love. The God in whom Christians believe should never, in the light of the cross, be looked upon as remote and untouched by our human pain. This God takes up death, and that means the *whole* of human history even in its deepest negativity, into his own inner life. This is what salvation means: not merely a negation but a fellowship. Church Fathers like Athanasius spoke of God becoming human so that we might participate in God. This means that God enters into real relations with his creatures and truly depends—not insofar as God is God but insofar as God freely chooses to be Creator—upon the free response of his creatures to his creative initiative in order to shape time.[4]

It is highly speculative, but can we imagine what the world in which we live today might be like had the response to Jesus been something other than rejection and crucifixion? That response two millennia ago has given shape to a history in which for the most part we have continued to crucify the innocent ones in our midst, including ourselves. Yet, the resurrection means that God remains faithful in his love even in the face of rejection. He does not suppress the contradiction in human experience (to do so would be to destroy us) but he suffers it for the sake of freedom. It is God's complete and total

---

4. I would stress the importance of analogy whenever we speak of the divine becoming, i.e., the absolute one-sideness of the relation. The creature in relation to God is both similar because entirely constituted by God in being and dissimilar because absolutely dependent in relatedness, while God *qua* God is only dissimilar because absolutely independent. Therefore, God can only be known on the basis of our relatedness to him and not in himself. However, the point about analogy is that we are saying something true about God and not merely indulging in anthropomorphisms. The above distinction is not intended to deny that God can and does enter into real relations with his creatures and so truly depends upon them *qua* Creator. What it does mean is that God's becoming is absolutely differentiated from human becoming "which rests on the individual incompletion of the changing subject, on the transition from potency to act . . ." Schoonenberg, *Christ* 84, n. 16. John H. Wright, S.J., "Divine Knowledge and Human Freedom," TS (1977): 450–477, employs a useful analogy when he speaks of "the God who dialogues" which involves the absolute free divine initiative, the free human response, and the divine response to the human response. One could say that Jesus' resurrection was the divine response to the human response of rejection. For a fuller development of these ideas, see chapter 5.

identity in the Son with the whole of human life—and especially with godlessness and godforsakenness—that makes it possible for us to accept the whole of our lives in the present and so to continue to trust in a promised future. Put simply, what Jesus reveals to each of us is that God loves *me* totally and unconditionally. He loves me for myself, not for anything I can say or do but simply because I am who I am, and he sets no conditions to that love. He does not say, '*if* you do such and such, *then* I will love you'. No, his love is the first act of creation and it never ceases to permeate all of creation. The realization of such love in the concrete experience of the gift of life that is mine is a tremendously freeing experience. It frees me to love as I have been loved: to love God for himself and without setting conditions to that love ('I will love you, God, *if* you are the kind of God I want . . .'); to love myself, accepting the gift of life that is mine, not seeking to live up to expectations—my own or others'—that alienate me from my true self, but embracing the gift that is mine and living it to the full; and, finally, to love others for themselves, because they are who they are, without setting conditions that would force them to live up to my expectations of who they should be.

From what has been said so far, one can say that the proclamation of Jesus' death and resurrection has the same intention as Jesus' own proclamation: to open us to the free acceptance of God's freely given and overwhelmingly generous love that commits us to life itself at the deepest level of our humanness. This is one level of identity between Jesus and the early Church, but the latter understood another level of identity as inseparable from this message, viz. the personal identity of Jesus himself. It is this same Jesus who proclaimed the Kingdom of God who is now proclaimed as Christ and Lord. Now identity involves a crucial difference: Jesus himself is the message. Is this a legitimate shift in focus? It can only be so if Jesus' fate (death *and* resurrection) is not only confirmatory of his prior mission and therefore revelatory in a purely noetic sense but is first of all determinative of who he is in an ontological sense.[5]

---

5. This is the approach taken by Pannenberg, *Jesus* 127–158. Jesus' person can only be understood as a *whole*. While the resurrection is the decisive event, the idea that Jesus had received divinity only as a consequence of his resurrection is not tenable. Rather, the resurrection event has *retroactive* power. Jesus did not simply become something that he previously had not been, but his pre-Easter claim was

In order to come to terms with this question, we must first consider what sorts of claims are being made for Jesus in the original
proclamation of his resurrection. Fuller maintains: ". . . what occurred in the 'visions' is not merely that God produced faith in the
resurrection. Rather, he revealed to them *Jesus* as the One he had
raised from the dead. The Easter testimony asserts an act of God not
merely upon the disciples but a prior act of God upon Jesus himself. . . ."[6] The first task is to investigate the earliest witnesses in order to find out what claims *they* were making. One may subsequently
choose to disagree with such claims, but at least one should be clear
that it is disagreement with the earliest tradition and not simply interpretation (*pace* Bultmann).

If something happened to Jesus and not merely to the disciples,
then this event has theological implications that move beyond the
question of soteriological continuity to that of explicit christological
judgments. Hence, in the following chapter, we will be concerned to
explore the transition to explicit christology in the light of the resurrection and how that christology develops from a more eschatological (imminent expectation of the end) to a more experiential
(continuing life in the Spirit) focus. Corresponding to this development, as Reginald Fuller has maintained in opposition to Oscar Cullmann,[7] there is already—prior to Paul's writings—a move from a
merely functional view (Jesus as God's agent) to ontic affirmations

---

confirmed by God. This confirmation is the new thing brought by the Easter event
(135). Yet, the retroactive power of Jesus' resurrection means that Jesus' essence is
established not only for our knowledge (noetic) but in its being (ontological). This implies a concept of essence that is contrary to the Greek philosophical tradition: ". . .
for thought that does not proceed from a concept of essence that transcends time, for
which the essence of a thing is not what persists in the succession of change, for
which, rather, the future is open in the sense that it will bring unpredictably new
things that nothing can resist as absolutely unchangeable—for such thought only the
future decides what something is." (136) Schematically, I would put it as follows: 'becoming' is a continuous process involving both identity and difference, while 'being'
is the terminus or end of the process and hence involves only identity. That is, at this
moment in the process, we both are and are not what we will be at the end of the
process. For a fuller development of Pannenberg's position, see chapter 5.

6. Fuller, *Foundations* 142 (italics mine).

7. Ibid. 247ff. For functional approaches to christology, see Oscar Cullmann,
The Christology of the New Testament (Philadelphia: Westminster, 1963); John A. T.
Robinson, *The Human Face of God* (Philadelphia: Westminster, 1973); and, more re-
cently Hans Kueng, *On Being a Christian* (New York: Doubleday, 1976).

(Jesus as *somehow* God's way of being human) which in turn raise ontological questions (how?). It will be maintained that it was a profound intuition of the early Christian communities, experienced primarily in worship and expressed in hymns, to move beyond phenomenological descriptions of Jesus' activity to affirmations about his ontic identity. Jesus' uniqueness as the definitive and irrevocable 'place' of God's self-communication in word[8] is not adequately grounded in a description of Jesus as the one who speaks the truth about the human condition. Jesus is God's Word because in his personal identity he *is* the truth about the human condition, especially at the moment of death. Only an identity in being with the divine can adequately ground the Christian *claim* that Jesus is unique among all the savior figures in human history. There are those who would dispute the need and the advisability of preserving that claim.[9] In my opinion, it is of the very essence of Christianity both for those who first received the revelation of Jesus' resurrection and who developed the implications of that revelation under the inspiration of Jesus' Spirit and for those who today would stand in continuity with that tradition.

B. The Divine Vindication: Resurrection

Reginald Fuller, in his book *The Formation of the Resurrection Narratives,*[10] offers one of the best critical studies on the New Testament data available today. In what follows, rather than repeat what he has already more than adequately treated, I will seek primarily to engage his book at certain critical points in order to outline my own somewhat distinctive view. There is certainly much more in which I agree with Fuller than disagree, but there are certain key points of difference that affect one's understanding of the whole.

---

8. This is the approach taken by Hodgson, *Jesus* 136ff.

9. Most recently, see John Hick (ed.), *The Myth of God Incarnate* (Philadelphia: Westminster, 1977) which denies that the idea of the incarnation is essential to Christianity.

10. Reginald H. Fuller, *The Formation of the Resurrection Narratives* (New York: Macmillan, 1971). See also S. H. Hooke, *The Resurrection of Christ as History and Experience* (London: Darton, Longman, & Todd, 1967); C. F. Evans, *Resurrection and the New Testament* (London: SCM, 1970); and Willi Marxsen, *The Resurrection of Jesus of Nazareth* (London: SCM, 1970).

The first thing to be noted is that the language of *egēgertai* (1 Cor. 15:4b) and *ēgerthē* (Mark 16:6; Luke 24:34) is derivative from late Jewish apocalyptic (cf. Isa. 26:19; Dan. 12:2–3; Enoch 51; 92:3). The divine passive denotes the interventive activity of God for those who are dead and in the grave. The word itself is a metaphor referring to the common experience of waking from sleep but, in the apocalyptic context, it connotes a transition from this age to the age to come. Hence, the notion of resurrection does not involve a return to this life in the manner of a resuscitated corpse (such as Lazarus who still had death ahead of him) but the transformation of one's personal existence beyond death. When Paul seeks to articulate the nature of this transformed existence, he makes use of a number of natural analogies, the most striking of which in my opinion is the phrase *sōma pneumatikon* (1 Cor. 15:44b). I interpret *sōma* to refer to the whole body-person, to the individual identity or self of the person in his or her entire psychosomatic existence. While *pneumatikon* can be understood generically as in the usual translation 'spiritual body', it is certainly rooted in Paul's theology of the Spirit of God. That is to say, in resurrection God's Spirit touches and transforms this body-person so completely that he or she enters into an utterly new existence which can be characterized in terms of the traditional understanding of Adam's and Eve's existence in the Garden of Eden, viz. as involving union with God (supernatural grace), harmony with oneself (integrity), and victory over death (immortality). Continuity should be stressed here both in the sense of identity (it is the *same* person) and in the sense of difference (the Spirit overcomes the alienation of that person from God, self, and others—what we call sin— and so effects a true transformation). What Paul is giving us, in effect, is a *theological* understanding of something that simply transcends our experience and can only be spoken about by way of analogy or metaphor.

If resurrection is beyond death, then by definition it is beyond history. As such it is more exact to speak of it not as an historical event but as a "meta-historical" event. Fuller's explanation of this term is worth quoting at length:

By this we do not mean to suggest that nothing transpired between God and Jesus, but rather that what took place between God and Jesus took place at the boundary between history and meta-history, between this age and the age to come. As such, the resurrection leaves only a negative mark within history: 'he is not here' (Mark 16:6). The positive aspect, 'he was raised', is not an event within history, but an event beginning at the end of history, and extending into the beyond-history. It is an event which can be known, not by direct observation, but only, as we shall see, by indirect revelatory disclosure within history.[11]

An historian, by reason of his methodological presuppositions, can only deal with the fact that shortly after Jesus' death some of his followers claimed that he had been raised from the dead and with the consequences that that claim has had upon subsequent human history, but he cannot verify or falsify the truth of the claim itself. Even the first witnesses could not directly observe the resurrection itself insofar as it occurs precisely at the end of history and the witnesses still stand within history. They were given an "indirect revelatory disclosure" (what we will treat shortly under the rubric of the appearances) to which the only response is either faith or unfaith. Peter and the rest were not exempted from faith because they saw. Rather, their 'seeing' was a 'believing seeing' (Ebeling). In turn, they could only proclaim what had been revealed to them and call others to believe not in themselves but in the revelation which they all preached. "Whether then it was I or they, so we preach and so you believed" (1 Cor. 15:11; note that *episteusate* forms an inclusion in vv. 2, 11).

One final important point before considering the texts in more detail is that the proclamation centers on "Jesus of Nazareth, the crucified one" (Mark 16:6b). The development of titles such as Lord and Christ (Acts 2:36; note *Christos* at 1 Cor. 15:3b and *ho Kyrios* at Luke 24:34) will be considered later. The important point here is that it was *this man* Jesus who was condemned as a blasphemer, crucified as a rebel, and died as one forsaken by God whom God has raised from the dead. The scandal is in the concrete particularity of

---

11. Fuller, *Formation* 23. Pannenberg, *Jesus* 98 tries to establish the resurrection as an historical event. See the criticism of this attempt in Evans, *Resurrection* 180ff. This is also developed further in chapter 5.

Jesus. It also grounds the uniqueness of this revelation, making it revelation in the strict sense *(eph' hapax),* for it could not be surmised from either nature or history (general revelation) but could only be known through revelatory disclosure and in no other way. Moreover, Jesus was raised as "the first fruits of those who have fallen asleep" (1 Cor. 15:20). By this, Paul means not only that he was the first instance in a series but that his resurrection is determinative for everyone else: "For as in Adam all die, so also in Christ shall all be made alive" (1 Cor. 15:22). This implies that the uniqueness of the revelation includes the uniqueness of Jesus himself, that the soteriological significance leads naturally to christological considerations for it is only by participating in Jesus' unique relation to his *Abbā* through the power of his Spirit that we can realize the freedom of the children of God (Gal. 4:4–7; Rom 8:14–17).

Keeping in mind the theological character of resurrection as apocalyptic and meta-historical and the decisive centrality of the name Jesus for the early kerygma, we must now look in greater detail at that earliest kerygma and how it developed into narratives.

(1) *Early kerygma.* The earliest text that we have is 1 Corinthians 15:3–8. Paul emphasizes at the outset, using technical rabbinic terms, that he is handing on a tradition which he has received. One can only agree with Fuller's balanced conclusion that in its core formulation we have a Hellenized form of an originally Palestinian tradition and therefore we should look for a Hellenistic Jewish community in close touch with Palestine. The likeliest candidate is Damascus, the first community with which Paul came into contact.[12] My difficulty with Fuller's analysis at this point is that he separates off the appearance formula from the first three formulae as having a different origin, viz. Paul's first visit to Jerusalem. He says: "The first three formulae are of a different character from the fourth. They are summaries of three basic incidents in the event of salvation: 'he died', 'he was buried', and 'he was raised', whereas the fourth formula is a list of appearances which validates the last of the three statements, rather than an event of salvation in its own right."[13] One

---

12. See the whole discussion in Fuller, *Formation* 10–14.
13. Ibid. 14.

could argue that 'buried' validates 'died' as much as 'appeared' validates 'raised', but my real contention is that it is highly questionable whether the appearance to Simon Peter is not an intrinsic and essential part of the earliest kerygma. In Fuller's own terms, how could the proclamation 'he was raised' be possible at all without a "revelatory disclosure"? I would suggest that the earliest formula of the kerygma is Luke 24:34: *hoti ontōs ēgerthē* [*ho kyrios*] *kai ōphthē Simōni!* It is interesting that Luke, with his penchant for developing narratives, knows no narrative of an appearance to Peter. Rather, he inserts the kerygmatic formula at a very awkward point in the Emmaus narrative and thereby preserves the primacy of Peter's experience, a primacy echoed throughout the tradition: 1 Corinthians 15:5; Mark 16:7; Matthew 16:17–19; John 20:2–10; John 21.

At this point, it will be helpful to look more carefully at the structure of Paul's formulae. We can omit from present consideration the developing theological motifs of the general fulfillment of scripture *(kata tas graphas),* the atoning significance of Jesus' death *(huper tōn hamartiōn hēmōn),* and the apocalyptic day of the Lord *(tē hēmera tē tritē).* We can also omit Paul's remark to the Corinthians that some of the five hundred have died, but we must retain his witness to his own experience of an appearance as he is the only one who testifies in his own case and so can give us some insight into the nature of such appearances. Granting these qualifications, we come up with the following basic structure:

> *hoti* [*Christos*] *apethanen*
> *kai hoti etaphē*
> *kai hoti egēgertai*
> *kai hoti ōphthē Kēpha*
>> *eita tois dōdeka*
>>> *epeita ōphthē epanō pentakosiois adelphois eph' hapax*
>>> *epeita ōphthē Jakōbō*
>> *eita tois apostolois pasin.*
> *eschaton de pantōn . . . ōphthē kamoi.*

What I am suggesting, in disagreement with Fuller, is that we have a chiastic structure following the *hoti* clause in reference to Peter. The appearances to Peter and Paul stand outside this structure so that the elements within this chiasm have their own special significance.

Fuller points out that the *hoti* is used to combine four different traditions, which is true, but structurally they are parallel to one another. The appearance to Peter is not parallel to the appearance to James, as Harnack and others have maintained. I would suggest that the original formula could have been a simple variant of Luke 24:34: *hoti egēgertai [ho Jēsous] kai ōphthē Kēpha!* The fourth *hoti* was inserted in order to maintain the parallelism with what preceded and at the same time allow the distinct tradition about the various appearances, formulated into the chiastic structure perhaps by Paul himself, to be attached to the earlier tradition about the appearance to Peter. This has the advantage of retaining and indeed emphasizing the insight that *hoti* combined different traditions. It is introduced at this point precisely in order to distinguish what had originally been together (raised-appeared to Simon) so that a different tradition could be combined with it. Since Peter and Paul lie outside that tradition, we will first consider the implications of their experience as revelatory and then return to the special significance of the chiastic structure.

We will simply accept Fuller's analysis that in the LXX *ōphthē* with the dative has the meaning of 'appeared' in the sense of a revelatory disclosure in which the emphasis rests upon the revelatory initiative of the one revealing and not upon the experience of the recipient.[14] Paul gives us the only first-hand account of such an experience in Galatians 1:11–17 and this is precisely the way he recounts it. It was God who was pleased, as a free gift of grace, *apokalypsai ton huion autou en emoi* (Gal. 1:16). There was a purpose in this: that Paul might preach him among the Gentiles. But the experience itself was not handed on to him by men nor was he taught it; the gospel that he preached came to him *di' apokalypseōs Jēsou Christou* (Gal. 1:12). This is all the more surprising because of the way he had persecuted the Church but it serves to emphasize the completely unexpected and unique character of the revelation. Paul states emphatically that he did not confer with flesh and blood nor did he even go to Jerusalem to confer with Peter and James until three years

---

14. Ibid. 30–32.

after the experience (Gal. 1:16–20). In other words, the only way that Paul could have known about it is through a revelation in the strict sense, i.e., not through nature or history but only through a divine communication of meaning.

It is important to note that, unlike Acts 9:1–22; 22:3–21; 26:1–23, Paul nowhere attempts to describe the experience. It may well have involved either a visible or an auditory experience or both, as Fuller suggests from his analysis of Acts, but what is decisive is the communication of meaning that centers upon Jesus as the one whom Paul was persecuting (Acts) and who is now revealed as the Son of God (Gal. 1:16). This revelation involves for Paul, as for all who receive it, both a being called to faith and a being sent on mission.

The tradition is unanimous, it seems to me, in asserting or at least inferring the priority of Peter in relation to this revelatory disclosure. We have no first-hand account from Peter but it is interesting to note that when he confesses Jesus as the Christ, the Son of the living God (the same confessional terms used by Paul at Gal. 1:12, 16) his experience is described in exactly the same terms as Paul used: ". . . flesh and blood has not revealed this to you, but my Father who is in heaven . . ." (Matthew 16:17b). Contra Fuller, I would maintain that the appearance to Peter is not only "church-founding" (Peter as the rock) but also "mission-inaugurating." In fact, the distinction is artificial and somewhat forced as Fuller uses it. In Paul's view, the fact that he too has seen the Lord makes him an apostle as much as the others whom he has named. One of his major concerns expressed at 1 Corinthians 1:1; 9:1–2; 15:8–10 is to claim legitimacy for his mission as an apostle. Yet, at the same time, he sees himself as the founder of the Church at Corinth (1 Cor. 3:10; 4:14–16; 9:1–2). In fact, the one leads to the other for his apostleship, grounded in seeing the Lord, is sealed by the existence of the community at Corinth, his 'workmanship in the Lord' (1 Cor. 9:1–2). The order would seem to be that one first has a personal experience of being called to faith that involves simultaneously a being sent on mission to proclaim the good news. That proclamation gives rise to the Church as the community of those who have responded in faith and who now come together in *koinonia* and *diakonia* in order to 'build up' the body. Yet, that Church does not exist for its own sake but for the sake of the mission which is its origin and goal. What is true of Paul is true of Peter and of the others whom he lists for he sees his apostleship as being in continuity with theirs and he continually insists that there is only one gospel, only one revelation (Gal. 1:6–9; 1 Cor. 15:1–2, 11).

While recognizing that everyone who is called to be an apostle by reason of the revelatory disclosure given to each has the same missionary and ecclesial vocation as Peter and Paul, still I would suggest that the special significance of Paul's chiastic structure may be to reflect the above-mentioned order of mission—Church—mission. Thus the Twelve, in close connection with Peter who is one of them, evoke the missionary command of Jesus which, in conjunction with the motif of doubt that must be overcome by believing, is the common element in the narratives at Matthew 28:16–20; Luke 24:44–49; John 20:19–23. Note that Paul uses the symbolic number Twelve rather than the more realistic use of the eleven in Matthew and Luke. Forming an inclusion with the Twelve is the reference to all the apostles which, for Paul, would be anyone else who has received a true revelatory disclosure. This generic reference indicates that Paul's concern is more symbolic than chronological (*pace* Fuller). 'All the apostles' is an inclusive term that parallels the symbolism of the Twelve and at the same time enables Paul to include his own experience of being called to faith and sent on mission. It is clear that the change to *epeita* and the reintroduction of the verb *ōphthē* sets off the appearance to the more than 500 brethren at one time as a distinct event. I am attracted to the view that this may represent an earlier stage of the Pentecost tradition—note the verbal connection of *pentakosiois* with *pentēkostēs* at Acts 2:1—in which there was a communal experience of the risen Lord in the Spirit which may well have been the foundational experience of the Church at Jerusalem. This would also help to explain the appearance to James, which is in perfect parallelism with the preceding, since James emerged as the leader of the Church at Jerusalem (Gal. 2:9–12; Acts 12:17; 15:13–21).

Mark 16:1–8 belongs to this section on the early kerygma because Mark, unlike the other Evangelists, has no narratives of the appearances but only the proclamation: *ēgerthē, ouk estin hōde!* The function of the angelophany is precisely to underline that this is a revelatory disclosure. This motif is found in the Old Testament, e.g., in Moses' experience at the burning bush: "And the angel of the Lord appeared [ōphthē] to him" (Ex. 3:2). The further details of the stone being rolled back and the appearance of the angel, highlighted even more by Matthew and Luke, are intended to underline this fact. Also, since v. 7 is obviously a Marcan interpolation, v. 8 following after v. 6 reads as a natural reaction of the women to the overwhelming experience of divine revelation. Their *tromos kai ekstasis* could be interpreted along the lines of Rudolf Otto's insight into the experience of the holy as a *mysterium tremendum et fascinosum,* at once terrifying and fascinating.

What is new in Mark's account is the tradition of the empty tomb. Does this belong to the early kerygma? Fuller's conclusion that there is an historical core to the tradition seems reasonable: "Our analysis suggests that this is the earliest form of tradition: As soon as possible after the sabbath, Mary Magdalene visited the tomb to give Jesus a proper burial, but discovered the stone rolled away and the tomb empty."[15] It seems very likely that Jesus' disciples, overcome by the devastating experience of his death on the cross, scattered in confusion and fear so that Jesus was buried by his enemies (Acts 13:29). Mary Magdalene (the one person to whom all traditions point), in her distraught state (John 20:1, 11–15), made her way to the tomb and found it empty. In itself, the empty tomb is an ambiguous fact. Did she go to the wrong tomb? Did someone steal the body? Did God truly raise Jesus from the dead? The fact that Paul knows nothing of the empty tomb indicates that the appearances were originally independent of the empty tomb tradition. Given the revelatory disclosure that Jesus had truly been raised, then that faith can give a proper interpretation to the ambiguous fact of the empty tomb. Thus, the empty tomb presupposes faith; it does not prove it. Given the faith, it can function like the narrative of the appearances to concretize that faith as a resurrection from the grave that is transformative of the whole body-person (cf. the analysis of *sōma* above). Once the early kerygma had been associated with Mary's story of the empty tomb, then it was natural to develop the legendary elements of the angelophany in order to affirm unequivocally its proper interpretation (note especially the apologetic devel-

---

15. Ibid. 56.

opment at Matthew 27:62–66; 28:11–15). It is worth noting that the empty tomb itself has never been called into question, only its interpretation. On the assumption that there was a tomb that was known, could the early Church have proclaimed Jesus' resurrection, in the context of how that would be understood by their contemporaries, if his body lay in a tomb?

One of the great puzzles in Mark is how to interpret v. 7. Fuller outlines the various interpretations of seeing Jesus in Galilee that have been proposed: that it is an appearance (Fuller's position because of the naming of Peter), the place of the missionary command to go out to the Gentiles (Matthew's interpretation), or even the place of the parousia. The problem with all of these suggestions is that they depend on evidence extrinsic to the Gospel. When faced with such a conundrum, it is usually best to look for an interpretation internal to the Gospel itself. There is no indication in the text that Mark knows of an appearance to Peter. The understanding of Galilee must depend not on Matthew's interpretation but on how Mark uses it in his text. And the view that Mark's Gospel is primarily apocalyptic in character is, it seems to me, a distortion. At this point, I will only suggest an alternative interpretation that would need to be substantiated by a critical analysis of the whole Gospel.

There are three elements in v. 7 that require explanation: the naming of Peter, the meaning of *proagei,* and the significance for Mark of Galilee.[16] In the first half of the Gospel, Galilee is the 'place' of Jesus' ministry, a place of mysterious revelation fraught with ambiguity for Jesus appears as one who teaches with authority and performs signs and wonders yet continually experiences rejection: the leaders plot to kill him (3:6), the people of Nazareth reject him (6:1–6a), the disciples persist in misunderstanding him (8:14–21). A turning point comes with Peter's confession at Caesarea Philippi (8:27–30). At this point, Jesus invokes the messianic secret and for the first

---

16. The use of *opsesthe* ('you will see') has been the basis for considering this a parousia reference (cp. Mark 13:26; 14:62; 9:1). Yet, as Fuller points out (63), the same verb is used in the tradition for the appearances (1 Cor. 9:1; Matthew 28:17; John 20:18, 25, 29). Moreover, Perrin, *Rediscovering* 181–185, has shown that the parousia use came from an earlier passion apologetic, which would be closer to the interpretation I am suggesting. In any case, nothing can be decided on the basis of *opsesthe* alone.

time gives content to his teaching. He interprets the title 'Christ' in the direction of the Son of Man, not the Son of Man who will come at the end of the age but the Son of Man who must suffer and die. Peter rebukes Jesus for this and Jesus *seeing his disciples* lashes Peter with the harshest words he uses in the entire tradition. This leads to a discourse on discipleship that centers on taking up one's cross and following Jesus. This entire section (8:31–10:52—the major teaching section of the Gospel) is articulated by three passion predictions accompanied in the second and third by a notice on the misunderstanding and *fear* (cp. 16:8) of the disciples which leads to a paranesis on discipleship. In the second prediction, it is mentioned that they are passing through Galilee but Jesus does not want anyone to know it because his concentration is now upon bringing the disciples to understand the true nature of his ministry in terms of suffering and death (9:30–32). The third prediction is particularly interesting for it is said that they were 'on the way' (*en tē hodō*—Mark's technical term for going to the cross) going up to Jerusalem and Jesus was going before *(proagōn)* them. This is the first use of *proagein* that interests us and it is immediately associated with the amazement and fear of the disciples (the same words used of the women at the tomb). While Peter is not explicitly mentioned here, certainly his rebuke of Jesus stands out as the most distinctive reaction among the disciples. This section ends with the healing of blind Bartimaeus who is Mark's paradigm of a true disciple (the story forms a contrasting inclusion with the gradual healing at Bethsaida at 8:22–26): Bartimaeus is commended for his faith which gives him his sight and he follows *(ēkolouthei)* Jesus on the way *(en tē hodō)*.

For Mark, Jesus' identity is only revealed through the concrete story of his way to the cross which culminates in the centurion's confession at 15:39. The question of who Jesus is is inextricably intertwined with the question of who we are as disciples. It is only by concretely taking up our own cross and following Jesus that we will discover his identity and so our own. Peter is presented throughout as the one who denies the cross. Thus, Mark sets the saying at 14:28 (which is cross-referenced at 16:7) about Jesus going before *(proaxō)* them into Galilee after the resurrection in the context of his prediction of the disciples' failure and, in the face of Peter's protestations to the contrary, of his prediction of Peter's denial (14:26–31). The meaning of 14:28 is obviously to inject a note of hope in the face of that failure. What Jesus is saying, in effect, is that it is only in the light of his death and resurrection that they will finally come to understand and accept the meaning of his ministry. Galilee as the 'place' of that ministry was necessarily fraught with ambiguity for Jesus, mighty in word and work, can only be properly understood in the light of the cross. At 16:7, which is Mark's version of the rehabilitation of the disciples and Peter, the reader is being told in effect to take another look at the ministry in Galilee in the light of the death-resurrection in order to understand Jesus on a deeper level than that of a mere wonder-worker *(theios anēr)* and so to understand your own Christian existence as well.

Yet, the ambiguity remains. For the women's fear with which the Gospel ends is equivalent to unbelief. Mark is throwing up a challenge to his community and to us as well. The resurrection does not remove all ambiguity and doubt. It is a call to faith which will enable us, like Bartimaeus, to see and to follow Jesus on the way.

(2) *Development of narratives.* The canonical gospels, unlike the apocryphal Gospel of Peter, do not try to describe the resurrection itself. Such a description would be impossible if, as we have maintained, the resurrection itself was a meta-historical event and therefore inaccessible to direct observation by witnesses who would still be standing within history. Hence, the earliest strata of the tradition do not attempt to narrate the resurrection but only to proclaim it. As we have seen from the above analysis, this proclamation was made possible by an indirect revelatory disclosure which was accessible to those still standing within history, viz. to Peter and the rest. This was a revelation in the strict sense, which is to say that there was no other way that the content of what was revealed could have been known to them; not the possibility of resurrection in general but the fact that *this man Jesus* had been raised from the dead. This revelatory experience did not exempt the recipients from faith but was precisely a call to faith that included a being sent on mission. It is interesting that all the Evangelists (Mark 16:8; Matthew 28:17; Luke 24:11, 25, 36–43; John 20:8–9, 24–29) make use of the motif of doubt and unbelief, for their own purposes to be sure, but it remained an element that could not be excised from the earliest memory of the appearances. Correlative to this, Paul's theology of justification by

faith as central and decisive for Christian existence could only have developed from his own experience of revelatory disclosure as a faith experience.

This is the earliest kerygma, but once Mary Magdalene's story of the empty tomb was associated with the earliest proclamation it was natural for narratives to develop, first in connection with the tomb as an angelophany whereby the basic kerygma is communicated and then, as christological thinking began to develop, as a Christophany independently of the tomb. In what follows, Matthew will be seen as representing the transitional stage in this development, Luke as carrying it to literal extremes, and John as representing something of a polemic against over-exaggerating its importance. In general, it is my contention that the narratives should not be understood as literal happenings but as ways of bringing out concretely the meaning of the revelation. Like the empty tomb, the appearance stories function to concretize the early Church's faith-image of the risen Lord. It should be noted that there is a certain freedom of belief at this point. All Christians are called in faith to believe that God has truly raised Jesus from the dead. And I believe that that must be interpreted, along the lines already indicated, as something that really happened to Jesus because this is the claim Peter, Paul, and all the apostles were making. My reason for rejecting a literal understanding of the appearance stories lies not only in their rather late and legendary character but primarily in the very nature of resurrection as apocalyptic, meta-historical event. The stories are difficult, if not impossible, to accept literally because the risen Jesus stands beyond death in an utterly transformed existence. As such, it seems unnecessary to imagine that he actually returned to this life in the manner of a resuscitated corpse who actually eats and drinks with his disciples. If he did so once, why did he not remain and establish his Kingdom as risen Lord upon the earth? Combined with the observation that the narratives are later developments and clearly legendary in character, it seems more reasonable to treat them, like the gospel form itself, as a mode of theological presentation.

For our present purposes, it is not necessary to offer an extensive and detailed analysis of the resurrection narratives in each author, but only to indicate the lines of development and what they contribute to our theological understanding. We will consider, in turn, Matthew 28, Luke 24, and John 20. John 21 and Mark 16:9–20, as much later developments with their own special concerns, need not be treated here.

A comparison of Matthew 28:1–8 with Mark 16:1–8 shows clearly the developing tendency to elaborate the legendary elements of the apocalyptic event in connection with the empty tomb. Aside from legendary embellishments, there are two key changes that Matthew makes: at the end of v. 7 he changes Mark's cross-reference to Jesus' prediction into a statement of the angel ("Behold, I have told you") and in v. 8 the women run to tell the disciples. Both prepare for what follows. The first allows for the transition from the angelophany to the parallel scene of the Christophany in vv. 9–10. Such a Christophany to the women is not known in Paul and Mark and so does not belong to the early tradition. Fuller remarks: "One can only conclude that the earlier tradition of the angelophany to the women had been later converted into a Christophany."[17] This Christophany marks the beginnings of the tendency first to associate the appearances with the empty tomb and to locate them in Jerusalem (Luke 24; John 20) and second to materialize the appearances by modeling them on encounters with Jesus during his earthly ministry (in this case already developed in the direction of the *theios anēr* as at Mark 5:6, 22). The second change, the women running to tell the disciples, prepares the way for the scene of the great commission on the mountain in Galilee (vv. 16–20). This is the culmination of Matthew's Gospel and is clearly impregnated with his own theological motifs. It is important to note that we do not have a *narrative* of an appearance here but a theological statement put in the words of an already exalted Lord speaking for all times to his Church. He now has "all authority" in the most comprehensive sense possible, i.e., "in heaven and on earth." Fuller maintains that Matthew has changed a "church-founding" appearance (to the Twelve) into a "mission-inaugurating" one. It is true that Jesus is giving a missionary charge to go out to all the nations, modeled very likely on the missionary charges of the earthly Jesus (cp. Matthew 10:5), but the artificiality of Fuller's distinction is demonstrated by the fact that the content of this commission is put entirely in ecclesial terms (a major motif

---

17. Fuller, *Formation* 78.

of the Gospel), viz. to make *disciples,* to baptize, to teach the new Torah, and to realize Jesus' communal presence (cp. Matthew 18:20) until the end of the age.

There are two conclusions to be drawn. The first is that Matthew's own version of the appearance in Galilee, which is his interpretation of Mark 16:7, stays close to the early kerygma. It is an appearance to the eleven which is revelatory (the mountain) involving a 'seeing' *(idontes)* to which the response is either belief (worship) or unbelief (doubt). Notice how he retains the motif at Mark 16:8 in his own way without elaborating on it. Finally, the appearance involves the recognition that it is Jesus (now exalted Lord who is with them to the end of the age) and that their call in faith is at once missionary and ecclesial. The second conclusion is that Matthew's distinctive Christophany, paralleling the angelophany that he has taken over from Mark, is the subdued beginning of a tendency to develop an 'epiphany' style of appearances of the risen but not yet ascended Lord at Jerusalem employing *theios anēr* traits.

It is in Luke, no doubt drawing upon earlier stories but using them for his own theological purposes, that we see this latter tendency carried to its most extreme in the canonical sources. Yet, it would be a mistake to see this as Luke's primary emphasis. He retains the basic kerygmatic formulae (24:19d–20 is reminiscent of Acts 2:22–23; 10:37–39; Luke 24:34 is the earliest formula; cp. 24:46) and his key concern is to develop the apologetic notion that Jesus' death and resurrection is in fulfillment of the divine plan *(dei)* as clearly manifest in "all the scriptures" (24:25–27, 44–46; cp. Paul's use of *kata tas graphas* at 1 Cor. 15:3–4). Also, the missionary command at 24:47–49 is similar to Matthew's in its implicit reference to baptism and in its being a mission to all nations. The Emmaus story is clearly folkloric in character, as Fuller shows. Jesus is presented as he would have been known to his disciples prior to his death: as one who walks with them on the way and explains the scriptures to them, as one who enters their homes and breaks bread with them. There are 'divine man' traits here, e.g., his sudden appearance and disappearance, but Luke has impregnated the story with his theological motifs of the divine plan in scripture and of the breaking of the bread and has climaxed it with the basic kerygma: "The Lord has truly been raised and has appeared to Simon!" He returns to his basic motif of scriptural fulfillment and introduces the missionary command and the expectation of the Spirit in vv. 44–49. Sandwiched in between (vv. 36–43) is a massively physical demonstration undoubtedly occasioned by the motif of doubt in the sources.

It is in these verses that the 'epiphany' style is carried to its most extreme and that the problem of what we are being asked to believe becomes most acute. In fact, as Fuller points out, it runs contrary to the early kerygma. His remarks are worth quoting at length:

> This new interpretation of the mode of the resurrection (resuscitation of the earthly body) is quite contrary to the apocalyptic framework of the earliest kerygma of 1 Corinthians 15:5, to Paul's concept of the *pneumatikon sōma* (see esp. 1 Cor. 15:35ff.) and to the presentation in Mark 16:1–8 and in Matthew 28:16–20. But it was made inevitable by the development of appearance narratives. We have already had an example of materialization in Matthew 28:9 which, however, is contrary to the general tenor of the Matthean presentation. For appearances could be narrated only by borrowing the traits of the earthly Jesus—he must walk, talk, eat, etc., as he had done in his earthly life. These features, at first conceived quite naively (as in the Emmaus story) are now drawn out and emphasized in the interests of apologetic.[18]

Three things should be noted here. First, this scene is clearly subordinate to the theological motifs derived from the basic kerygma that Luke has received. Second, Luke makes use of these narratives for his own theological scheme of salvation history in which the resurrection functions as a bridge between the time of Jesus' earthly ministry and the time of the exalted Lord's presence to the Church. Luke is the only author to make a clear distinction between the resurrection and the ascension. And third, the intention of this physical demonstration is to make a theological point, viz. that it is the *same Jesus* whom the disciples knew prior to his death who continues to live beyond death. The narratives, then, function to concretize that

---

18. Ibid. 115.

fundamental religious truth that is present on all levels of the tradition. Luke undoubtedly received these narratives in a more primitive form from his sources. He probably accepted them as factual and made use of them for his own theological purposes (cp. the same procedure in the infancy narratives). Does the likelihood that he accepted them as factual mean that we must do the same? An analogy could be drawn to the story of Adam and Eve in Genesis. In order to accept the religious truth that the story embodies, it is not necessary to accept the story itself as literal fact. Yet, it is important to realize that the religious truth is not simply an idea of universal import but is itself a *fact,* viz. the fact that God has created the world as good and that evil has entered into that creation through human sinfulness. The important question both there and here is: what is the *indispensable* fact that is the very essence and ground of our faith commitment? In the case of the resurrection, it is the fact that God has truly raised this man Jesus from the dead. One way, indeed the best way, of communicating that fact is by telling stories.

John, like Luke, retains the primacy of the basic kerygma and makes use of the appearance stories for his own theological purposes. One of those purposes, perhaps the primary one, is to offer a polemic in the context of his own community against over-exaggerating the importance of seeing the Lord in order to believe. Taking the various pericopae of John 20 in the order in which they are presented, I will simply highlight the factors that suggest such a motif.

John 20:2–10, the story of Peter and the disciple whom Jesus loved running to the tomb, is interpolated into the story of Mary Magdalene at the tomb. Its purpose, it seems to me, is to provide an inclusion between v. 8 and v. 29. The beloved disciple functions in John as the one who has the correct insight into what is going on. In this case, it is emphasized that he is the one (not Peter) who believed simply on the basis of the empty tomb without benefit of an appearance or of an explanation of the scriptures. But, it was he alone of the disciples who was present at the foot of the cross and who saw Jesus' side pierced so that blood and water came out and who, by implication then, was the one who bore witness to it that we might believe (John 19:26, 34–35). This is important, for in John Jesus' exaltation (ascension?) takes place on the cross (John 12:32–33). John is similar to Mark in that the true revelation of Jesus is on the cross. If one understands that, then one has no need of massive physical demonstrations and so is blessed for not seeing yet believing (v. 29).

The subsequent pericopae reinforce this basic theme. John 20:11–18, the scene with Mary Magdalene, is a revelatory encounter in which Mary recognizes Jesus but misunderstands the nature of the encounter. When Jesus says to her: *mē mou haptou* ('do not cling to me': v. 17), we have a piece of Johannine irony in which Jesus is saying, in effect, do not misunderstand this revelatory encounter as a return of your earthly teacher (*rabbouni*) to resume the same kind of relationship that existed during his earthly ministry. That person is a figure of the past. The reason given, *oupō gar anabebēka pros ton patera* ('for I have not yet ascended to the Father'), would then mean that Mary's misunderstanding is preventing the completion of Jesus' work, i.e., as long as she continues to misunderstand the nature of this encounter his work *(katabasis)* is not yet complete and therefore he cannot yet be said to have 'ascended' *(anabasis)*. Therefore, she is to tell the brethren that he is in the process of ascending which leads into the next pericope.

In John 20:19–23, Jesus appears to the disciples and immediately shows them his hands and his side, i.e., he points to the cross as the 'place' whereby they might recognize him. It was on the cross, at the moment of his death, that he handed over the Spirit (John 19:30). Hence, the following missionary command refers back to the cross where Jesus breathed forth his Spirit and won forgiveness. Now he breathes that Spirit upon the disciples and gives them the mission of forgiveness. The important point, for our purposes, is that the focus of this scene is on the cross. Their reception of the Spirit gives them the correct understanding of the cross in terms of their mission. Once this is done, Jesus' work could be said to be completed so that he has ascended to the Father—were it not for doubting Thomas.

The final scene, John 20:24–29, is intended to form an inclusion with the first scene and to emphasize polemically that a proper understanding of the cross is sufficient for faith. John does not deny the tradition of physical demonstration (Thomas is invited to touch his hands and side, although there is obvious irony in the exact repetition of his words) but he does downgrade the importance of such physical demonstrations. Thomas does not touch but sees, yet "blessed are those who not seeing still have believed." That this scene concludes Jesus' work is shown in the fact that Thomas' confession of faith transcends even what he sees: *ho kyrios mou kai ho theos mou!*

With this we bring to a conclusion our investigation of the early witnesses to the resurrection in order to find out what claims they were making. The most essential and ineradicable affirmation of their faith is that it was this man Jesus who has truly been raised and that he now lives an utterly transformed existence beyond death. This affirmation has implications for Jesus' personal identity as that was experienced prior to his death and continued to be experienced in the faith community. We must now investigate how the event of Jesus' death and resurrection, understood initially and most fundamentally on the soteriological level, developed into explicit christology.

CHAPTER FOUR

The Proclaimer as Proclaimed

The eschatological event of Jesus' death-resurrection brings us quite literally to the crux of Christian understanding: the question of continuity between the Jesus of history and the Christ of faith. A proper understanding of continuity within historical process involves both identity and difference. Identity emphasizes the truth of the traditional dogma of incarnation that "Jesus did not become the Son of God only after his death, but was and is Son of God already as the historical Jesus." Hence, "The faith of the days after Easter knows itself to be nothing else but the right understanding of the Jesus of the days before Easter."[1] On the other hand, the difference lies not simply in the fact that Jesus' cause can now continue as proclaimable without limitation (Ebeling, Marxsen) but that something new is now being proclaimed, a 'new creation' which is first constitutive of Jesus himself in his personal identity and only so revelatory to us of who he is (Pannenberg). This is to say that the truth of the incarnation, the basis or ground for our speaking of his unity with God,[2] can only be known through the revelation of his life as a *whole*. From this perspective, incarnation is not seen to be the starting point but rather the conclusion of a christology. In what follows, we must hold these two aspects of identity and difference in a tensive unity if we are to maintain as equally valid Jesus' proclamation of the Kingdom for all human persons and the Church's proclamation of Jesus as the unique savior of the world.

---

1. Gerhard Ebeling, "The Question of the Historical Jesus and the Problem of Christology," *Word and Faith* 298, 302. Cp. Marxsen, *Resurrection*, who summarizes this approach in his famous phrase: "Die Sache Jesu geht weiter."
2. This is the approach taken by Pannenberg, *Jesus* 53ff. See above. 92–94.

Our concern, as mentioned in the last chapter, is twofold: to explore the transition from the soteriological concerns of Jesus to the explicit christology of the early Church and to investigate the development of christology in the light of subsequent experience. We wish not only to analyze the various stages of the development historically but also to ask the more fundamental questions of why such a vital move was made and whether or not it can be justified theologically. Hence, it must be recalled at the outset that Jesus' ministry was prophetic in character. He spoke in terms of crisis/resolution. The crisis of his present experience of rejection would have its resolution in the divine activity of vindication prophetically symbolized by the apocalyptic image of 'the day of the Son of Man'. This vindication included his disciples insofar as he gave them his mission to proclaim the Kingdom of God. As they were associated with him in his rejection, so they would be with him in his vindication. It must be remembered that it was they who forsook him and fled in fear at his arrest. The memory of Jesus' word must have had a particularly shattering poignancy for Simon Peter: "Whoever acknowledges me before men will be acknowledged before the angels of God, but the one who denies me before men will be denied before the angels of God" (Luke 12:8–9 par, as reconstructed by Perrin).

For the early Church in the person of Peter and the rest, the ultimate crisis was Jesus' rejection on the cross and the resolution of that crisis came in the revelatory disclosure that the Father had indeed raised Jesus from the dead. As we have seen, it was the conviction of the earliest proclamation of the resurrection that it was Jesus, the Nazarene, the crucified one (Mark 16:6b) who was raised. This means that the divine vindication took the form of God acting in Jesus. This was begun in Jesus' eschatological proclamation of the Kingdom, consummated in the decisive eschatological event of his death-resurrection, and would continue in the Church's eschatological proclamation until the consummation of all things.[3] The effect of this upon the disciples was the realization that their own vindication would only be possible if they could resume the fellowship they had

---

3. See Fuller, *Foundations* 142–143.

with Jesus prior to his death.[4] This would explain the emphasis upon this motif in the resurrection narratives. However, such fellowship was not a simple return to the relationship as it had been for the event of Jesus' resurrection was an apocalyptic event. It was this event that made it possible for the early Church to identify Jesus with the Son of Man in apocalyptic terms. It was the combination of Jesus' use of the apocalyptic image of the Son of Man and the apocalyptic event of resurrection as something that happened to Jesus which enabled the early Church to take the step to an explicit christology. Keeping in mind then the conclusions that we have reached so far in our study, we must now investigate more closely this "transition from the soteriological use of the name Son of Man in Jesus' teaching to the christological understanding in the primitive community."[5]

---

4. Toedt, *Son of Man* 253–265. See also "Excursus III: Discussion of the concept 'fellowship with Jesus'," 306–311.

5. Ibid. 226–231. I am relying heavily here on Toedt's analysis and Fuller's use of it, but with my own modifications. It is important to note the hypothetical character of this reconstruction. It is dependent upon the distinction between "Jewish" and "Hellenistic" categories as proposed by Wilhelm Bousset in his *Kyrios Christos: Geschichte des Christusglaubens von den Anfangen des Christentums bis Irenaeus* (Goettingen: Vandenhoeck und Ruprecht, 1913; rev. ed. 1921, 1965; ET 1970 by Abingdon). This distinction was employed extensively by Rudolf Bultmann and modified into three categories (Palestinian-Jewish, Hellenistic-Jewish, and Hellenistic-Gentile) by Ferdinand Hahn in *Titles*. It is this latter categorization that Reginald Fuller in *Foundations* uses extensively. Larry W. Hurtado, "New Testament Christology: A Critique of Bousset's Influence," TS 40 (1979) 306–317, maintains that the contemporary discussion has moved beyond Bousset and has rendered questionable at least three of his positions: "Bousset's view of early Christianity as divisible into the two pre-Pauline stages of Jewish Christianity and Hellenistic Christianity, his view of the earliest form of Christology as an apocalyptic Son of Man Christology, and his contention that the Kyrios title reflected a Christology that was possible only in a non-Palestinian setting dominated by pagan religious influence" (307). Since these are close to the positions being developed in this chapter, a few comments seem in order. First, while I would agree that the cultural background of early Christianity cannot be reduced to "rigid categories" because there was obviously Greek-speaking influence in Palestine, I think the categories are useful for reconstructing 'tendencies', i.e., the earliest followers of Jesus, being Palestinian fishermen, etc., would tend to be 'more' Palestinian and hence more resistant to hellenizing, while the emerging experience of the Hellenistic missions, both Jewish and Gentile, would tend to be 'more' Hellenistic and hence less resistant to new developments. It is not necessary to draw a straight chronological line here, but simply to see the possibility of real diversity based upon different environmental predispositions. The categories are useful as providing

A. KERYGMA OF THE EARLIEST CHURCH:
PALESTINIAN JUDAISM

Our concern is with the beginnings of christology, with what John A. T. Robinson has termed "the most primitive Christology of all." Fuller sets the scene: "Jesus had declared that his own eschatological word and deed would be vindicated by the Son of Man at the end. Now his word and deed had received preliminary yet certain vindication by the act of God in the resurrection. The earliest Church expressed this new-born conviction by identifying Jesus with the Son of Man who was to come."[6] Fuller, following Toedt, accepts Luke 12:8 par, along with all those future sayings that make a distinction between Jesus and the Son of Man, as authentic sayings that go back to Jesus. If our earlier analysis is correct, Jesus used the image of Son of Man as a prophetic symbol of the *divine activity,* not of his own or someone else's activity. My difficulty with Luke 12:8 par as it stands is that it is already a *personalized* use of the Son of Man imagery. Hence, following Toedt but with that modification, I would suggest the following sequence. Once the earliest community made the move from the soteriological use of the image to the chris-

---

a 'framework' to study this diversity. Moreover, I would agree with Hurtado's conclusions that more attention should be given in the study of New Testament christology to Old Testament background and to the earthly Jesus. The titles must be understood in relation to the *whole* of the Jesus experience from creation to parousia, as I am attempting to do in this book. Hence, they should not become the sole focus of christology. My second comment is to agree that Son of Man is not a pre-Christian *title* with a clear and distinct meaning. In chapter 2, I have indicated that the expression is a cipher to be filled with content and have tried to show how Jesus might have used it as a symbol for divine vindication. I would still maintain that it provides our most solid link in understanding the earliest development of the use of titles for Jesus. Finally, my third comment is that the possibility of an equivalence in theological content between *Mārêh* and *Kyrios* (indefinite) or between *Mārya* and *ho Kyrios* (definite/emphatic), while it cautions us against a too rigid separation between Aramaic and Greek, still does not vitiate the real differences between the two in terms of their 'tendencies'. Moreover, in closer agreement with Hurtado's point, I will seek to show that the earliest christological judgment that Jesus is the Son of Man already contains the whole of christology *in nuce. Mārêh* is an extension of that. In this connection, I would add to Hurtado's list of Old Testament background and earthly Jesus, the crucial importance of worship in the Spirit.

6. Fuller, *Foundations* 143–144. Cf. J. A. T. Robinson, "The Most Primitive Christology of All?" *Twelve New Testament Studies* (London: SCM Press, 1962) 139–153.

tological judgment that Jesus is the Son of Man, then it sought to apply that insight in closest connection with Jesus' own usage. The image had come from Jesus, hence it remains always on his own lips. The image was used by Jesus for soteriological purposes, hence the earliest application of it was to sayings of Jesus that maintained what Toedt calls the "differentiating way of speaking." Thus, the earliest application would very likely be Luke 12:8 par which, as a personalized use of the image, has already moved from Jesus' focus upon the divine activity to a focus upon an individual figure who, in the light of the resurrection, could only be Jesus.

The second step, in close connection with the first, is derived from the experience of the resurrection as an apocalyptic event. If Jesus' word about the divine vindication led to his identification as the Son of Man, then in apocalyptic terms he is the Son of Man who will come at the end of the age for divine judgment. Fuller, referring to the work of Ernst Kaesemann on the subject, says: "It is faith in Jesus which gives rise to the apocalyptic elaboration in earliest Christianity."[7] Contra Fuller, I would maintain that it was at this stage that all the sayings about the coming Son of Man were formed. This eliminates the need for the somewhat arbitrary distinction he makes between the earliest Church preserving some of the sayings and forming new 'future' sayings which then go through elaboration with apocalyptic imagery and Old Testament phraseology. As was pointed out earlier, there is an obvious parallel to this process in the apocalyptic Book of Enoch wherein Enoch becomes the Son of Man by reason of his translation to heaven.[8]

This creativity raises again the question: was the early Church's step beyond what had been expressed by Jesus to an explicit christology an arbitrary one? The answer lies, as previously indicated, in how one understands the resurrection: did the disciples truly receive a revelatory disclosure about something that happened to Jesus in the twofold sense of confirming his earthly ministry and of consti-

---

7. Fuller, *Foundations* 144. Cf. Ernst Kaesemann, "The Beginnings of Christian Theology," in *Apocalypticism* 17–46. This entire volume is an excellent study of the subject of apocalypticism.

8. See above, 66–67. Cf. also Martin Hengel, *The Son of God* (Philadelphia: Fortress, 1976) 46–47 on the later rabbinic use of Enoch (Metatron) in Jewish mysticism and 60–66 on parallels between Enoch and early christology.

tuting him in a transformed existence? The first sense gave rise to the earliest christology we can trace; the second to the development of christology as the early community reflected in the Spirit about the implications of the resurrection for the person of Jesus. Toedt sees the earliest stage as a response to Jesus' own words:

> For the authority of the one who had uttered the words of promise on earth had been confirmed by the Easter event in a way which, leading to a new understanding of his person, gave the impetus for Christological cognition. This post-Easter cognition then referred to the pre-Easter words of promise uttered by Jesus himself. The community built upon the foundation of this promise the Christological cognition that the one who gave the promise will himself be the guarantor for its fulfillment, i.e., that Jesus will come as the Son of Man.[9]

This confirmation of Jesus as the Son of Man who will come led naturally to the kind of elaboration that Fuller speaks of in terms of apocalyptic imagery and Old Testament phraseology. Yet, as Toedt insists, the community exercised considerable caution. The identification of Jesus with the coming Son of Man did not mean a simple transferral of the heavenly attributes of the Son of Man to the earthly ministry. Rather, a clear distinction was maintained between the apocalyptic Son of Man who is to come at the end of the age for judgment and the earthly Son of Man who had authority (*exousia*) to forgive sins (Mark 2:10), to set himself above the sabbath (Mark 2:28), to befriend tax-collectors and sinners in the name of the Kingdom (Matthew 11:19 par), to call disciples to follow him at great personal sacrifice (Matthew 8:20 par), and who himself led the way by coming not to be served but to serve (Mark 10:45a; cp. Luke 22:27b). It is interesting that all of these 'present' sayings occur in the context of Jesus' conflict with his contemporaries. As the one who was rejected and vindicated, he is now seen always to have had such authority. Hence, at its earliest stage, christology developed two foci, the future

---

9. Toedt, *Son of Man* 230.

coming and the earthly ministry. While the urgent expectation of Jesus' imminent return did not lead immediately to reflection upon Jesus' present activity, so that the resurrection may have been thought of at this stage "merely as inaugurating a brief interval of inactivity before the parousia,"[10] nonetheless a continuity between the present and post-Easter Jesus has been established which will prove fruitful for further reflection. Toedt expresses well what is the essential ground for such continuity: "The new basis which by means of the Christological cognition of the post-Easter community was recognized as the foundation on which this continuity could be established was Jesus' *person.*"[11]

This continuity, based irrevocably now in the person of Jesus, developed in two distinct but finally inseparable directions. The first, as reflected in the Q material, was primarily concerned to continue to teach the teaching of Jesus. The second, as reflected in the writings of Paul and Mark, centered upon the passion kerygma. Toedt illustrates the difference by pointing out that Mark focuses upon the gospel *of* or *about* Jesus Christ (1:1; 13:10) in which the central teaching is the passion kerygma (8:31–10:45). In the Q material, however, the disciples are commissioned to continue Jesus' proclamation of the Kingdom (Matthew 10:7 par). "The post-Easter community, continuing to preach the message of the approach of God's kingdom, accordingly looked for the speedy coming of the Son of Man (Matthew 10:23). They founded this expectation on Jesus' own teaching."[12] It is worth noting here that this source (Q) is primarily a collection of Jesus' sayings and that, among other things, it has preserved the expression that we traced back to Jesus at the end of chapter two, viz. 'the day of the Son of Man' (Luke 17:24 par). In this material the redemptive significance of Jesus' death has not been recognized and developed. The resurrection, understood as the divine vindication of Jesus, is not what was preached but what *enabled* the early community to continue the teaching of Jesus as the one who always had authority (*exousia*) and as the one who will come

---

10. Fuller, *Foundations* 154. Cp. Toedt, *Son of Man* 273–274 for a good summary of the two foci in Q.

11. Toedt, *Son of Man* 231.

12. Ibid. 249–250.

again to fulfill his promises. But this is already a profound and significant christology that will necessitate further development. Jesus himself, in his own person, is now understood to be the decisive (eschatological) activity of God for his people. He is the one who with full authority had bestowed fellowship on earth and had restored that fellowship with his disciples by continuing to call them into the Kingdom after his death, a Kingdom that will be consummated by his return in sovereign authority as the Son of Man.[13]

At this juncture, it will be helpful to articulate some of the principles that I see already implied at this originating stage of christological development as they will be operative in the discussion of the subsequent stages. First, the move from Jesus' soteriological concerns to the explicit christological judgment of his disciples could only be made in the light of the resurrection, but this means that christology is rooted in soteriology and must always remain so. To be true to Jesus is to recognize that he proclaimed not himself but the Kingdom of God. Christology is but the deepest expression of soteriology, of God's saving activity, because it affirms the *radical* character of God's personal involvement in the creative-salvific process. Hence, it must always be in service to the fundamental proclamation of salvation. Second, maintaining the distinction between Jesus' open and universal call into the Kingdom, illustrated by his table-fellowship, and his particular call into the special fellowship of being a disciple who 'follows' Jesus and receives from him the commission to continue his ministry, christology is seen as a very specific and explicit response of *disciples* to the mystery of Jesus as revealed in the whole of his life understood now in the light of the resurrec-

---

13. Ibid. 253–269. Toedt discusses the texts in the Q material that articulate this Son of Man christology. He concludes (268–269): "In our enquiry into the Q material we met with the same motifs which we found in the Son of Man sayings. We found ourselves within the same self-contained sphere of concepts in which the Christological significance of Jesus in view of his sovereignty as the coming Son of Man and of his acting on earth with full authority was dominant. The concepts of the passion kerygma remained outside this sphere. Thus the Q material proved to be an independent source of Christological cognition. From it a Christology has flowed that is clearly distinguished by the name Son of Man as used both for the coming Lord and for the Lord acting on earth. Son of Man Christology and Q belong together both in their concepts and in their history of tradition." See also his summary, 273–274, and Excursus III referred to in n. 4.

tion. This response is a true and valid one but its purpose is not to perpetuate itself as the only possible way of bringing to expression the mystery of Jesus; rather, the purpose of any and every christology is to articulate in explicit but culturally conditioned terms the mystery of salvation for all persons, a mystery which transcends every expression of it and which Jesus personally embodies in his relation to his Father. Third, once the crucial step has been made to christological judgment at this initial stage, there is an inner necessity to develop all the implications of this initial insight. It is a matter of consistency.[14] Once one identifies the eschatological activity of God with the person of Jesus, one logically includes *all* the activity of God. This led the early Church to explore the relationship of Jesus to other intermediary figures both from within the heritage of Palestinian Judaism and from more directly hellenistic modes of thought as missionaries moved more and more into the Greek-speaking world. The christological development, as we shall see, was from eschatology to protology, schematically from a focus upon the parousia, moving backwards through Jesus' death-resurrection, baptism, and conception, finally to pre-existence. The purpose in all this development is simply to articulate what was already contained in the initial insight, viz. Jesus' identity with the divine activity, an identity that for the early Church could not be satisfactorily articulated in merely functional terms but demanded an identity-in-being. The end illumines the beginning and vice versa. Hence, it is possible to schematize this development, as Fuller does, but the historical sequence is not so important as the theological judgment which justifies such a move in the first place.

Keeping these principles in mind, we move on to the next step in the development. Still within Palestinian Judaism, it is the move from the earthly authority of Jesus whose teaching must be continued to the beginnings of the focus upon the redemptive significance of the cross itself. At the outset, it should be noted that the move from the vindication and confirmation of the proclaimer to the trans-

---

14. Hengel, *Son of God* 67, speaks of an "inner consistency." He concludes his discussion of this as follows (71): "*Thus there was an inner necessity about the introduction of the idea of pre-existence into christology.* Eberhard Juengel is quite right when, from the standpoint of a systematic theologian, he passes the judgment: 'It was more a matter of consistency than of mythology'."

formative power (both for the world and for Jesus himself) of the event of death-resurrection was not an innovation but, as developed in the previous chapter, was already contained in the experience of that event and only needed further reflection in the Spirit to bring out the implications. With regard to the cross, if Jesus could have used the enigmatic phrase *bar 'enāšā* to refer to the crisis of rejection that he was experiencing in his ministry,[15] then it was natural and normal for the earliest community—once it had established the titular usage of the apocalyptic Son of Man for Jesus—to apply that title not only to his earthly ministry but to the cross as well. The simplest and earliest form would be to take over the saying that may well have come from Jesus himself, viz. Mark 9:31a (cp. 14:21, 41).[16] To this would be attached, post-factum, the references to 'being killed' and to 'rising', thus forming the passion predictions as we know them in Mark. The apologetic motif of scriptural fulfillment would follow almost immediately as the passion is that which most needed explanation. The earliest text was probably Psalm 118:22 (cf. Mark 8:31; 9:12) because its motif of rejection and vindication would lie closest to the events as they were experienced. This also corresponds to the reactive formula in the kerygmatic speeches in Acts: 'you killed him, but God raised him' (Acts 2:23b–24, etc.).

Moreover, if Jesus himself, as suggested in chapter two, saw his own impending death as somehow directly operative in the salvific activity of God bringing the Kingdom to its consummation (Mark 14:25), his earliest followers would very quickly have seen the actual event of the cross in explicitly soteriological terms. The earliest form of this may have derived simply from the popular idea of vicarious atonement by death and been expressed in such formulae as 'Jesus died for our sins' (*huper tōn hamartiōn hēmōn*; 1 Cor. 15:3) or 'for us' *(huper hēmōn)*, an idea that clearly had its roots already in such actions as Jesus' table-fellowship with tax-collectors and sinners. It was a short step to apply the most striking text in the Old Testament, Isaiah 53, to this insight (Mark 10:45b; 14:24). Thus, we have the be-

---

15. See above, 63–66, for the discussion of Jesus' awareness of his death.

16. See the discussion and references of Fuller, *Foundations* 151–155, who follows Toedt, *Son of Man*, and Hahn, *Titles*, in his analysis of the suffering Son of Man. In what follows, I am principally indebted to his exposition.

ginnings of reflection upon the passion kerygma for its own sake. However, this is not an arbitrary imposition. It is rooted in Jesus' own awareness of the salvific activity of God in his ministry.

Thus far we have been considering the development of the Son of Man christology as "the most primitive christology of all," rooted in Jesus' own usage of the 'day of the Son of Man' and enabled to develop out of the earliest experience of his death and resurrection. It looks to Jesus as the one who will return as the Son of Man and as the one who continues to exercise authority through his earthly ministry and death. At this stage, nothing is said about Jesus' activity between the resurrection and the parousia nor have the implications for the totality of God's revelatory and saving activity been drawn out. Toedt makes the point that the elements of exaltation and pre-existence are absent from the synoptic sayings concerning the Son of Man. Pre-existence is not alluded to at all and exaltation (Luke 22:69; Mark 14:62) is first derived from another sphere of christological cognition (*Kyrios*).[17] We must now consider these other spheres of christological cognition, heavily influenced as they are by the move of the early Church from its Palestinian origins to the more Hellenistic milieu of its missions, but first a word must be said about what Fuller terms "the terminological shift" that occurred already within the Palestinian milieu.

At the outset, he offers the basic reason for the shift:

'Son of Man' was not a satisfactory term for kerygmatic proclamation, for confession of faith, or for use in Christian instruction and worship. For it naturally lent itself to use only in sayings of Jesus. Other terms had to be found for these purposes, and already in Palestinian Christianity these terms replace 'Son of Man' to cover Jesus' earthly ministry and his coming again.[18]

Note that the two-foci pattern remains but that new titles are employed to express it. The title that corresponds most closely to the

---

17. Toedt, *Son of Man* 284–292. See above, 68–69, especially n. 47, for the discussion of this.

18. Fuller, *Foundations* 155.

two foci of earthly ministry and future coming is the Aramaic word
for 'my lord' (*mari*) or 'our lord' (*marana*), which would have been
used as a title of respect by Jesus' disciples during his ministry and
which became the liturgical prayer of the early Church's expectation:
marana tha (1 Cor. 16:22; Rev. 22:20; Did. 10:6). A more problematic shift is the use of *Mašiah*. Hengel maintains that "the resurrection by itself is inadequate to explain the origin of Jesus'
messiahship." He appeals to N. A. Dahl and to J. Jeremias who
claim that the early Church could only have proclaimed a crucified
Messiah if Jesus himself had been crucified for messianic claims.[19] It
is certainly true that the charge against Jesus nailed to the cross,
'King of the Jews', has good claims to historicity, but this is a Ro-
man mockery of Jewish pretensions. Jesus rejected the title of *Mašiah* during his earthly ministry because of its openness to popular
misconceptions about the nature of his mission.[20] The early Church
applied the title to Jesus in the changed situation of the resurrection
as an equivalent for the apocalyptic Son of Man. The reason, most
likely, was to be able to proclaim Jesus to the Jews as the fulfillment
of all their eschatological expectations. The implications of this decision for the development of christology are evident: "The Church
could either continue to reject the whole concept, as Jesus had done,
or alternatively it could take the bull by the horns and Christianize
it. It chose the latter course, with far-reaching consequences for later
christological development, particularly, as we shall see, in Hellenistic Jewish Christianity."[21]

The evidence for this christology is primarily Acts 3:20–21 (cp.
Mark 14:61–62), which is certainly a more primitive christology than
Acts 2:36. Here the focus is not on the resurrection in itself but on
the parousia: " . . . that he may send the Christ appointed for you,
Jesus, whom heaven must receive until the time. . . . " The following
vv. 22–23 give the earthly focus of this Palestinian christology by re-

---

19. Hengel, *Son of God* 62. References are to N. A. Dahl, "Der gekreuzigte
Messias," in *Der historische Jesus und der kerygmatische Christus,* ed. H. Ristow &
K. Matthiae (Berlin: Evangelische Verlaganstalt, 1960) 161, and to Jeremias, *Procla-
mation* 255.

20. See above, 37, especially n. 4.

21. Fuller, *Foundations* 159.

ferring to the prophet like Moses (Deut. 18:15–19) who is God's glorified servant (v. 13 = Isa. 52:13) 'raised up' (v. 26 = Deut. 18:15)
for his earthly mission. As with the Son of Man and in the light of
the *titulus* on the cross, it was but a short step to applying *Mašiah*
to the suffering of Jesus (1 Cor. 15:3b; Acts 3:18) and to developing
the notion of the suffering servant from Isaiah 53. Finally, two other
titles, associated with messianic expectations, reflect the two foci of
this stage of development, viz. Son of God and Son of David. The
most important text here, stripped of its Hellenistic antithesis between *sarx* and *pneuma,* is Romans 1:3: " . . . born of the seed of David, appointed Son of God from the resurrection of the dead . . ."
(as reconstructed by Fuller). Fuller interprets *horisthentos* ("appointed") not as enthronement to an exalted state but as predestination
to an eschatological role at the parousia, citing parallel usage at Acts
3:20; 10:42; 17:31. Such a usage of Son of God for the parousia finds
possible support at Mark 14:61–62 (both Christ and Son of God are
interpreted in the direction of the coming Son of Man, but this text
has a long and complicated history as we have seen), at Luke 1:32
(if the 'Kingdom of our father David' at Mark 11:10 and here has
truly been reinterpreted in a parousianic sense), and at 1 Thessalon-
ians 1:10 (on the assumption that 'Son' here refers to Son of God).
At any rate, this will quickly be superseded by the notion of the exalted and pre-existent Son of God. Fuller's attempt to interpret Son
of David in a parousia sense as well is not convincing. The texts he
adduces do not employ the title (Mark 11:10; Luke 1:32) and the appeal to the genealogies and the birth at Bethlehem precisely emphasize the physical, earthly focus, as does Romans 1:3. Hence, it would
be better to see Son of David as parallel to the Mosaic Servant-
Prophet. There is an intriguing parallel in the fact that Moses was
conceived of not only as prophet but also as king.[22]

This brief review of Fuller's section on "the terminological
shift" is sufficient to make the point clear that the early Church

---

22. Ibid. 162–164. On the concept of Moses, especially as applied in the Gospel
of John, see Wayne A. Meeks, *The Prophet-King* (Leiden: Brill, 1967). It is true that
in John the Mosaic figure has replaced the Davidic, but I am suggesting that at this
earlier stage of beginnings there was a simple parallelism that had not yet led to con-
flicting interpretations.

made a decision of far-reaching significance not only in its initial christological judgment but in its willingness to carry that further by the application of other titles besides the Son of Man. Once the initial insight of Jesus' identity with the divine activity had been attained, then a whole range of possibilities from within the heritage of Israel became grist for the christological mill. The individual titles are not as important as the basic insight. Hence, a christology of the New Testament should never be based on the titles alone but on the whole development that we have analyzed in earlier chapters. Moreover, there can be a danger of seeking to oversystematize the development in Western terms. Hengel offers a well-taken caution: "Ancient man did not think analytically or make differentiations within the realm of myth in the way that we do, but combined and accumulated his ideas in a 'multiplicity of approximations'. The more titles were applied to the risen Christ, the more possible it was to celebrate the uniqueness of his saving work."[23] What is most important is the christological judgment that initially opened up this "multiplicity of approximations." No title can exhaust the mystery of Jesus' identity with God. Nonetheless, this should not discourage us from seeking to understand how the Church moved from more Palestinian to more Hellenistic expressions of faith and whether such a development was a deepening of its perception of the mystery. It is my contention that, while this development was conditioned by the external circumstances of mission, it was *necessitated* by the internal dynamics of theological judgment. The two foci of the earliest Palestinian kerygma were remarkably close to the ministry of Jesus with his proclamation of the Kingdom and his expectation of vindication symbolized by the 'day of the Son of Man'. The resurrection had enabled the early Church to proclaim Jesus in terms of a future but imminent parousia. Very quickly, it was called by outer circumstances and inner need to reflect more deeply upon the resurrection itself as a *present* reality, i.e., as the living presence of Jesus continuing to act in the midst of his Church. It is to that development that we now turn.

---

23. Hengel, *Son of God* 57.

B. HELLENISTIC MISSIONS:
JEWISH AND GENTILE

The move from a more Palestinian to a more Hellenistic christology is basically a move from an Aramaic-speaking to a Greek-
speaking environment. Very quickly (cf. Acts 6:1ff.), the Church
moved out from Palestine into the diaspora where the Hellenistic influence was much stronger on the Jewish consciousness. It was already present in Palestine as well, but more likely to be resisted
there. Moreover, instead of the Hebrew masoretic text, the Jews of
the diaspora used the Greek Septuagint (LXX) text of the Old Testament. As Fuller says: "Here lies the main clue to the christological
development in early Hellenistic-Jewish Christianity."[24]

The crucial shift in perspective can be seen if one compares Acts
3:20–21, with its focus upon the parousia, with Acts 2:33–36, with
its focus upon the present exaltation and active reigning (" . . . *he* has
poured out this which you see and hear . . . ") of the one who has
become Lord and Christ from the moment of his ascension to the
right hand of God. This shift was made possible by the application
of Psalm 110:1 to Jesus. The title *Kyrios* could only be applied to Jesus on the basis of the LXX version of this text wherein the same
word can be used both for God and Jesus. Hence, this shift takes
place within a Hellenistic-Jewish provenance. The deeper reason,
however, is to be found in a basic dissatisfaction with a continuing
focus upon the parousia as time passed and the parousia was delayed.
Inseparable from this was the ongoing experience of the Spirit in the
here and now. In fact, the Spirit should be seen as the essential and
indispensable key to this entire development. The root experience of
the resurrection, as we have seen, was that it was Jesus who had been
raised and that this event was transformative of Jesus himself
through the power of the Holy Spirit (*sōma pneumatikon:* 1 Cor.
15:44b).[25]

It was the experience of Jesus' Spirit active in the midst of the
community that gave rise to the basic confession of faith: KYRIOS
IĒSOUS! It was that same experience that led to the close association

---

24. Fuller, *Foundations* 183.
25. See above, 81–84.

of the title *Kyrios* with *Christos* (with its root meaning of one 'anointed' by the Spirit) and with Son of God (Rom. 1:3–4 = appointed now in power through the Spirit of holiness: *en dunamei kata pneuma hagiōsunēs*). Note that Paul combines all three titles in his text: *peri tou huiou autou . . . Iēsou Christou tou kyriou hēmōn.* Even Son of Man is later combined with this theme of exaltation (Mark 14:62 par).[26]

The shift from the focus upon the parousia to the focus upon the present active rule of the exalted Lord in the Spirit did not lead to a denigration of the earthly work of Jesus but to a modification by way of a sharper contrast, as is evident in Rom. 1:3–4: *kata sarka . . . kata pneuma.* The title Son of David is not applicable to the exalted state as the controversy story at Mark 12:35–37 makes clear. Yet, the title does have positive significance for the earthly ministry of Jesus, as the healing narratives and the infancy narratives (especially the genealogies) indicate. The title *Christos* is used sparingly of the earthly ministry (perhaps reflecting the memory that it was only legitimated after the resurrection), but when it is used it represents, like Son of David, a terminological shift from Mosaic Servant-Prophet. Its applicability would come from the memory that Jesus' ministry was in the power of the Spirit; hence he was the 'anointed one'. The most interesting title, because it quickly gained ascendancy for the *whole* of Jesus' life, is Son of God. Not only is Jesus 'appointed' Son of God through the Spirit from the resurrection (Rom. 1:3–4), but his ministry in the Spirit (cf. Acts 10:38) is seen to be a permanent charismatic endowment that identifies him as Son of God in the transfiguration, temptation, and baptismal narratives (possibly replacing an original servant motif: *pais*) and constitutes him as such even from the moment of his conception in the infancy narratives (in contrast to his physical descent from David).

Fuller characterizes the christology of the Hellenistic-Jewish Mission as a two-stage christology: the exalted Lord and the earthly work. There is a contrast but, at the same time, a higher evaluation of the earthly ministry, especially as Son of God becomes applicable to the whole history of Jesus from his conception through his baptism and ministry to his resurrection. This may seem far removed

---

26. See above, 69, especially n. 47.

from Jesus himself but actually it is rooted in Jesus' own ministry as the Spirit-endowed eschatological prophet (which has its deepest dimension in his personal relation to his *Abbā*) and in the early Church's experience of the resurrection as a transformation of Jesus in the power of that same Spirit, which power is now reaching into their own lives and causing them to exclaim: KYRIOS IĒSOUS! The move back to the origins of Jesus—truly Son of God because conceived through the creative power of the Spirit—is an attempt to express "in terms intelligible to the Hellenistic-Jewish world that the whole history of Jesus is God's saving, eschatological act, 'his presence and his very self'."[27] This is still expressed in functional terms (God's action is carried out *through* the exalted Jesus), but the move to identity in terms of origins unavoidably opens the way to ontic considerations (identity-in-being). As we come now to these developments, it must be emphasized once again that the key remains the experience of the Spirit: rooted in Jesus' ministry, revealed as the power of the resurrection, experienced within the community in worship, and expressed by the community in christological hymns.

In understanding the early Church's move from a two-stage to a three-stage (pre-existence—incarnation—exaltation) christology, the important issue is the introduction of the idea of pre-existence, for once that is given it has a transformative effect upon all the titles employed prior to this insight and it opens the way to a full affirmation of incarnation. Externally, the occasion for this development was the ever-deepening involvement of *Jewish* missionaries in the Gentile world. Influences would include both the syncretistic tendencies already present within Hellenistic Judaism (exemplified by Philo) and the natural missionary desire to engage the concerns of those missionized (e.g., a more cosmic concern with fate as the power that holds the human race in thrall). Internally, it was a question again of consistency with the initial christological insight that identified Jesus with the decisive (eschatological) activity of God. At issue here is the fact that the identification is not simply with the activity of God in a functional sense but with the being of God in an ontic sense. We will consider each of these dimensions in turn: first, the

---

27. Fuller, *Foundations* 197.

external, historical development, with a particular focus upon the sources in Hellenistic Judaism from which the idea of pre-existence was derived, and second, the internal, theological judgment that necessitated the move from a functional to an ontic christology.

There is a growing consensus among scholars[28] that the appropriate place to look for the sources (or background) for this christological development is not in a hypothetically reconstructed Gnostic-Redeemer Myth (Bultmann) but in the more immediate and abundant speculations on Wisdom (*sophia*) to be found within Hellenistic Judaism. The chief sources from the Old Testament itself are to be found, interestingly enough, in poems dedicated to Wisdom: Job 28:23–28; Proverbs 1–9, especially 8:22–21; Baruch 3:9–4.4; Sir 1; 4:11–19; 6:18–31; 14:20–15:10; and especially 24:3–22; Wisdom 6–10. Fuller follows Wilckens in suggesting that this concept was influenced by an ancient oriental myth, the borrowing being more restrained in the Old Testament itself and more uninhibited in the apocalyptic writings of Late Judaism, exemplified especially by Eth. Enoch 42. The analysis of these sources yields a mythic pattern of Wisdom as a pre-existent agent of creation and revelation who descends from heaven into this world, experiences rejection, and returns to heaven. Wisdom 9:1b–2a draws a parallel between *sophia* and *logos*. Philo develops the Wisdom speculation in terms of the Logos. Correspondingly, rabbinic speculation develops in terms of the Torah. The pattern was there as a christological tool for the early Church. But it should be noted at the outset that this pattern was basically a creative and revelatory myth. Fuller insists, quite rightly, that our sources within Hellenistic Judaism, including Philo's further speculations on the First or Heavenly Man and on the High Priest (cp. Hebrews), give us no redeemer myth in the proper sense. When the Logos concept is employed in the Prologue to John, the notion of pre-existence (vv. 1–2) and the functions of creation (vv. 3–5) and of revelation (vv. 10–12a, reinterpreted by the interpolations of the final redactor regarding John the Baptist) are clearly derived from

---

28. Ibid. 72–75, 93–97; Hengel, *Son of God* 21–56; Raymond E. Brown, *The Gospel According to John I–XII* (New York: Doubleday, 1966) LII–LXVI, CXXII–CXXVIII, 519–524 (Appendix II: The 'Word').

the pattern. But, when the hymn goes on in v. 14 to say *ho logos sarx egeneto,* it breaks the pattern and introduces the distinctively Christian concept of incarnation.

Fuller locates this three-stage christology in a number of early hymns which he reconstructs from their present contexts and places within the life of the community prior to the writings of any New Testament authors as we now possess them. This indicates that this level of christological insight was reached rather quickly in the consciousness of the early Church. The hymnic character of this christology is important for it suggests that the identification of Jesus with the divine originally emerged from the experience of the community in worship (in baptismal and/or eucharistic liturgies). "No one can say 'Jesus is Lord' except by the Holy Spirit" (1 Cor. 12:3). That Spirit, then and now, is experienced primarily in worship. A good indicator of what one truly believes is the way that one prays, both individually and in community. These hymns were simply the community's expression in poetic form of what was being experienced in worship. Such a grounding of belief (doctrine) in the concrete, lived experience of the faith community—being as it is the very origin of christology—must always remain the touchstone of future developments from that day to this.

What was it that the community brought to expression? Accepting Fuller's reconstructions as generally adequate, my purpose here is not to repeat his argumentation but simply to emphasize the more important dimensions that emerge at this stage of the Church's christological consciousness. The first hymn he treats is from Philippians 2:6–11.

Presupposed throughout this hymn is the Hellenistic world view, with its three storied universe consisting of heaven, earth, and underworld (v. 10). The lower world is under the thrall of the 'powers' and needs redemption. This redemption is brought through a revelation which comes from the world above and ascends to it again. This is the pattern of the sophia myth. Our hymn asserts that in the Christ event this redemptive revelation has occurred.[29]

29. Fuller, *Foundations* 207.

Fuller sees five phases of the Redeemer's existence in this hymn: pre-existence, becoming incarnate, incarnate life, re-ascension, and exalted state. In its notion of pre-existence, the hymn goes somewhat beyond the sophia myth insofar as it speaks not simply of a hypostatization of God but of a 'mode of being' (*morphē*) which is interpreted to mean a state of equality with God (*einai isa theō*). This is further confirmed by the fact that the Redeemer freely chose (*ekenōsen heauton*) to exchange the divine mode of being (*morphē theou*) for that of a slave (*morphē doulou*). This latter, understood as an entry into the sphere of human bondage under the 'powers' (which, for Paul, became sin, law, and death), is still derivative from the sophia myth. It is precisely at this point that the hymn introduces the distinctively Christian notion of incarnation when it goes on to say that he was 'born' (*genomenos*) 'in the likeness of men' (*en homoiōmati anthrōpōn*). The emphasis upon being born assures his ontic identity with the rest of mankind (cp. Gal. 4:4; Rom. 1:3; John 1:14), while the word 'likeness' maintains his distinctiveness from all other men. Lest this be taken in a docetic sense, the hymn immediately restates it: 'being found in fashion as a man' (*schēmati heuretheis hōs anthrōpos*). The word *schēmati* leaves room for the idea that more than merely a man is here, but the word *anthrōpos* assures that he is really a man, especially as this is immediately articulated in terms of his human, historical experience of humiliation and obedience unto death, which Paul further specifies as death on the cross.

Fuller maintains that the original sophia-anthropos myth has been split into two: the sophia part being used for pre-existence, descent, and ascent and the anthropos part being adapted to the specifically Christian notion of the Redeemer's incarnate life as a reversal of the First Man's fall (Christ as *anthrōpos* always being intended as a contrast to Adam: cp. the development of this idea at 1 Cor. 15:20–49; Rom. 5:12–17). In any case, the reference especially to his death shows that the mythic elements have been adapted to the concrete history of Jesus. His exaltation (the resurrection is not mentioned) is in contrast to his humiliation, for it is precisely in his obedience unto death that he overcomes the power of death (and hence every power) and so receives the name that is above (*huper*) every name in the entire universe. This results in a cosmic worship of Jesus using the definitive Christian confession of faith: KYRIOS

IĒSOUS CHRISTOS! Here, as Fuller notes, we have moved beyond a functional identity between the exalted One and Yahweh to an ontic identity. The pre-existent One (in mode of being, divine) as the incarnate One (in mode of being, human) is given 'the Name', i.e., an identity with the divine mode of being that calls for worship. The difference for Christians between pre-existence and incarnation-exaltation is that it is now *Jesus* who has this name.

With the analysis of Philippians 2:6–11, we have the essential elements of this three-stage pattern. The other hymns that Fuller treats emphasize one or another dimension of this pattern, so in what follows I will only make brief mention of the more distinctive features. Colossians 1:15–20 speaks of the pre-existent One as the 'image' (*eikōn*) of the invisible God who is *active* in the creation and preservation of the world. The redemptive turning point is the resurrection, the basic contrast being between the 'first born' (*prōtotokos*) of all creation and the 'first born' from the dead, but exaltation is implied in the fact that henceforth all the fullness (*plēroma*) of God was pleased to dwell in him and so he became the reconciliation point for the entire universe. Through a chiastic structure 1 Timothy 3:16 sets up a series of parallel statements about the earthly and heavenly existence of Jesus, but what is interesting is that the earthly, incarnate life is not seen here as a kenosis but as an epiphany of the divine glory. Likewise, 1 Peter 1:20 has the pattern of pre-existence and epiphany which Bultmann maintains belongs with 3:18–22, a hymn which has a contrasting pattern ('flesh'/'spirit') and which culminates in resurrection-exaltation and cosmic power. Hebrews 1:3–4 is more difficult to reconstruct but it does contain characteristic elements of the hymnic pattern, viz. pre-existence in a divine mode of being, preservation of the universe, purification for sins and exaltation leading to triumph over the powers.

Finally, John 1:1–18 contains a hymn of four strophes (vv. 1–2, 3–5, 10–12a, and 14, 16 taken together)[30] which deals successively with the relationship of the Logos to God (pre-existent identity in being), to creation, to revelation in the world, and to the Christian community. The pattern of the pre-existent One's creative and re-

---

30. Here I am following the analysis of Brown, *John* 1–37, which differs somewhat from Fuller's analysis.

velatory functions is directly derivative from the sophia myth interpreted as the Logos. The incarnation of the Logos is the specifically
Christian adaptation of the myth. It is conceived again not as a kenosis but as an epiphany of the divine glory (*doxan hōs monogenous
para patros*), the divine *plēroma*. Fuller makes the point that insofar
as 'only Son' (*monogenēs*) is Wisdom vocabulary (cf. Wis. 7:22) this
hymn is the first to employ the sophia myth not only for the pre-existent state but also for the incarnate life. This may well have been
the origin within the Johannine school of the christology of Jesus as
personified Wisdom that runs throughout the Gospel of John.[31]

It is important to note that the titles of Jesus play almost no part
in the christological development of these hymns. In fact, the only
title employed is *Kyrios* in the Philippians hymn (*Christos* already
having been pretty much reduced to the level of a proper name). The
ontic use of this title is symptomatic of the transformative effect that
the pre-existence—incarnation motif will now have upon all the titles. For example, Son of Man is employed in John to express pre-
existence—descent—ascent (*katabasis—anabasis* christology: cf.
John 3:13; 6:62). The most important title, Son of God, will now be
interpreted as referring to Jesus' personal identity in being with the
divine. This is most clearly the case in the whole first chapter of Hebrews as well as in the *leitmotif* of John: Jesus' personal identity with
the Father (John 10:30 and throughout the gospel). Note that the
reference to the 'only Son' (*monogenēs*) in the hymnic part of the
Prologue is immediately interpreted as a parallel to the divinity of
the Logos (v. 1: *theos ēn ho Logos* / /v. 18: *monogenēs theos*). This
theme of the Son's divinity is developed throughout the gospel and
culminates in the ultimate christological confession on the lips of
Thomas: *ho kyrios mou kai ho theos mou* (John 20:28). Not only is
the Son *theos,* but the identification through his glorification is so
complete that he can now be given the title normally reserved for the
Father alone: *ho theos*. Moreover, once pre-existence is given, the
'sending' of the Son, originally derived from prophetic mission, takes
on a different meaning (cf. Gal. 4:4–5; Rom. 1:3; 8:3; John 3:16).

---

31. Ibid. CXXII–CXXV. Brown offers numerous points of comparison to sub-
stantiate this view.

At this point, are we not far removed from the historical ministry of Jesus? Fuller thinks not:

> Jesus had understood his work as the proleptic presence of the coming salvation. From the very first the post-Easter church had proclaimed his victory as the eschatological act of God. Thus the quintessence of the Christian message is variously interpreted to the succeeding environments of the Christian mission. But it was essentially the same message throughout, the message of the divine salvation in Jesus of Nazareth.[32]

This serves to make sense of the external, historical development, but does it really explain the necessity of moving from functional to ontic statements? *That* the early Church made such a move is clear, but what justifies it theologically? Fuller remarks:

> It may, of course, be argued that this ontic language is merely the translation into Greek terms (and mythological terms at that) of what the earlier functional Christologies were affirming. This is true, but it is not the whole truth. For it is not just a quirk of the Greek mind, but a universal human apperception, that action implies prior being—even if, as is also true, being is only apprehended in action.[33]

---

32. Fuller, *Foundations* 232–233.
33. Ibid. 248. Russell F. Aldwinckle, *More Than Man. A Study in Christology* (Grand Rapids: Eerdmans, 1976) 55, offers a criticism of posing the question in terms of "functional" versus "ontic" which is worth quoting: "What Cullmann and Fuller call functional Christology, then, does not really evade the question of the nature of the reality involved. What or who is functioning? The answer can only be: God is functioning in this activity manifested through Jesus of Nazareth. The real question is therefore not 'functional' versus 'ontic', but whether the activity of God in Jesus is such as to justify faith in giving to Jesus an absolutely unique role in the locus of the divine activity without parallel elsewhere. Fuller's threefold pattern seems to show that the church was led irresistibly to this conclusion. Was it merely wishful thinking or was it authentic discernment? Was it only human reflection or response to a divine self-disclosure? The answer to these questions will determine the meaning we give to the term 'divinity' as applied to Jesus." He then raises the question of language, of whether the language of descent and ascent, preexistence, etc., the "models" of the early Church, have enduring value for us today or whether we can find other models.

Hence, the identification of Jesus' person with the eschatological activity of God (Son of Man) implies an identity in being that the early Church gradually makes explicit.

If this is so, then the question becomes: what kind of language is employed to make such affirmations? Hengel quite correctly calls attention to the difference between the metaphorical language of the New Testament and the metaphysical language of the later Fathers and Councils:

> As in the case of the relationship between a personified hypostasis and purely metaphorical language, the transition here from mere 'ideal' pre-existence (that is, to some extent only in the thought of God) to 'real' pre-existence is fluid. Moreover, the concept of pre-existence is not yet understood in the sense it later acquires during the Arian dispute as uncreatedness and timeless, eternal being with God. In the first place it denotes a 'being before the creation of the world'.[34]

In either case, the attempt is being made to bring to expression the ultimate Christian symbol, viz. JESUS ('Yahweh saves'). Jesus is the 'locus' of God's salvific activity from creation to parousia. Therefore, his identification with Wisdom as mediator of creation and salvation is intended to express conclusively the unsurpassability and finality of God's self-communication in Jesus.[35] Yet, it must be asked whether metaphorical language—growing as it does in this case out of the story of Yahweh's dealings with Israel—speaks about reality, i.e., about the way things *are*. Only if the very identity of God, the personal reality of the divine, is given in Jesus can it be said that God has communicated himself in a definitive and final (*eph' hapax*) way that will not again be superseded in some future event.[36] This means that the only God we know is the God who reveals himself in Jesus. Identity-in-being is a grounding in fact (the real) that serves to con-

---

34. Hengel, *Son of God* 69–70.
35. Ibid. 72.
36. This is the approach to revelation taken by Pannenberg, *Jesus* 127–133. We will return to his views later.

trol all *merely* mythological and/or legendary tendencies. Does the metaphorical language of the New Testament accomplish that?

Hengel underlines the importance of metaphor: "In reality, theology will never be able to dispense with the language of 'myth', with its transcendent metaphors, and at this very point we would do well to learn from the example of the greatest Greek 'theologian', Plato. The 'Son of God' has become an established, unalienable metaphor of Christian theology. . . ."[37] It would be well, in the light of this quote, to distinguish symbol as metaphor from its possibly 'mythical' expression, as Hengel tends to identify the two. Jesus used the phrase 'Kingdom of God' as a symbol for the final and definitive activity of God on behalf of his people. As we have seen,[38] his favorite way of expressing what he meant by this symbol was in telling stories. Norman Perrin understands 'Kingdom of God' as a symbol that evokes the *myth* of God acting as King on behalf of his people. A parable in his analysis can be a simile that is essentially illustrative or a metaphor that is essentially participative. I would maintain that Jesus, by his *metaphorical* use of parable, interprets the symbol away from a 'merely mythical' understanding and toward the concreteness of human experience. As Perrin puts it: " . . . the secularity, the concrete everydayness of the parables is very important because this element of the parables becomes an *interpretation* of the Kingdom: the hearers are challenged to recognize the reality that is mediated by the myth in terms of the concrete actuality of the everyday."[39] In this sense, it can be said that the myth has been 'broken' (Paul Tillich), that it has become history (A. von Harnack).

Parables are metaphors, but they are indispensable metaphors. They are not a means to gain information about something else (as when they are allegorized or moralized), so that once the point is gained they can be dispensed with. Rather, they are metaphors about ordinary, everyday human life which are intended to draw the listener to participate, to 'enter into', that world precisely as parabolic.[40] Jesus, in his use of parables, was saying: 'The Kingdom of God

---

37. Hengel, *Son of God* 92–93. Likewise, Pannenberg, *Jesus* 187, speaks of the resurrection as an "absolute metaphor."
38. See above, 42–47.
39. Perrin, *Language* 202. See also pp. 16–32, 55–56, 202–203.
40. See the discussion of this in Crossan, *Parables* 7–22.

is a man sowing seed in his field. . . . ' Likewise, the early Church, in the light of Jesus' whole life, death, and resurrection, was saying in effect (especially in its use of the gospel form): 'The Kingdom of God *is* the Son of God laying down his life for his friends. . . .' Jesus himself has now become the symbol of God's final and definitive activity on behalf of his people and therefore his story has now become the parable of God. This means that Jesus himself, as a person, is indispensable to the personal identity of God in our world. As with Jesus' parables, the story itself *is* the reality, the way things are. One cannot simply dispense with the story once one has gained the item of information that Jesus is the Son of God. To do so is to distort the reality itself, viz. the concrete, personal existence of Jesus himself. 'Son of God' is a symbol that has come to narrated metaphorical expression in the gospel form. It is my contention that we must always retain the primacy of the metaphor in christology, i.e., the primacy of Jesus in his concrete, personal history. The subsequent developments of the Fathers and the Councils are legitimate but can become distorted if the resultant theologoumena are disengaged from their original unity in the man Jesus. It is to this question that we now turn.

C. CHRIST OR APOLLO:
THE EMERGENCE OF HELLENISM

The basic patterns of christology that developed from the earliest kerygma were employed in different ways by the NT authors themselves. The total pattern does not appear in its entirety in any one author, but each uses elements of the pattern for his own purposes.[41] The christologies of Paul and Mark, with their emphases upon the cross, are more kenotic in orientation; Matthew and Luke represent a transition to a greater emphasis upon the glory of Jesus as the Son of God (the man conceived by the power of the Spirit who receives 'all authority' at his resurrection); while John, with his emphasis upon the Word become flesh as the manifestation of the glory

---

41. See Fuller, *Foundations* 243–247, for outlines of the three basic patterns and for his comments on the relation of the full pattern as reconstructed to the individual authors of the New Testament.

of God, is fully epiphanic in orientation. Yet, even for John, the emphasis upon the flesh concretized in the gospel form is intended to oppose any disengagement of the *Logos* from the concrete story of Jesus. It is not necessary for our present purposes to do a detailed analysis of the different authors in the New Testament, but simply to point out that there is tremendous diversity in their christologies. After the New Testament, one element within this diversity emerged as the point of focal interest, viz. *ho logos sarx egeneto* (John 1:14).

The writings of the Fathers are surely much more complex and diverse than this might suggest, but the point remains valid that with the emergence of the *Logos* speculation (starting with the Apologists) and the development of the controversies between the *Logos-Sarx* christology of the Alexandrian school and the *Logos-Anthropos* christology of the Antiochene school culminating in the Council of Chalcedon (451),[42] the intellectual preoccupation from the Apostolic Age to Chalcedon was a concentration upon the *Logos* as the central christological concept. My contention is that this is legitimate, but *only* insofar as the *Logos* is not disengaged from the concrete story of Jesus. Hence, this development, which represents as it were a mathematical point of concentration within a broader perspective, must be recontextualized by the concrete history of Jesus if it is to be properly understood. This, I believe, is what many contemporary writers in christology are seeking to do, as I shall attempt to demonstrate in the next chapter.

As Grillmeier points out, the intent of the first four Councils of the Church was not to 'hellenize' Christianity, but to remain true to the heritage of the New Testament itself.[43] On the one hand, the Fathers were seeking to remain true to the biblical and apostolic tradition within the framework of a *regula fidei*. On the other hand, they could only do this by engaging the world in which they lived, seeking to demonstrate both compatibility with Jewish monotheism and, correspondingly, incompatibility with pagan polytheism. To do this, they chose a path that is unavoidable, given the nature of Chris-

---

42. The best single volume treatment of this whole development is Aloys Grillmeier, S. J., *Christ in Christian Tradition. Volume One: From the Apostolic Age to Chalcedon (451).* (Atlanta: John Knox Press, 1975².)

43. Ibid. 106–108.

tian faith, viz. to engage the world in which they lived in the spheres of its own legitimacy.[44] Hence, they attempted " . . . to maintain the mystery inherent in the basic data of the Christian revelation by a limited use of Hellenistic or contemporary concepts and language and to avoid the distortions of Hellenization. To see the chronic Hellenization of Christianity in these dogmas themselves (A. v. Harnack) is to mistake the first intention of the dogmatic statements."[45]

While this remains true, it must also be affirmed that one can accept Chalcedonian orthodoxy (the fullness of humanity and divinity within the unity of one person) without accepting the intellectual framework in which it is expressed. The language of Chalcedon has its origins in the *Logos* speculations of the second century, beginning with the Apologists (Justin Martyr) and culminating in Origen, in whose middle Platonism all subsequent developments (both orthodox and heretical) could find their inspiration.[46] The most important factor for understanding the development of christology up to the compromise statement of Chalcedon is the crucial decision made at the Council of Nicaea (325), under the influence of anti-Arian polemic, to separate the trinitarian and incarnational issues and to concentrate on the former.[47] In so doing, they introduced a tendency to separate conceptually the pre-existence of the Son of God from the concrete existence of Jesus. The notion of pre-existence is derivative from the three-stage pattern already present in the New Testament, but it is not commonly employed by this time in terms of the concrete history of God's dealings with his people from creation to parousia. Rather it is understood in terms of the pre-existence speculations of Origen. It is understandable how, in the given situation of repudiating the pre-existence concept of Arianism, the Fathers would engage the issue with the same language (though, it should be noted, the Nicene creed does not use the term *Logos* but rather employs the scriptual titles *kyrios, christos, huios tou theou,*

44. See above, 1–4.

45. Grillmeier, *Christ* 107–108.

46. Ibid. 138–149; Piet Smulders, S. J., *The Fathers on Christology* (DePere, Wisconsin: St. Norbert Abbey Press, 1968) 39–52, and especially 48–52, lines up in a convenient summary the dangers inherent in Origen's speculations which led to various heretical extremes; see also Schoonenberg, *Christ* 54–56.

47. Grillmeier, *Christ* 246–248, 272–273.

monogenēs, theos in reference to Jesus). In affirming the divinity of Jesus, they were affirming the *lectio difficilior*, as Grillmeier puts it, of the biblical and apostolic tradition. Yet, they were affirming it within a given intellectual milieu that would control subsequent christological belief and thought.

The Nicene creed calls us to affirm in faith the full divinity of Jesus. That is clearly the intent of the Council and is not at issue here. But, what is at issue is whether we who live in a quite different intellectual and cultural milieu—one that is heavily influenced by historical consciousness—need to accept as well the understanding of reality that is the matrix out of which this affirmation of Jesus' divinity came. Pannenberg expresses the problem well:

> The concept of preexistence stands under the suspicion of conceptually separating Jesus' community with God as a special *being* (the preexistent Son of God) and his temporal appearance. The two distinct things are then reunited through the idea that the divine being has, in the incarnation, joined himself at a particular point in time with the earthly corporeality of the man Jesus. Thus the distinction between a preexistent divine being and the man Jesus or his earthly appearance conceptually divides precisely that which belongs together in Jesus' existence. This constitutes the mythical element of the incarnational Christology: it conceptually divides the eternal Son of God and the earthly, human appearance of Jesus, which together constitute the concrete existence of Jesus, into two separate beings. Therefore, what is thus divided must be subsequently brought together again.

In describing this process of conceptual division and reuniting, he gives a vivid description of the thought-world of popular middle Platonism. It is

> an example of an intellectual bent that likes to find the prototypal eternal occasionally effective in the flux of things and events and also in other ways. Indeed, the uniqueness

of mythical thinking in general is that it separates the essence of reality as a special, prototypal essence from the appearance in order to reunite the two through a dramatic process especially conceived for the purpose.[48]

Pannenberg's point is not to deny the necessity of distinguishing the humanity and divinity in Jesus, but to insist upon the necessity of seeing these two aspects always as belonging to a single, concrete life. To do so, one must not disengage the concept of incarnation from the biblical understanding of God's concrete activity in the history of Israel culminating in the personal history of Jesus. This approach will occupy us when we consider the contemporary christologies of Schoonenberg, Pannenberg, Moltmann, and Hodgson (Ebeling) in the next chapter.

The development from Nicaea to Chalcedon can be schematically summarized in terms of the christological emphases of the first four ecumenical Councils: Nicaea (325) defined the fullness of divinity, Constantinople I (381) the fullness of humanity, Ephesus (431) the unity of person ('one and the same'), and Chalcedon (451) the inviolable distinction and the inseparable unity of the humanity and the divinity. Chalcedon, as a compromise document which culminated a long history of debate and struggle, has remained the touchstone of christological orthodoxy down to the present day. One may seek to interpret Chalcedon, but one cannot ignore it and remain in continuity with Christian self-understanding. The next chapter will seek to offer a reinterpretation of Chalcedon in the light of at least one approach to the contemporary understanding of reality. At this point I am only concerned to emphasize with Karl Rahner that Chalcedon is not only an end, but a beginning.[49] It has set the parameters within which all subsequent interpretation must operate but it has not in any sense excluded subsequent interpretation by canonizing only one, e.g., the enhypostatic interpretation of Leontius of Byzantium (d. 543) which has a history of its own. The interpretation will al-

---

48. Pannenberg, *Jesus* 154–155.
49. Karl Rahner, "Chalkedon—Ende oder Anfang?" in *Das Konzil von Chalkedon* III, ed. A. Grillmeier & H. Bacht (Wuerzburg: 1962³) 3–49. Grillmeier, *Christ* 555–557, agrees with Rahner.

ways depend on the understanding of reality that one is willing to accept and, as the history of philosophy shows, these are many and diverse. Hence, we must look to Chalcedon for the credal affirmation of our faith but not necessarily for our philosophical understanding.

Like the New Testament hymns, the conciliar creeds have their originating ground not in philosophical speculation but in the communal experience of worship. In doxological statements, "the praise of the eternal God on the basis of his deeds,"[50] we reach the limit of human expression beyond which nothing more can be said. The cry of Thomas, *ho kyrios mou kai ho theos mou!* (John 20:28), is precisely an expression of a limit-experience that swallows up his ego-centered appeal in which he tried to experience in his own terms, and hence to control, the reality of the risen Jesus. Doxological statements are "final" statements as Pannenberg, following Edmund Schlink, emphasizes strongly. If the story of Jesus, centering upon the event of the resurrection, is truly identified with the one God, then one is affirming something, however proleptically, about the totality of reality, i.e, about the way things *are*. As expressions in worship of a limit-experience, such statements cannot be used as logical premises from which one could deduce further conclusions, e.g., the historical activity of God. This is why the incarnation must be seen as the conclusion of christology, as indeed is evident in the gradual historical development toward this creed, rather than as the starting point. Again and again, it must be emphasized that it is the concrete experience of Jesus' story as the parable of God, a story that is self-involving insofar as it articulates the hearer's own personal experience, which gives rise to the doxology: KYRIOS IĒSOUS CHRISTOS!

At this point, one must hold in tensive unity God's self-involvement and our own. Unless one describes 'myth' so broadly that it in-

---

50. Pannenberg, *Jesus* 184, follows "Edmund Schlink's distinction between kerygmatic and doxological forms of expression. Kerygmatic statements speak of definite earthly events that are understood as events that come from God, and in this sense they speak of 'God's acts'. Doxological statements, on the other hand, intend primarily to speak of God's eternal essence. They are the praise of the eternal God on the basis of his deeds."

cludes both fact and fantasy,[51] that it can refer not only to a prototypal divine reality but also to the concreteness and historicity of the man Jesus, it becomes necessary as we have seen to differentiate myth and parable. Pannenberg distinguishes "myths concerning prototypal events in the divine sphere" from the kerygma of Jesus' resurrection. He recognizes that they both have a *metaphorical structure* in common, but he sees the distinction to lie

> in the fact that the expectation of a future resurrection of the dead represents the adequate expression—precisely again in the contemporary situation in anthropological research—of the question beyond death which is inalienably a part of human existence. It is metaphorical, and, to be sure, in the sense of the 'absolute metaphor' which is the sole appropriate expression for a definite subject matter, and is neither interchangeable with other images nor reducible to a separate, rational kernel.[52]

In other words, like the parables of Jesus, the story of his victory over death draws each person who hears it ever more deeply *into* the concreteness and particularity of his or her own experience, in this case the decisive experience of death. Yet, myths could do the same. Any approach to the divine reality—whether mythical or mystical or theological—which effectively alienates one from one's own humanness, which promises salvation by 'escape' from the human condition rather than by entering more deeply into it, is antithetical to what Jesus is all about. Discipleship means that Jesus' story is now our story as well. It is only by taking up our cross and following him that we can in any legitimate sense exclaim: Truly, this man was Son of God! Nonetheless, this emphasis upon the existential meaning of Je-

---

51. Perrin, *Language* 22, so defines myth: "Myth is a word that is notoriously difficult to define, but in the case of the myth of God acting as king I like Alan Watts's statement, as quoted by Philip Wheelwright: 'Myth is to be defined as a complex of stories—some no doubt fact, and some fantasy—which, for various reasons, human beings regard as demonstrations of the inner meaning of the universe and of human life'." Reference to Wheelwright, *Metaphor* 130.

52. Pannenberg, *Jesus* 187.

sus for our own personal experience must never lead us to forget the prior actuality of Jesus' personal relation to the Father as that which makes our own freedom from death possible.

The reflections upon contemporary christology that follow must be understood in this context. We have already reached the ultimate of what can be said in the doxology of Thomas. We must ever and again return to that primordial experience of the risen Jesus. What follows is an attempt to express in very human terms the implications of *that* experience. "The doctrine of the Trinity formulates the concept held by finite men of the God who is revealed in Jesus. . . . Our thought experiences the infinity of God, but does not comprehend it."[53]

---

53. Ibid. 183–184.

CHAPTER FIVE

Contemporary Approaches
to Christology

So far in our study, we have sought to articulate through an historical-analytical approach the development of christology from the proclamation of Jesus to the dogmatic statement of Chalcedon. Inevitably, along the way, there have intruded synthetic questions regarding starting points, judgments, and conclusions. It is time now to seek to organize the material analyzed in a more consciously synthetic manner. We will seek to do this in conversation with four contemporary approaches to christology that have been influenced by the type of analysis offered in the preceding chapters.

Avery Dulles, in a recent article,[1] has offered a typological analysis of contemporary approaches. He identifies five: (1) dogmatic, (2) historical, (3) biblical-kerygmatic, (4) liturgical-sacramental, and (5) secular-dialogic. The fourth approach, with its emphasis upon the experience of the community in worship, is seen to be necessary for giving depth, vitality, and realism to christology but to be inadequate for a complete christology. Therefore, it is seen at least as a supplement to the other three. While agreeing that the experience in worship is not of itself adequate for constructing a christology, I would put much greater stress on the indispensable character of such experience as both the origin and the goal of every christology. This is rooted in the historical Jesus whose whole life was always understood by the New Testament authors as primarily a living worship of the Father and it is that which made possible the christological

---

1. Avery Dulles, S. J., "Contemporary Approaches to Christology: Analysis and Reflections," *Living Light* 13 (1976) 119–144.

development of the early community from the revelatory experience of the death-resurrection to the culminating affirmation of Jesus' divinity. The fifth approach, with its emphasis upon engaging the understanding of reality and the concerns of the contemporary world, is of course indispensable for anyone who is seriously concerned about doing theology today. It is the concern of all the authors treated in this chapter. Dulles asks whether, with their emphasis upon the full humanity of a Jesus fully inserted into the history of the world, they have gone to the other extreme: "Do they, at least unintentionally, undermine the church's faith in the true divinity of Jesus and thus leave us, in the last analysis, without true contact with God's redeeming presence?"[2] It is the question of this chapter.

In his section on method in christology, Dulles proposes ten theses, one positive and one cautionary for each of the approaches. His final conclusion is that the five approaches can "be integrated through a method of convergence and discernment." One must recognize both the mutual interdependence and the distinctive peculiarities of each approach, but the final goal is an integrated christology. "An adequate Christology, in my opinion, must draw on both the Jesus of history and the Christ of faith; it must exploit both the original deposit and the ongoing tradition; it must reflect on the present experience of the church in worship and also on the exigencies of proclamation to the world of our day."[3] While agreeing with this insight, this chapter will seek to achieve such integration by entering into dialogue with four contemporary theologians, who by their choice of a starting point, represent the four dimensions that must be integrated into an adequate christology, viz. incarnation, resurrection, crucifixion, and historical Jesus. We will begin where we ended our analysis, with the Chalcedonian affirmation of incarnation and a contemporary reinterpretation of it, and then move backwards through resurrection and crucifixion to the historical Jesus. With each of these dimensions, we will ask why the author in question chose this particular starting point and what are the implications of such a starting point for an integrated christology. In so doing, we will be seeking to make a theological judgment as to which starting

---

2. Ibid. 132.
3. Ibid. 144.

point is the best for integrating the other dimensions and so arriving at a fully adequate christology for today.

Before entering into a detailed analysis of the authors in question it will be helpful to discuss two preliminary concerns that they have in common. The first is a general presupposition with regard to the starting point for any and every contemporary christology and the second is the recognition of the importance of analogy whenever we speak about God.

To return to the point with which we began this study[4] and which has been presumed throughout, all the authors we are considering would agree that a contemporary christology must begin from below, i.e., from the human and historical. This does not mean from a general theory about what it is to be human (which is just as abstract as starting from a general theory about what it is to be divine) but from the concrete, personal existence of Jesus of Nazareth. It is true that for our understanding of Jesus, as for that of his contemporaries, he did not exist in a vacuum. If we are to apply words like 'God' and 'man' to him, then we must have some awareness of what those words mean in the context of human experience and human history. Jesus proclaims the God of Israel and calls for the human response of faith, but the important point being made here is that he reveals something utterly new and unheard-of in the divine-human relationship simply by being the person he was in all his concreteness and particularity. What Jesus reveals to us is precisely what it is to be human and we can only know that by entering ever more deeply into relationship with his own unique self. The hermeneutical key to this approach can be expressed in the formula: "known as man, confessed as God."[5] Among other things, this means that no matter what starting point we choose for our christology we must give Jesus room to be Jesus, i.e., that we must recognize a development from

---

4. See above, 4–7.
5. This is a formula taken from Ansfried Hulsbosch, "Jezus Christus, gekend als mens, beleden als Zoon Gods," *Tijdschrift voor Theologie* 6 (1966) 250–273, which Robert North, S.J., "Soul-Body Unity and God-Man Unity," TS 30 (1969) 27–60, uses as a starting point for his illuminating review of the Dutch discussion on christology involving Hulsbosch, Schillebeeckx, and Schoonenberg. For a somewhat expanded version of this article, see Robert North, S.J., *In Search of the Human Jesus* (New York: Corpus Books, 1970).

the earthly Jesus to the risen Lord and that we must not allow what we say about his identity with the divine to cancel out his humanness. For Schoonenberg, "Jesus' divine sonship is his human-ness to the utmost."[6]

The second point, the recognition of the importance of analogy, is an indispensable corollary to the above presupposition. Put simply it is the recognition that all of our language about God is very human language, that any and every christology is a very human attempt to bring to expression a mystery that simply transcends the limitations of human systems of thought expressed in human words. We have already pointed out, in the context of discussing the notion of a crucified God, the importance of analogy whenever we speak of the divine becoming.[7] We shall return to this, but two points need to be stressed initially and kept in mind in the discussions that follow: first, God can only be known on the basis of our relatedness to him (creature—Creator) and not in himself, i.e., in any sense apart from that relationship; and second, the claim of analogy is that we are saying something true about God and not merely indulging in anthropomorphisms. Peter Baelz, in his reply to the question of Maurice Wiles: "Does christology rest on a mistake?" rightly emphasizes that the Christian faith is committed to the attempt to find a middle way between anthropomorphism and sheer agnosticism. "Now there is an important—and, I should add, still living—tradition in Christian theology which seeks to avoid the dilemma of anthropomorphism or agnosticism by treading a kind of middle way. There is, it is claimed, an analogical use of language by which we can say certain things about God and say them intelligibly, even though we cannot fully grasp what it is that we are saying."[8] Peter Hodgson, in his discussion of the homologous relationship between the word of God and human word—a discussion to which we shall return—recognizes the indispensable importance of analogy. "The insistence upon homology in this context is not intended to deny the valid use of

6. Schoonenberg, *Christ* 7.
7. See above, 78, especially n. 4.
8. Peter R. Baelz, "A Deliberate Mistake?" in *Christ, Faith and History: Cambridge Studies in Christology,* ed. S. W. Sykes and J. P. Clayton (Cambridge: University Press, 1972) 24.

analogy in second-order language *about* God. *We* can speak about God only analogically and metaphorically; yet God, when he speaks, does so homologically."[9]

Christology is second-order language about God. Like myth and parable, it has a metaphorical structure. The employment of analogy is an explicit and conscious attempt to move the metaphorical language of the New Testament in the direction of metaphysical discourse. It is the recognition that only identity-in-being can control all *merely* mythological and/or legendary tendencies. The assumption of this chapter is that such language can only be employed in closest connection with the concrete, personal history of Jesus. One cannot dispense with the metaphorical structure. Just as Jesus interpreted the Kingdom by his parabolic appeal to the concrete actuality of the everyday, so the christological developments that we have analyzed can only be interpreted by appeal to the concrete actuality of Jesus.[10] We are not being called away from human experience but more deeply into it, indeed into its very center.

With these two assumptions clearly in mind, we turn now to the question of reinterpreting the conciliar, dogmatic tradition, particularly the Council of Chalcedon. With Avery Dulles,[11] we agree that "the dogmatic tradition furnishes indispensable guidelines for theology," which in christology means that we must always affirm the fullness of humanity and divinity in the unity of person. But, we also agree that such dogmas "must be understood with reference to their biblical basis and reinterpreted according to sound hermeneutical principles," the basic principle being the hermeneutical circle which recognizes the indispensable need not only of present understanding to interpret the past but equally of past understanding to interpret the present. One of the more interesting and controversial attempts to reinterpret Chalcedon has come from Piet Schoonenberg of the University of Nijmegen. He does this by seeking to situate the more abstract and speculative formulations of Chalcedon within the concrete patterns of God's salvific activity in the history of Israel culminating in the history of Jesus.

---

9. Hodgson, *Jesus* 102, n. 101.
10. See above, 122–125, 125–132.
11. Dulles, "Contemporary Approaches" 132–134.

A. Incarnation (Piet Schoonenberg)

There is a profound unity to Schoonenberg's approach to theology which must be clearly understood if one is to avoid misinterpreting him. In his introductory remarks to *The Christ,* a book which, as he notes, contains two theological studies written for different purposes, he articulates what is at the heart of that unity. "The two studies presented in this book are both written from the same viewpoint—a believing viewpoint. God does not compete, God does not alienate. He does not dehumanize us, but makes us fully human, ultimately through his Word become man. As I have written elsewhere: our divinization is our humanization. Now I can add to that: Jesus' divine sonship is his human-ness to the utmost."[12] The fundamental insight—whether one is speaking of God in relation to creation in general or in relation to the more particular covenant gift of grace or in relation to the person of Jesus—is that God is not competing, but fulfilling. The unity lies in the creative intention of God who from beginning to end intends only the good of creation. Any concept of God that would see him as somehow alienating us from our own humanness is antithetical to this approach. It is Schoonenberg's contention that many false dilemmas in theology have been created by setting up just such an opposition.

In his first study, appropriately entitled "God or Man: A False Dilemma," he spells out the implications of this insight for God's activity in creation and in the covenant relationship of grace. What is important here is his strong emphasis upon *God's initiative.* ". . . everything is to be explained by factors within the world, but in the coming into effect of these factors God has the initiative, he *is* the initiative. This is precisely what the words 'God is Creator' mean."[13] The world can be spoken of not only as the effect of God's causality but also as the embodiment of God's intention. Therefore, God's creative activity should not be conceived as apart from or parallel to or in competition with the world's activity but as that which is effectively realized in and through the world. God realizes his intention by giving to his creatures their own being and activity precisely as

---

12. Schoonenberg, *Christ* 7.
13. Ibid. 28–29.

their own such that his intention is mediated through the activity of his creatures. Such a view of God's immanence can only be maintained on the basis of his absolute transcendence whereby he is not one cause among or alongside others but is the "supremely active"[14] who embraces the whole of created reality precisely as it is in its concrete condition.

In these terms, the classic problem of the relationship between divine knowledge and human freedom can be seen to be a false dilemma. Furthermore, grace is seen simply as the ever more profound initiative of God within the creative process whereby he freely gives himself to those creatures who can freely respond in dialogue and so enter into a relationship of love. Finally, this emphasis upon the divine initiative has important consequences for understanding Schoonenberg's christology. His position has often been characterized as adoptionism, but if this is meant to imply an emphasis upon human initiative such that Jesus is first merely a man and then subsequently elevated by God to a special role,[15] such a charge misses his emphasis upon the divine initiative. Schoonenberg's position is that Jesus is permeated totally, in everything from the beginning, with the fullness of the godhead (Col. 2:9). As we shall see, this still raises questions about how that divine presence in Jesus is to be understood, but his emphasis upon the divine initiative should lay to rest all charges of a naive adoptionism. The real question is the way (ontologically) that God's creative activity is operative in Jesus as distinct from creation in general and other graced individuals in particular.

---

14. Wright, "God Who Dialogues," uses this expression as the *leitmotif* of his argument. His article offers a profound metaphysical grounding for what Schoonenberg is trying to say here. Schoonenberg frequently uses Wright's image of 'dialogue' to describe divine-human relationship.

15. Aldwinckle, *More Than Man* 150, in defending a position similar to Schoonenberg's that the fullness of God dwells in Jesus, denies the charge of adoptionism as follows: "The weakness behind all forms of adoptionism lies in its often unspoken premise that the initiative in becoming aware of the divine presence rests solely on the manward side. This, however, is not true, even of many lesser figures than Jesus. On biblical assumptions, it would not in any case make sense. If any man is able to 'know' the presence of God, not in a merely intellectual sense but in an existentialist sense in which the whole of the human person is involved, this can be only because God lets Himself be known and experienced in this sense. God gives Himself to the creature according to the measure in which the latter is able to receive Him."

Schoonenberg begins his second study, entitled "God and Man, or God in Man?", with a review of the Chalcedonian pattern and his objections against it. His basic objection is that the two-nature pattern is abstract and essentialistic, that it gives rise to a tendency to ignore the radical dissimilarity between the divine and the human natures so that they can easily be conceived in some kind of competitive relationship. This results in a de-emphasis of Jesus' historical particularity, both his place in the history of salvation and his own personal history of salvation (the New Testament distinction is not between two natures but between the earthly and glorified life of Jesus), with consequent distortions of his humanity. Again, the insight is operative that God is not competing, but fulfilling, and that whatever we say of Jesus must be in terms of the full realization of his humanness. Hence, while Schoonenberg begins with an analysis of Chalcedon and is concerned to maintain the truth in that traditional pattern, his real starting point—which then is a reinterpretation of Chalcedon as traditionally understood—is the complete humanness of Jesus rather than the divinity of the *Logos*. He does this by considering first, from a more atemporal point of view, "the man who is God's Son," and then, from a more human and historical point of view, "the earthly and glorified life of Christ as a man." Our concern in what follows is primarily with the first as this constitutes his reinterpretation of Chalcedon. He will conclude his argument by calling his position "the theory of the enhypostasia of the Word."[16] It is worth noting that he thereby preserves not only the hypostatic language of Chalcedon but also the enhypostatic language of subsequent interpretations of Chalcedon (Leontius of Byzantium, *et al.*). By way of anticipation, our main criticism of Schoonenberg's position will be that if he takes the language of hypostasis seriously, then he must mean by it an 'identity-in-being' and not a 'mere' christology of God's presence. This necessity of speaking in ontological terms will be reinforced by Pannenberg's approach, as we shall see, but let us now investigate how Schoonenberg arrives at his conclusion.

(1) *Starting point.* Schoonenberg begins with a point that is de-

---

16. Schoonenberg, *Christ* 89. For a recent endorsement of Schoonenberg's basic position, see Gerard S. Sloyan, "Some Problems in Modern Christology," in *A World More Human—A Church More Christian* (Staten Island: Alba, 1973).

ceptively simple and can be stated briefly. He starts from the self-evident fact, universally accepted, that Jesus is 'one and the same' person. This is the strongest affirmation of Chalcedon which, in its credal definition (DS 301–302), repeats eight times that Jesus is 'one and the same' or the 'same'. The christological problem arises, of course, when one seeks to predicate both humanity and divinity of this one person. Schoonenberg's second step is crucial to his whole argument, viz. that in this dual predication we should begin with that which is better known to us: the humanity of Jesus. The point is the completeness or fullness of that humanity. If Jesus is to be fully human, then he must have everything that is *essentially* constitutive of the human and that means, above all, human personhood. His divine sonship must be approached in the context of this basic assumption.

Note that he is operating here on an *a priori* assumption of what it is to be human. I would agree with the basic thrust of his argument that we should begin with that which is better known to us ("known as man, confessed as God") and with the idea that there are certain general structural characteristics of humanity that can be culled from the ongoing experiences of human beings in the world. I would agree further with the arguments that he brings to bear on his position, particularly the argument from the Fathers that Jesus must be fully one with us if he is to redeem us ('what is not assumed, is not healed') which applies above all to the personal reality of being human. This argument is grounded in the insight explored above that God's creative activity works in and through the mediation of created reality in such wise that he seeks to bring that created reality to the fullness of its own proper being. Jesus could not even *be* a man in this world if he did not have a human, created act of being and if he did not come to the full realization of that humanness by living through the concrete, historical process of becoming that is constitutive of human personhood. But, at the same time, I would offer the caution that we must remain open to the possibility of Jesus' uniqueness as a man. If Jesus truly reveals to us what it is to be human—which revelation is truly redemptive from within the concrete actuality of being-human-in-the-world—then we must be open to the fact that we do not know what it is to be fully human until Jesus reveals it to us, and that he does this simply by being the kind of man he was in all his concreteness and particularity. Hence, I would agree with the principle that if Jesus is not unique—dissimilar where he is most completely one with us, i.e., in his *humanity*—redemption would be frustrated.[17] Schoonenberg will speak later of "the human transcendence of Jesus Christ as a man" as a consequence of his re-interpretation of Chalcedon, so we shall return to the theme of Jesus' uniqueness as a man. First, we must see how he develops his rein-terpretation from the above starting point. Taking our clue from the Nicene separation of the trinitarian and incarnational issues, we shall consider first the question of person in trinitarian theory and then the question of the hypostasis of the Word in the man Jesus.

(2) *Person in trinitarian theory.* "Jesus Christ is one person. He is a human person. Can he then still be called a divine person? He is so called in the Chalcedonian pattern, but not precisely in the in-dividual formula of Chalcedon itself—only by those who prepared and elaborated Chalcedon."[18] Unless we wish a schizophrenic Jesus, we cannot maintain that he is a human person who is then somehow in dialogue with himself as a divine person. The oneness of Jesus as a person is the unquestionable basis of any christology. As Schoon-enberg points out, it is no answer simply to deny the problem on the basis of the incommensurability and non-numerability of the divine and the human. We must still ask how the divine in Christ relates to the human person Jesus. Nor does any kenotic theory which would maintain that the divine person somehow withdraws or with-holds some of his divine attributes—Schoonenberg calls this position "an inverted Monophysitism and an inverted Alexandrian christol-ogy"—afford an answer, although as we shall see a careful interpre-

---

17. John McIntyre, *The Shape of Christology* (London: SCM Press, 1966) 37.

18. Schoonenberg, *Christ* 74–75. Schoonenberg is invoking here a principle of minimal interpretation. In effect, he is saying that we are only bound in faith to what the creed explicitly affirms and not to the intellectual milieu in which it was formu-lated. The milieu can help us to interpret what the text meant to those who formulated it, but it also leaves us free to reinterpret the text from within our own contemporary milieu. This is not to deny continuity with the basic affirmations of the faith through the centuries, but it is an attempt to recognize that the interpretations of such affir-mations have gone through real change in varying socio-cultural contexts and hence that we should not impose more than is minimally necessary for continuity in faith. Those who do not accept such a principle of minimal interpretation will, of course, reject Schoonenberg's reinterpretation as illegitimate from the start.

tation of the kenotic language in Philippians 2:6–11 can offer helpful insights into our problem. We come closer to a solution in the trinitarian doctrine of Thomas Aquinas, but this doctrine precisely raises the problem of what we mean by 'person' when applied to the inner-trinitarian life.

The term *hypostasis,* which was employed by the Fathers and early Councils and so passed on to scholastic theology, means "reality standing by itself." It led to the definition of 'person' by Boethius as *individua substantia rationalis naturae* and by Richard of St. Victor as *rationalis naturae incommunicabilis existentia,* both of which were employed by Thomas Aquinas in his doctrine on the Trinity.[19] The focus of these definitions is on the "existing in itself" of the person, on the proper individuality and inalienability of the subject: it is the basic insight that I am I and not someone else. While this is valid as far as it goes, it too narrowly restricts what we normally mean by the word 'person'. It is true that the reference to a rational nature in each of the definitions is intended to preserve the realities of consciousness and freedom as constitutive of a person existing in oneself but, when applied to the Trinity, such a notion of person must be eliminated in order to preserve the unity of the one divine life which realizes the consciousness and freedom common to all three. Hence, according to our normal understanding of person, the Trinity could more properly be called one person as Augustine's famous analogy[20] makes clear. This can be visualized schematically as follows:

one divine life:	FATHER (origin)───▶ SON (logos)───▶ SPIRIT (love)
one person: MIND:	REMEMBERING (God) KNOWING (God) LOVING (God)
differentiation (of persons):	JESUS

---

19. Ibid. 78. Cf. Thomas Aquinas, ST I, q.29, a.1 & 3, ad 4um; Boethius, *Tractatus* V, c. 5; Richard of St. Victor, *De Trinitate* IV, 18 & 23.

20. Augustine in books VIII to XV of the *De Trinitate* offers a number of images of the Trinity by way of analogy from the psychological nature of the human person. J. N. D. Kelly, *Early Christian Doctrines* (New York: Harper & Row, 1960²) 277–278, offers an excellent summary of Augustine's subtly varied use of the analogy: "It has often been assumed that Augustine's principal Trinitarian analogy in the *De Trinitate* is that disclosed by his analysis of the idea of love (his starting-point is the

This is my own schematization, not Schoonenberg's, but in the course of his argument he cites the christological consequence that Schillebeeckx draws from the Thomist concept of person in trinitarian theory, viz. ". . . that the Son is conscious of his sonship not in a divine but only in his human consciousness."[21] Central then to Schoonenberg's position, one with which I would agree, is that the scriptural data of Jesus' relation to the Father as an 'I' to a 'Thou' is only possible in and through the human personhood of Jesus. Therefore, such a differentiation of the trinitarian life into an 'I-Thou' can only take place at a particular point of time within the creative process. Moreover, to predicate person of the divine *Logos* is at best analogous to predicating person of the human Jesus. In fact, the term as applied to the Trinity is so reductive as to be equivocal

---

Johannine dictum that God is love) into the lover (*amans*), the object loved (*quod amatur*), and the love (*amor*) which unites, or strives to unite, them. Yet, while expounding this analogy, he himself reckons that it affords only an initial step towards our understanding of the Trinity (*coepit utcumque . . . apparere*), at best a momentary glimpse of It (*eluxit paullulum*). His discussion of it is quite brief, and forms no more than a transition to what he considers his all-important analogy, based on the inner man, viz. the mind's activity as directed upon itself or, better still, upon God. This analogy fascinated him all his life, so that in such an early work as the *Confessions* (397-8) we find him pondering the triad of being, knowing and willing (*esse, nosse, velle*). In the *De Trinitate* he elaborates it at length in three successive stages, the resulting trinities being (a) the mind, its knowledge of itself, and its love of itself; (b) memory or, more properly, the mind's latent knowledge of itself, understanding, i.e., its apprehension of itself in the light of the eternal reasons, and the will, or love of itself, by which this process of self-knowledge is set in motion; and (c) the mind as remembering, knowing and loving God Himself. Each of these, in different degrees, reveals three real elements which, according to Augustine's metaphysic of personality, are coordinate and therefore equal, and at the same time essentially one; each of them throws light on the mutual relations of the divine Persons. It is the last of the three analogies, however, which Augustine deems most satisfactory. The three factors disclosed in the second 'are not three lives but one life, not three minds but one mind, and consequently are not three substances but one substance'; but he reasons that it is only when the mind has focused itself with all its powers of remembering, understanding and loving on its Creator, that the image it bears of Him, corrupted as it is by sin, can be fully restored." The quotation of Augustine is from *De Trinitate* X, 18. Kelly goes on to describe Augustine's awareness of the immense limitations of this analogy. He also notes that for Augustine the members of the Trinity are persons, whereas they are not so in the human mind.

21. Schoonenberg, *Christ* 79. See E. Schillebeeckx, "Het bewustzijnleven van Christus," *Tijdschrift voor Theologie* 1 (1961) 227–251, especially 241.

and so significant contemporary theologians search for other language to speak of the inner-trinitarian life.[22]

(3) *The hypostasis of the Word in the man Jesus.* This brings Schoonenberg to the approach which he considers conclusive and which he discusses under the heading "hermeneutics of the pre-existence texts." His position quite simply is that the language of pre-existence is derivative from the concrete, personal history of Jesus and not the other way around. Even the conciliar creeds set everything in apposition to the "one Lord Jesus Christ." His proposal is that ". . . we put the theological and the magisterial discussion on the Son as divine, transcendent, and pre-existent person back in the context it originally had and thus interpret it according to what it meant in that context."[23] This context not only includes the oneness of Jesus as a human person with his own personal history—such that whatever we say of him as divine can never nullify his humanness—but also the whole history of God's salvific activity in and through the creative process. He states a principle that also is operative in Pannenberg's approach: "Where God's Trinity and especially the divine person of the Word are concerned, we must first establish that we do not know the Trinity outside its revelation and that this revelation occurs in the Word that is flesh and in the Spirit which is poured out. . . ."[24] However, unlike Pannenberg, he thinks that this should lead to an agnosticism with regard to a pre-existent Trinity (pre-existence being understood as a temporal image for transcendence, not as implying a 'before' or 'after' in God). One can neither affirm it nor deny it because it is not contained in God's revelation. The only God we know is the one who becomes triune through the process of history. Therefore, it is better to speak of the pre-history of the *Logos* (creation—covenant—incarnation) than of pre-existence. The *Logos* is the creative power of God whereby he has progressively made

---

22. Karl Barth, *Church Dogmatics* I, 1 (Edinburgh: T & T Clark, 1936) 400–440, prefers the phrase "modes of being or existence." Karl Rahner, *The Trinity* (New York: Herder & Herder, 1970) 103–115, prefers "manners or modes of subsistence." See also the remarks of Pannenberg, *Jesus* 179–183 and of Hodgson, *Jesus* 119–130.

23. Schoonenberg, *Christ* 80

24. Ibid. 82.

the history of what he has created profoundly his own.[25] We will now seek to unpack some of the implications of this position.

The weakness of Schoonenberg's agnosticism lies, it seems to me, in the concept of revelation that is implied. If revelation is not *self*-revelation in the strict sense, then it becomes a sort of positivistic communication of bits of information about the world and God remains as uninvolved as ever. The gut issue is how radically we are willing to conceive God's personal self-involvement in his creation. We will return to this notion of revelation when we treat Pannenberg, but for the moment I would like to focus upon a problem which Schoonenberg's agnosticism allows him to ignore. Granted for the moment that the revelation in Christ is a true revelation of the eternal essence of God as a threefold unity, the problem arises as to how we are to understand the activity of the *Logos* who does not somehow disengage himself from the Father in order to become man. The problem is that the Father must retain his own personal center of knowing and willing over against the human personhood of the Son if he is to be a 'Thou' in relation to Jesus' 'I'. This means that

---

25. This notion is not new in the history of theology. The idea of the pre-history of the *Logos,* with the emphasis upon the salvific *oikonomia* whereby the *Logos* progressively identifies with each age, is already found—prior to the more speculative *Logos* doctrine of Origen—in the *Logos* doctrine of the Apologists Justin and Tatian. It is also in Hippolytus who was influenced by Irenaeus' doctrine of the universal *oikonomia* in the history of revelation. See Grillmeier, *Christ* 106–117. On this level of the creative power of God, one could as well speak of the *Spirit* as of the *Logos.* There is a renewed interest in reviving a Spirit christology. For example, see Philip J. Rosato, S.J., "Spirit Christology," TS 38 (1977) 423–449. Insofar as this is meant simply to emphasize dimensions obscured by a more abstract and speculative *Logos* christology, e.g., the biblical, eschatological, and soteriological dimensions, this could be done by a revitalized *Logos* christology. The problem with *replacing* a *Logos* christology with a Spirit christology (which is not Rosato's position) is that it tends to obscure the traditional distinction—already clear in John's gospel—between Jesus and the Spirit. Moreover, it tends toward a subordinationist type of christology in which the Spirit 'possesses' or 'indwells' Jesus. G. W. H. Lampe, "The Holy Spirit and the Person of Christ," in *Cambridge Studies* 124, proposes just such a christology when he says that Jesus *is* God not 'substantivally' nor 'adjectivally' but 'adverbially': "By the mutual interaction of the Spirit's influence and the free response of the human spirit such a unity of will and operation was established that in all his actions the human Jesus acted divinely." We will treat further the place of the Spirit when we come to Pannenberg's christology. Rosato, "Spirit Christology" 438–444, offers a good comparison of the more Spirit-oriented approach of Walter Kasper as distinct from the more historical approach of Pannenberg. Both agree, however, on the centrality of the resurrection for christology.

the *Logos* must be understood to function both as the Father's own self-consciousness within the trinitarian life (what makes God be God in absolute independence) and as the Father's self-expression in the Son (what makes God be Creator).

The key to understanding this lies, it seems to me, in the distinction between God as God and God as Creator, a distinction first introduced in chapter three when discussing the meaning of Jesus' crucifixion as involving a *stasis* within God. This distinction needs to be explored more fully now. It should be noted at the outset that it has nothing to do with the antecedent and consequent nature of God in process thought. The distinction we are proposing is from our human point of view an abstraction, for the only God we know is the God who has involved himself in the creative process. Yet, it is not meant to deny that such involvement is truly self-revelation of the essence of God. Rather, it is intended to preserve the absolute independence and transcendence of God precisely in our talk about God as Creator involved in the creative process. The distinction could be put this way: what makes God be God in no way involves him in the creative process (creation being the free initiative of God, he would remain God whether he had ever chosen to create or not). On the other hand, what makes God be Creator *does* involve him in the creative process. Schoonenberg objects to the idea of a pre-existent Trinity because he claims it is argued "via a concept of God's immutability that is open to criticism." If immutability means that God remains God no matter what happens within creation, then I would retain the concept. But, the real issue is whether we understand God's revelation as a personal *self-involvement* that affects his very identity as Creator.

Out of his free divine initiative, God has created the world as we know it, not a static world but a world, as Schoonenberg describes it, that is continually being created as it moves through the successive stages of its evolutionary development until there emerges that which changes *chronos* into *kairos,* the evolutionary process of nature into the open possibilities of history, viz. human freedom. God's creative activity continues or the world would cease to exist, but now he can more properly be spoken of as the "God who dialogues," for the absolute free divine initiative seeks to engage a free human response. This means, as we saw when discussing the crucifixion, that God enters into real relations with his creatures and truly depends—not insofar as God is God but insofar as God freely chooses to be Creator—upon the free response of his creatures to his creative initiative in order to shape time. One might even go so far as to say that he has freely *subjected* himself to his creation by creating one who can himself create his own future. The history of his dealings with his people Israel is best described as a covenantal relationship in which he remains faithful to his promises (and therefore true to his own nature as love) even in the face of continued rejection of that love. The response of rejection gives shape to that history as much as the initiative of love, a history of rejection that finally culminated in the crucifixion of his beloved Son, to whom they would not listen. As we have seen, the resurrection is the divine response to that human response: God remains God, faithful in his love in the face of rejection, but deeply affected as Creator by that rejection.

The manhood of Jesus is best understood, it seems to me, in terms of the free initiative of God as Creator and the free response of Jesus as creature, i.e., in terms of the dialogue between Father and Son. C.F.D. Moule offers an important insight into this creative process in his interpretation of the word *kenōsis* in Philippians 2:6–11. The mythic pattern of the Redeemer freely choosing to exchange the divine mode of being for that of a slave (as we interpreted it following Fuller) should not be interpreted, as in many 'kenotic' theories, to mean that "... the pre-existent Son of God voluntarily emptied himself of divine prerogatives for a time, in order to share to the full the human lot, and resumed his full capacities only after the death on the cross." Rather than emphasize the contrast between humiliation and exaltation, Moule sees in this hymn—and also in John and Hebrews—a paradoxical identification between the two which "... recognizes what is ordinarily called 'emptying' as really 'fulfilling': *kenōsis* actually *is plērōsis;* which means that the human limitations of Jesus are seen as a positive expression of his divinity rather than as a curtailment of it ..."[26] He appeals by way of exam-

---

26. C. F. D. Moule, "The Manhood of Jesus in the New Testament," in *Cambridge Studies* 96–98. For our interpretation of Philippians 2:6–11, see above, 118–120. Moltmann, *Crucified* 205, speaking of the cross as the incarnation of God in reference to Philippians 2, offers a similar description: "Humiliation to the point of death on the cross corresponds to God's nature in the contradiction of abandonment. When

ple to an artist or craftsman who accepts and makes positive use of the limitations of his medium. Once he has chosen his medium, he must work within its limitations but in such wise that he seeks to exploit its possibilities to the *full.* As applied to God, Moule calls this "creative fulfillment-by-self-limitation." The incarnation, then, is seen as ". . . a positive filling, not a negative emptying. . . ." I would go further and say that such a view almost demands incarnation as a logical necessity: not that God *has* to create in this way but that only God has the creative power to become completely one in being with his creation while remaining God in absolute transcendence. Like Moule, Russell F. Aldwinckle also sees the necessity for some kind of divine self-limitation if we are to understand how God can become man without ceasing to be God. Putting the emphasis upon the divine initiative, he offers a helpful description of how this creative activity might take place: "God gives Himself to the creature according to the measure in which the latter is able to receive Him. If this is granted, then it is at least possible to conceive in principle that God could give Himself wholly to a man and a man give himself wholly to God in a way which would produce *a new and unique actuality,* i.e., a human personality which was a transparent medium of the real presence and the saving activity of God Himself."[27]

Jesus, then, is filled with all the fullness of God (Col. 1:19; 2:9). But, this must be understood as a new actuality not only in creation

---

the crucified Jesus is called the 'image of the invisible God', the meaning is that *this* is God, and God is like *this.* God is not greater than he is in this humiliation. God is not more glorious that he is in this self-surrender. God is not more powerful than he is in this helplessness. God is not more divine than he is in this humanity. The nucleus of everything that Christian theology says about 'God' is to be found in this Christ event."

27. Aldwinckle, *More Than Man* 150 (italics mine). He goes on to describe the human experience of such a new actuality: "If such a relationship between the human and the divine is in fact possible, then what kind of experience would be involved on the human side? It would show the marks of genuine and authentic creaturehood and of humble and freely chosen dependence upon the Eternal Father. At the same time, the man would speak and act with the sovereign authority and confidence of One who knows that the Father's presence is with Him and in Him and that the Father's will is being truly done in and through Him. This paradoxical combination of human weakness and divine authority is precisely what we find in the gospel records of the life and ministry of Jesus of Nazareth." Ibid. 151. See 97–98 for his discussion of divine self-limitation.

but in the Creator. Through the creative power of his *Logos,* the Father creates the human personhood of Jesus as a new reality *within* the divine life. North, summarizing Schoonenberg's earlier response to Hulsbosch on the pre-existence formulas, remarks:

> . . . all these formulas . . . leave open *some* possibility that the existence of God as Son from all eternity is in relation to his eventual human nature. However, after Nicaea and Constantinople, formulations taken from Origen and Hippolytus lost their emphasis on what had been originally paramount: the Logos is such in relation to creation, the Son is such with relation to his Incarnation . . . '*Pater generat Filium incarnando eum*' or '*ab aeterno generat Filium incarnandum*'.[28]

Later, in *The Christ,* he reiterates his agnosticism as to whether the Word existing from eternity is directed to becoming flesh (*verbum incarnandum*) or originates only through becoming flesh (*verbum incarnatum*). Again, this agnosticism seems rather forced and unnecessary. If God is personal, then he must be from all eternity his own center of knowing and willing; if he is Creator, then he must have both that creative power within himself which we call the *Logos* and he must be able to communicate that power to his creation. Hence, what remains eternal (in answer to the Fathers' opposition to the notion that 'there was a time when he was not') is the eternal nature of the divine life as a threefold unity; what changes is the hypostatization that goes beyond that of Wisdom in the Old Testament insofar as this man Jesus is alone of all creation the *plērōsis* of created possibility. Only in this sense can it be said that God becomes triune.

Schoonenberg's discussion of "divine becoming"—the idea that God really changes in relation to his creatures, that he becomes more *our* God—is important and helpful at this point. It need not be tied to process thought, though Schoonenberg is attracted in this direction. The basic insight is that there is real change in God because,

---

28. North, *Search* 49. See also his conclusion, 59. The discussion on Schoonenberg's idea of pre-existence is found on 44–50. Cp. Schoonenberg, *Christ* 86.

contrary to the position of scholastic theology, God enters into *real* relations with his creatures. The opposition of scholasticism was based on the fear that such an idea would reduce God to the level of a creature (even though real relations of equality were posited within the Trinity). Hence, if we are to speak of a divine becoming, the possibility of change in God must be absolutely differentiated from human becoming ". . . which rests on the individual incompletion of the changing subject, on the transition from potency to act, on growth in the broadest sense of the word. This all must indeed be excluded from our concept of God, if we wish God to be seen as God."[29] God does not change for his own fulfillment, but for ours: to bring his creation to the fullest realization of its possibilities. Such a God is not the unmoved Mover of Aristotle but the covenantal God of Abraham, Isaac, and Jacob-Israel, the "God who dialogues." Such a God profoundly affects our lives by his divine initiatives and is in turn profoundly affected by our human response. Such a God changes not through limitation or imperfection but through the abundance of his love, which is his very nature. Such a God, through his own free divine initiative, ". . . becomes Trinity through communicating himself in a total way to, and being present in, the man Jesus as Word, and through being in the Church as Spirit."[30] Such a God is so completely involved and identified with his creation that his very creative power, his *Logos,* has become flesh, one in being with a human person, the man Jesus. This new creation has profound implications for both partners in the dialogue, for Jesus in his identity as a man and for the Father in his identity as Creator. We must now reflect more deeply on each of these in turn.

The implication for Jesus is that his personhood is analogous to ours. Schoonenberg calls his position "the theory of the enhypostasia of the Word." It is my contention that he must take the metaphysical implications of such language with the utmost seriousness if he wish-

---

29. Schoonenberg, *Christ* 84, n. 16, where he summarizes his earlier article "Christus zonder tweeheid," *Tijdschrift voor Theologie* 6 (1966) 289–306. See above, 78, n. 4. Schoonenberg appeals further to the formula of Karl Rahner that "God changes in the Other" from his article "Current Problems in Christology," *Theological Investigations* I (New York: Seabury, 1963) 181.

30. Schoonenberg, *Christ* 85, n. 16.

es to propose an adequate christology. He summarizes his reinterpretation of Chalcedon as follows:

> The concept developed here regarding Christ's being-person is a reversal of the Chalcedonian pattern insofar as it is influenced by neo-Chalcedonism, which has become our current christology. Now not the human but the divine nature in Christ is anhypostatic, with the proviso, moreover, that this is valid inasmuch as we do not know the person of the Word outside the man Jesus. However, it is primarily not the human nature which is enhypostatic in the divine person, but the divine nature in the human person.[31]

The value of such a reversal is that it steadfastly refuses to locate the divinity of Jesus outside the humanity. Jesus can be called God only by his being man in a special way. He is the human measure of the divine, the humanity of God, such that the mystery of his divinity is not above or beneath the man Jesus but precisely in his being-man itself.[32]

Yet, such a reversal must not be allowed to obscure the emphasis upon the divine initiative with which we began this whole discussion. Once again, it is not a question of choosing between competing alternatives: Jesus as "divinized man" ('man has become God') or as "humanized God" ('God has become man').[33] Rather, it is a question of the divine initiative within the creative process taking place in such a manner that God is seen not as competing but as bringing to

---

31. Ibid. 87.

32. For a discussion of this approach, see North, *Search* 27–35. Especially interesting is Schillebeeckx's interpretation of Aquinas in this vein: "This man himself *is* the person of the Son of God . . . so that in him humanity itself attains an unimaginable fulfillment (*Sum. theol.* 3, q.3, a.1, ad 1m: '*non Deus sed homo perficitur*')." Ibid. 34 (North's paraphrase).

33. William E. May in his Preface to North, *Search* 4–8, feels that the formula of Hulsbosch: "The divinity of Jesus *consists in* the perfection of his humanity" implies that man has become God rather than that God has become man. Although this is a possible interpretation, I do not think it is the intention of Schoonenberg for the reasons given, particularly as the objection operates out of the dualistic assumption of competition between the divine and the human. For my part, I would prefer to say that the divinity of Jesus *constitutes* the perfection of his humanity.

fulfillment creation itself. But the order is important. It is the Father's initiative, identifying his creative Word with the man Jesus, which makes Jesus fully—and hence uniquely—human. Because Jesus is the humanity of God, he is a divinized man, not in the sense that he somehow ceases to be a man but in the sense that he realizes within creation the deepest personalization possible. It is because Jesus is the Word that he is unique as a man, i.e., his uniqueness as a man is not constitutive of the incarnation—otherwise Jesus would not be a man but something else, a *tertium quid*—but is a consequence of the incarnation. In this there is nothing lacking to the humanity of Jesus. Rather, Jesus reveals to us what ultimately constitutes the fulfillment of human personhood: union with the divine. From this perspective, it is rather we who are lacking in the fullness of what it is to be human, it is we who are not yet fully personalized in our existence as relational beings. Precisely what Jesus redeems or saves is the personal dimension, simply by being the man he was. This is what Schoonenberg's insight into the uniqueness of Jesus as "the human final completion" should mean.

Schoonenberg's position may be characterized by many as radical. In my opinion, it is not radical enough. Precisely at the point where he should spell out the breathtaking implications of his "theory of the enhypostasia of the Word" as that which makes Christianity radically distinctive in its understanding of God's personal involvement in the world, he retreats to a mere "christology of God's presence." His final position can be summarized by saying that this man is permeated totally (in everything from the beginning) with the fullness of the godhead. But, this is too close to the indwelling framework of the Antiochene school and implies a quantitative rather than a qualitative distinction between Jesus and ourselves.[34] He would be

---

34. Schoonenberg, *Christ* 89, 93, 97 prefers to speak in the language of "whole" as distinct from "partial," taking as his favorite text Colossians 1:19; 2:9. His difficulty in answering the questions as to whether Jesus differs essentially or accidentally and whether his transcendence is absolute or relative (Ibid. 97) seems to me to rest on a failure to employ analogy. His appeal to process theology would suggest that he sees a difference only in degree and not in kind. I think *Time Magazine* (Feb. 27, 1978) 44–45 is correct in its article "New Debate Over Jesus' Divinity" when it reports: "In 1972 the Vatican's Congregation for the Doctrine of the Faith issued its most recent declaration on Christology. It defined as an error the theory that God was only 'pres-

better served here if he stayed with the notion of the enhypostasis of the Word as meaning a real ontic identity of Jesus with the divine. He comes closest to such language in the course of justifying his theory with further arguments:

> . . . it is not the personhood itself which becomes problematical in God, but the existence of still other persons in God, opposed to his original personhood, as the Son (and the Holy Spirit) to the Father. For if an opposition in God still persists, and not in a thought construction but in reality, then it is obvious that this occurs through a limitation, and thus there cannot be a limitation in God except insofar as *he identifies himself with a creature.* On the one hand, then, as we argued above, a merging of the human person in a divine person through a real anhypostasia or 'ecstasy of being' would nullify human personhood. On the other hand, the *self-identification of God's being with a human person* brings about precisely in God himself a new person and thus a plurality of persons.[35]

This statement by itself is a perfectly acceptable articulation of the theory of enhypostasis, but only if it is intended to say more than mere presence.

Schillebeeckx, in disagreement with Hulsbosch, affirms the need for the hypostatic formula (though he prefers "hypostatic *unity* rather than *union*") precisely because ". . . the dogmatic confession of hypostatic union never was meant to express anything other than the implications of *Jesus' unique mode of being man,* a uniqueness which would have to remain a mere meaningless word unless the hypostatic formula had been found." And further (as North summarizes his position): "In the case of Jesus, God did not merely 'creatively posit' or infuse the being of a particular human subjectivity as he does for

---

ent in the highest degree in the human person Jesus', including the version in which Jesus is 'God' in the sense that in 'his human person God is supremely present'. Though no names were mentioned, this was aimed primarily at Schoonenberg." The ET of the Vatican declaration is in *The Catholic Mind* 70 (1972) 61–64.

35. Schoonenberg, *Christ* 88 (italics mine).

every man, but he creatively posited this special human subjectivity as his own. This is what ought to be called the 'hypostatic unity'." Finally: "If you conjure away the hypostatic unity, the absoluteness of Jesus' human uniqueness is taken away. He would then be only one in a row of religious geniuses who have in fact brought men nearer to God."[36] What is radical in Christian faith is the conviction that God has come near to us, as near as he can, by identifying himself with a creature, the man Jesus. Through identifying his *Logos* with this human "mode of being" and thus making this human subjectivity his own, he has not only brought created reality to the definitively unique fullness of its possibilities—no further or greater perfection is conceivable beyond oneness in being with the divine—but he has also created a new reality within his own divine life, a Son who through his human consciousness can be a 'Thou' in relation to the Father's 'I'. In this way, God freely chooses to become triune. But, this means that the hypostatization of the *Logos* in the human personhood of Jesus has implications not only for Jesus but for the Father as well. It is here, I believe, that Schoonenberg's theory must be brought to its most radical expression.

If we take Jesus' humanness seriously, then the unavoidable implication, it seems to me, is that the Father truly risks his personal identity *as Creator* in the free obedience of his Son. This is what I meant when I said earlier that we must give Jesus room to be Jesus, i.e., that we must recognize a development from the earthly Jesus to the risen Lord and that we must not allow what we say about his identity with the divine to cancel out his humanness. We have seen that God as Creator works in and through the limitations and possibilities of his medium. This means, in the case of human freedom, that he takes our human response to his initiative with the utmost seriousness. It makes a profound difference to him as Creator how we respond, for our response gives shape to his creation as an ongoing process moving toward its future consummation. As suggested in our discussion on the crucifixion, the world in which we live today

---

36. E. Schillebeeckx, "Persoonlijke openbaringsgestalte van de Vader," *Tijdschrift voor Theologie* 6 (1966) 283. The translation and the summaries are from North, *Search* 52–53, 55 (italics mine). See 50–57 for his whole discussion of Schillebeeckx's position.

would be far different if our response to Jesus had been something other than rejection. But, Jesus' mission was not only to call *us* to respond to the Father's love. He himself had first to say *Amēn* to his *Abbā*. If we do not admit this, then I do not think that we can take Jesus' humanness seriously; then God is not truly working in and through his humanness but is only using it as an extrinsic instrument for the sake of something else. Hence, things *could* have happened differently in the earthly ministry of Jesus: his temptations were real! The question, finally, is: to what extent is Jesus' humanity operative in our salvation, i.e., to what extent does his humanness truly *mediate* our salvation, and, correspondingly, to what extent are we willing to conceive God's risk in creating human freedom?

We know that Jesus remained faithful to the mission given him by the Father, not by any psychologizing of Jesus' interior states of mind but by the theological fact, given to us in revelation, that the Father embraced his Son in the moment of his death, that he raised him up, made him Lord and Christ, and gave him the Name which is above every name. And so, the letter to the Hebrews can affirm that we have a high priest who can suffer with us in our weaknesses, one tempted in all things, like us, except that he did not sin (*chōris hamartias:* Heb. 4:15). There is only one mediator, the *man* Jesus (1 Tim. 2:5), because in him alone has the created response to the divine love been lived out in perfect fidelity, in him alone has the alienation between the divine and the human been perfectly overcome. As we will see in treating Pannenberg, we know this for the whole of his life in the light of the resurrection, an event which constitutes him ontologically in his eternal union with the Father. But, if that union has cosmic implications, as claimed particularly in the letters to the Colossians and the Ephesians, then one should not shrink from speculation about the equally cosmic implications of Jesus' possible rejection of his mission, for such speculation serves the useful purpose of heightening our awareness of how *real* the stakes were in Jesus' fidelity. Jesus is God's Word because in his personal identity he is the truth about the human condition, especially at the moment of death. Had that truth been turned into the lie of human sinfulness, of human rejection, then the identification of God's creative power, his *Logos,* with the man Jesus would have resulted not in salvation but in dissolution, cosmic destruction, the end of creation as we on this planet have known it. I believe this possibility, speculative as it is, must be stated so strongly and so radically if we are to appreciate fully the profound difference that Jesus' victory has made to our human condition. It is in this sense that the Father truly risks his personal identity as Creator in the free obedience of his Son.

In all of this, the humanity of Jesus remains God's self-expression in the world (*Logos ensarkos*), God's human 'way of being', or we do not have a self-involving God who moves us to repentance through his own suffering. It is the depth of the Father's suffering in the sacrifice of his Son, a sacrifice which he once asked Abraham to make of his beloved son (Gen. 22:1–2) and which he at the decisive moment in human history asks of himself and of his Son in filial obedience to his will, which is the truly radical and startling claim of Christian faith. With remarkable insight, Juergen Moltmann articulates the fundamental difference between Jews and Christians, both of whom look for redemption and both of whom experience the world in which we live today as unredeemed. "Does redemption depend upon the repentance of man? If it does, redemption will never come. If it does not, it seems to be irrelevant to men. The Jewish answer could be described by saying that God forces Israel to repent through suffering. The Christian answer is that God brings the sinner, whether a Jew or a Gentile, to repentance through his own suffering in the cross of Jesus."[37] The Father works creatively in and through the limitations and possibilities of created reality, in and through the very humanness of his Son, in order to bring to expression from within the most perfect possible realization of human personhood: the complete union with himself that overcomes all separation and alienation between the divine and the human, the redemption of humanity. The deepest intuition of scripture and tradition is this: God is personally involved in our human condition in such wise that he is affected deeply within his own divine life by our human response, a response that came to its critical and culminating expression in the personal history of Jesus.

---

37. Moltmann, *Crucified* 102. But see his more recent *The Church in the Power of the Spirit* (New York: Harper & Row, 1977) 61–62, where he modifies this position with a quote from Franz Rosenzweig. The Jews also recognize the suffering of God in their experience. I would still maintain that Christians bring this insight to its most radical expression.

Hence, while Schoonenberg begins his study of christology with the Chalcedonian formulation of incarnation because he wishes to meet head on the traditional problematic, his real starting point, as already indicated, is the complete humanness of Jesus, his concrete personal history, rather than the divinity of the *Logos*. In his second section, then, on "the earthly and glorified life of Christ as a man," he develops this history. We have given our version of it in the preceding chapters. In speaking of the reality of Jesus' temptations (which is always the touchstone of any approach to christology), he offers a concluding statement that catches the spirit of this whole section:

> Here what we have often illustrated again comes to the fore: it is necessary to include adoption christology in incarnation christology. Jesus' divine sonship is at the same time with his manhood a reality-in-becoming: the whole fullness of the Godhead takes possession of him more and more, by affirming Jesus in obedience and by making him conquer sin and Satan.[38]

Although I dislike the use of the term 'adoption' here, I take Schoonenberg to mean this not in the naive sense discussed above but in the sense that Jesus, who is one in being with the Father from the very beginning of his created existence, grows into his relationship with the Father in such wise that his full identity as the Son (incarnation) can be properly understood only as the conclusion to the *whole* of his earthly and glorified life. What Schoonenberg objects to is the phrase *viator simul et comprehensor* insofar as this would rob Jesus of the concreteness and particularity of his personal history. His final completion can only come at the end, at the eschatological culmination of God's creative activity, which he must arrive at by personally taking up his cross and going 'on the way' (Mark 10:52) in fulfillment of the Father's will.

The implication for an integrated christology, an approach which Schoonenberg then shares with the other authors that we will now consider, is that the concrete personal history of Jesus is basic

---

38. Schoonenberg, *Christ* 146.

and essential to the affirmation of his divinity. The proclamation of Jesus' obedience even unto death (kerygma) is the indispensable basis for affirming his divinity (doxology).[39] For Wolfhart Pannenberg, the possibility of making such a proclamation depends on the event of Jesus' resurrection. In discussing the position of the new quest that faith must have "support in the historical Jesus himself" (Ebeling), he remarks: "One can agree completely with this assertion. The only question that remains is, What is really *the decisive factor* in Jesus' life and proclamation upon which faith is based?"[40]

B. RESURRECTION (WOLFHART PANNENBERG)

As with Schoonenberg, we are not concerned here to deal with all the issues in christology which Pannenberg raises—many of which we have dealt with in our own way in the preceding chapters—but rather we are concerned to analyze and evaluate the central insight of his approach, the starting point that conditions his conclusions, as a help to us in achieving an integrated christology. Hence, we will focus primarily upon Part One (chapters 3–4) of his book *Jesus—God and Man* which he entitles "The Knowledge of Jesus' Divinity." Prior to that, however, we must discuss a fundamental methodological presupposition of Pannenberg with which we are in basic disagreement, as a comparison of our first chapter on the question of faith and history with Pannenberg's first chapter on the task and method of christology, which he entitles "The Starting Point," would demonstrate.

---

39. From another perspective, that of liberation theology, Jon Sobrino, S.J., *Christology at the Crossroads* (Maryknoll, N.Y.: Orbis, 1978) 311–345, employs the distinction of Schlink and Pannenberg between kerygmatic (he prefers 'historical') statements and doxological statements to interpret the meaning and value of christological dogmas. He uses this to differentiate his approach from that of traditional christology: "Thus the Christology elaborated here maintains the dogmatic statements, but it offers a different approach to understanding them. Instead of beginning with the doxological affirmation of the incarnation of the eternal Son in Jesus of Nazareth (the theology of *descent*), it ends up with the doxological statement that this Jesus of Nazareth is the eternal Son. Both approaches involve a shift from the historical to the doxological. The advantage of my approach here over that of the traditional Christology of descent is that it regards the history of Jesus as basic and essential to the dogmatic assertion that Christ is the eternal Son." Ibid. 337.

40. Pannenberg, *Jesus* 24 (italics mine). The reference is to Ebeling, *Nature* 46.

In discussing what he sees as an "irreconcilable tension" in two opinions of Paul Althaus, he offers a clear summary of his own position.

> *Either* the statement is valid that knowledge about the history as it happened, which is presupposed by faith, is 'not yet knowledge of God's revelation in the events. This knowledge comes into existence with faith itself' *or* . . . Christology has to ask and show the extent to which the history of Jesus forms the basis of faith in him. How else is the history of Jesus supposed to substantiate faith in him except by showing itself to be the revelation of God? Only when its revelatory character is not something additional to the events but, rather, is inherent in them can the events form the basis of faith. Christology has to show just this. Thus the task of Christology is to establish the true understanding of Jesus' significance from his history, which can be described comprehensively by saying that in this man God is revealed.[41]

For Pannenberg, as is well known, history itself is revelatory and there is no revelation of God outside of history. Therefore, if the resurrection is to be a revelatory event, it must be an historical event.

There is no question that the history of Jesus is revelatory of God and I would agree with Pannenberg that what makes the *whole* of that history truly revelatory is the decisive (eschatological) event of Jesus' resurrection. My principal disagreement is in his attempt to establish the resurrection itself as an *historical* event. I prefer Fuller's notion that it is a meta-historical event that can only be known through revelation in the strict sense of being communicated solely out of the creative initiative of God through an indirect revelatory disclosure. In my opinion, this in fact coheres better with Pannenberg's emphasis upon the resurrection as an apocalyptic event, an

---

41. Pannenberg, *Jesus* 30 (italics mine). The quote is from Paul Althaus, *Fact and Faith in the Kerygma Today* (Muhlenberg Press, 1959) 34. The other horn of the dilemma is a reference to Paul Althaus, *Die Christliche Wahrheit* (Guetersloh: Bertelsmann, 1962⁶) 424, which Pannenberg quotes on 29.

event which in its positive aspect as transformation of Jesus does not occur within history but begins at the end of history and extends into the beyond-history.[42] At the end of his discussion of the appearances (primarily appealing to Paul), he offers an interesting, if convoluted, statement of what he means by the resurrection as an historical event. For the sake of clarity, I quote it leaving out two important qualifiers to which I shall return below.

> Thus the resurrection of Jesus would be designated as a his-
> torical event in this sense: If the emergence of primitive
> Christianity . . . can be understood . . . only if one examines
> it in the light of the eschatological hope for a resurrection
> from the dead, then that which is so designated is a histori-
> cal event, even if we do not know anything more particular
> about it.[43]

If all Pannenberg means by this is that shortly after Jesus' death some of his followers (who still stand on this side of death and so within history) claimed that he had been raised from the dead and that this claim has had a profound effect upon subsequent human history, then I would agree that these elements are historical. But, he apparently means more than that.

The first qualifier omitted above is the fact that Paul traces the origins of Christianity back to the appearances at 1 Corinthians 15:3–8 as intending "to give proof by means of witnesses for the facticity of Jesus' resurrection." He disputes the contemporary assumption that this is not "a historical proof in the modern sense" by distinguishing "historical curiosity" from "inner involvement." He claims that Paul argues from the latter. I have two problems with this. The first is that the question of history in the modern sense is precisely our question, a legitimate question arising out of a nine-teenth-century concern. We ignore the methodological limitations of what contemporary historians mean by the word history and historical proof at our theological peril (see above, chapter one).

---

42. See above, 82–83, for our analysis of the resurrection as apocalyptic and me-tahistorical.

43. Pannenberg, *Jesus* 98. His discussion of the appearances is on 89–99. See above, 83–88, for our discussion of the appearances as revelatory disclosures in faith.

My second problem is that Paul's own account of the appearances is better understood as an experience of a revelatory disclosure involving both a being called to faith and a being sent on mission (see above, chapter three) than as a historical proof in any sense. Paul is concerned to claim the facticity of Jesus' resurrection by means of witnesses. Hence, I would agree with this statement of Pannenberg's further on: "The Easter appearances are not to be explained from the Easter faith of the disciples; rather, conversely, the Easter faith of the disciples is to be explained from the appearances." Pannenberg's concern throughout is with the "reliability of the report," with its objectivity and certainty so that our faith is not based on subjective illusion, but this is no less the concern of Bultmann who seeks to ground the faith objectively in the creative activity of God inspiring the first witnesses to understand the true meaning of the cross. The kind of objectivity and certainty that faith claims cannot be grounded in history alone for it makes claims that transcend the competence of history, viz. claims about the divine activity. Pannenberg's approach would subordinate faith to a kind of totalitarian concept of history. By way of contrast, our approach in chapter one saw historical knowledge functioning in a subordinate but indispensable way in relation to faith knowledge. The two have tasks that are distinguishable but inter-related.

The second qualifier omitted above is an appeal to "critical examination of the tradition," Pannenberg's characteristic history of the transmission of traditions (*Traditionsgeschichte*). We have sought to offer such a history in the preceding chapters. Our conclusion is that such a history moves us to the recognition of the resurrection as the decisive (eschatological) event that is transformative of the entire history precisely because it occurs at the end of history (proleptically). If "the end of the world is already present in Jesus' resurrection," as Pannenberg phrases it in his section on the significance of the resurrection, then how can it be historical? What remains within history is our movement toward this end through being called to faith and sent on mission which constitutes the history of Christianity.

Moreover, if the confirmation of Jesus is historical in Pannenberg's sense, then it should be open to any neutral observer and not just to believers, i.e., to the enemies of Jesus as well as to his followers. Yet, the tradition is unanimous in depicting the experience of the appearances as faith experiences. In my opinion, faith knowledge is a necessity *within* history (for those of us who still stand on this side of death) precisely because of the limitations of historical knowledge. Faith, then, *is* a kind of historical certainty but clearly distinctive as related to historical knowledge in the modern sense of the word. For Pannenberg, on the other hand, there is no faith knowledge of revelatory *events* independently of historical knowledge, for he equates what really happened as historical. Consider the following: "There is no justification for affirming Jesus' resurrection as an event that really happened, if it is not to be affirmed as a historical event as such. Whether or not a particular event happened two thousand years ago is not made certain by faith but only by historical research, to the extent that certainty can be attained at all about questions of this kind." And further, as evidence of the totalitarian notion that events only happen in history: "If one claims to possess other means in addition to the instruments of historical criticism which are given priority over historical criticism in case of conflict, then one is led to contest the right of the historical method in principle." But, is it necessary for historical method to claim to be the only way of knowing rather than to admit that what it knows is limited precisely by the method itself? This final quote shows the extent to which Pannenberg has subordinated faith knowledge to historical knowledge: "If, however, historical study declares itself unable to establish what 'really' happened on Easter, then all the more, faith is not able to do so; for faith cannot ascertain anything certain about events of the past that would perhaps be inaccessible to the historian."[44]

In my opinion, Pannenberg himself is caught in a dilemma. Either his appeal to historical knowledge alone would effectively eliminate that which has always been considered essential to Christian understanding, viz. the creative initiative of God active in such events as virginal conception, nature miracles, and above all resurrection (we should not arbitrarily limit the potential of God's creative involvement in our world) or his notion of history must be so expanded methodologically for theological reasons that it would be unrecognizable by contemporary historians. The only resolution of

---

44. Pannenberg, *Jesus* 99, 109.

this dilemma that I can see is to maintain the clear differentiation between history and faith as proposed in the first chapter. Although this is a fundamental disagreement with Pannenberg over epistemological presuppositions, it need not affect the usefulness of Pannenberg's central insight for an integrated christology.

For Pannenberg, if the task of christology is to show that in this man (in all his concrete, historical particularity) God is revealed, then the method of christology must take as its starting point that which uniquely constitutes him in his humanness, viz. his unity with God. The decisive factor for the whole of his activity on earth lies in his relationship to God, and this must be understood first in terms of Jesus himself, of his person, if we are to understand properly his significance for us which is inherent in his history.[45] Hence, Pannenberg discusses in Part One of his book "the knowledge of Jesus' divinity." Only after that, does he discuss the man Jesus as the fulfillment of human destiny in part two and the relationship of his divinity and humanity in part three. We will concentrate here on the first part, considering first the nature of his starting point and then its implications for Jesus' personal identity and for his personal relation to the Father and to the Spirit.

(1) *Starting point.* The question is, what is the decisive factor, the ground, of Jesus' unity with God? For Pannenberg, it is not the authority of Jesus' earthly word and work taken by itself, but it is the resurrection understood as the confirmation by God of Jesus' claim to authority during his earthly ministry. This accords well with our analysis of Jesus as prophet who experiences the crisis of rejection in his ministry and prophetically proclaims the resolution of that crisis in the Father's vindication of him. As Fuller speaks of Jesus' message as proclaiming "the proleptic presence of the future Kingdom of God," so Pannenberg refers to "the proleptic structure

---

45. Ibid. 30 (on task) and 36 (on method). In chapter two, "Christology and Soteriology," Pannenberg discusses the importance of not detaching Jesus' significance for us from the concrete actuality of his person (as Bultmann particularly tends to do). While advocating earlier that christology is rooted in soteriology and must always remain so, I am in complete agreement with Pannenberg that what constitutes Jesus' salvific significance is precisely his personal relation to the Father as the perfectly obedient Son. Otherwise, his humanness would not be truly operative in our salvation as we proposed earlier. This is to maintain again that christology is but the deepest expression of soteriology.

of Jesus' claim to authority."[46] This means that while the Kingdom of God is truly being realized during the earthly ministry of Jesus, it is at the same time in process toward its full realization so that everything depends finally on the connection between Jesus' claim and the Father's vindication or confirmation of that claim.

Hence, it is only through the revelation of his life *as a whole,* and therefore focally in his destiny or fate, that we have a basis or ground for speaking of his unity with God, his divinity. To repeat an insight of Fuller's used earlier: "The church's Christology was a response to its total encounter with Jesus, not only in his earthly history but also in its (the church's) continuing life."[47] The definitive transitional point between Jesus and the early community is, as we have seen, his fate (death *and* resurrection). The important point for understanding the development of christology in the early Church is Pannenberg's contention, which we will presently develop, that the resurrection is not only revelatory to us of who Jesus is in a noetic sense but is first of all determinative of who Jesus is in an *ontological* sense. Over against those who in one way or another would reduce the definitive salvific activity of God to the earthly ministry of Jesus and so would tend to ignore the central and constitutive character of the resurrection, Pannenberg affirms the resurrection as the definitive reality for Jesus himself in his personal identity and, only so, for us as well.

Once Pannenberg explores the biblical understanding of resurrection (which we have treated in our chapter three) and the historical problem, he goes on to discuss the implications of his starting point in his chapter four: "Jesus' Divinity in Relation to the Father's Divinity." He offers the following thesis as a summary of the chapter: "In his revelational unity with God, which constitutes Jesus' own divinity, Jesus at the same time still remains distinct from God as his Father. The beginning of the doctrine of the Trinity lies in this."[48] Agreeing with his basic starting point, we will now look at his development of these implications.

---

46. Ibid. 66. Fuller, *Foundations* 104 (see above, 43).

47. Fuller, *Foundations* 15 (see above, 24).

48. Pannenberg, *Jesus* 115. His discussion of "The Mode of God's Presence in Jesus" is on 115–133.

(2) *Jesus' personal identity.* The operative word in the above thesis is *revelational.* Pannenberg, in discussing various theories about how God is present in Jesus, prefers the term "revelational presence" which for him goes beyond a *mere* presence of the Spirit or of an appearance and implies an identity of essence, a 'substantial' presence. "That appearance and essence belong together is expressed by the concept of 'revelation' as self-revelation." He sees this restriction of the concept to *self*-revelation in the strict sense to be modern (having its roots in Hegel and being widely accepted in contemporary theology). Yet, even the Old Testament and New Testament go beyond the notion of revelation as "the making known of the most varied sorts of information" to the extent that all happenings began to be perceived as a single great historical unity that would bring the full knowledge of Yahweh only at the end of history, an idea that apocalyptic expressed through the image of the glory of God. Peter Hodgson points out that ". . . it is misleading to speak of God's revelation as *self*-revelation—as though there were a divine self to be revealed prior to and apart from the event of revelation itself. It is better to speak of God's *indirect* self-*communication* in his unconcealment of the world."[49] He sees this as a clearer expression of Pannenberg's idea that God's self-revelation occurs indirectly through God's acts in history. God is not the 'object' of revelation but rather he 'unveils' the possibility of authentic human existence in the world. Likewise, Fuller speaks of the appearances as an "indirect revelatory disclosure." What is disclosed in the resurrection, as we have seen, is *Jesus* as the human final completion, as the full realization of God's creative intent for our humanness. Yet, Pannenberg is surely right in his view that the resurrection, as the apocalyptic event that reveals the end of all created reality, does truly and properly reveal to us something about God himself in his personal identity as Father and as Son. He indicates "three steps that lead materially from the concept of revelation to the knowledge of Jesus' divinity."[50]

The concept of self-revelation in reference to God can only be applied to a revelatory event that is final and definitive and so truly revelatory of God's essential identity. Such an event is the resurrec-

---

49. Hodgson, *Jesus* 130.
50. Pannenberg, *Jesus* 129–130.

tion. First, the beginning of the *end of all things* is revealed proleptically in Jesus' resurrection. Second, the resurrection is a *single*
revelation, which I take to mean that God can tell us no more about
himself than what he tells us in this definitive event, viz. that at the
moment of death he will embrace us. Otherwise, he would not be
fully and completely revealed but only partially. I might add that
since death is for us the ultimate limit-experience, only the actual experience of death itself will open to us the possibility of further revelation. The limitation here is from the side of our being created
human beings still within historical process. What God tells us about
himself is how he personally gives meaning to the whole of that process by embracing it in its entirety. Third, the resurrection reveals that
Jesus belongs to the very essence of God himself. God's *personal
identity* is revealed in Jesus or, once again, God would not be revealing himself in the strict sense. As Moltmann emphasizes, 'God' is
what takes place between Jesus and the Father on the cross. We cannot presume, as does both theism and atheism, that we know what
the word 'God' means prior to or apart from the concrete personal
existence of Jesus of Nazareth, for in him God is experienced in a
new, and indeed startling, way as a new creation. God is a question
for which the answer comes only through the particular experience
of reality as a whole. As Pannenberg puts it:

> . . . Jesus belongs to the definition of God and thus to his
> divinity, to his essence. The essence of God is not accessible
> at all without Jesus Christ. God is *essentially* 'the God . . .
> who gives life to the dead' (Rom. 4:17) because he is the
> one 'who raised Jesus from the dead' (Rom. 8:11). We do
> not first know who God is and then also something about
> Jesus, but only in connection with Jesus do we know that
> the ground of all reality about whom every man inquires,
> openly or concealed, consciously or unconsciously, is in its
> real essence identical with the God of Israel.[51]

Pannenberg notes that Paul in the above-quoted text (Rom.
4:17) immediately combines God's creative power with his life-giving

---

51. Ibid. 130 (italics mine).

power over death. He comments that the true nature of God as Creator is revealed in Jesus' resurrection. It is important to note that, throughout his discussion, when he speaks of God's essence, he is not speaking of God as God (in the sense of our distinction above) but of God as Creator. That is, he is not using a concept of essence that transcends time but one that allows God to be seen as involved in the temporal process as Creator. In my own terms I would summarize Pannenberg's three steps as follows: God as Creator embraces the *whole* of created reality. The only God we know is the God who personally involves himself in the creative process. If there is a 'moment' in that process which can properly be described as final and definitive for the whole of creation (viz. resurrection), then that moment is *the* revelation of the very essence of God as Creator.

What does all this tell us about Jesus' personal identity? about his essential unity with God? Does Jesus *become* one with God *only* at his resurrection? or at his transfiguration? baptism? conception? or was he already one with God in a pre-existent state? Pannenberg insists that these events must not be taken in isolation (as if one would cancel out the other) but that Jesus' person can be understood only as a *whole*. While the resurrection is the decisive event, "the idea that Jesus had received divinity only as a consequence of his resurrection is not tenable." Rather, the resurrection has *retroactive* power. "Jesus did not simply become something that he previously had not been, but his pre-Easter claim was confirmed by God. This confirmation, the manifestation of Jesus' 'divine Sonship' by God, is the new thing brought by the Easter event."[52] The retroactive power of Jesus' resurrection means that Jesus' essence is established not only for our knowledge (noetic) but in its being (ontological). This implies, as noted above, a concept of essence that is contrary to the Greek philosophical tradition:

. . . for thought that does not proceed from a concept of essence that transcends time, for which the essence of a thing is not what persists in the succession of change, for which, rather, the future is open in the sense that it will bring unpredictably new things that nothing can resist as absolutely

---

52. Ibid. 135.

unchangeable—for such thought only the future decides what something is.[53]

This concept of essence is not something uniquely or peculiarly applicable to Jesus but is, as Pannenberg puts it, "a matter of universal ontological relevance." Schematically, I would put his position into the following terms:

'becoming' = a continuous process involving *both* identity and
            difference;
'being' = the terminus (or *end*) of the process, i.e., *only* iden-
            tity.

For example, in our human experience at this moment in the process (and this applies to creation as a whole), we both are and are not what we will be at the end of the process. As we shall see more fully in our section on Hodgson, our identity as human persons, human personhood, consists of the event of gathering and being gathered into presence through word as the power of the *future* that deeply involves us in time and space and only so opens us to transcendence. What can be said of creation in general and human personhood in particular applies above all to that one in whom creation comes to its full realization. Again, as we saw with Schoonenberg, such a way of conceiving Jesus' divine sonship allows us to take his humanness with the utmost seriousness, principally to understand that humanness as truly mediating our salvation through a freely given obedience. Jesus' identity as the Son is a "reality-in-becoming." One in being with the Father, he still grows into his relationship with the Father in such wise that his full identity as the Son can be properly understood only as the conclusion to the *whole* of his life.

Hence, for both Schoonenberg and Pannenberg, incarnation is the conclusion not the starting point of a christology. The resurrection does not simply confirm Jesus' message; rather it throws light on his person as a whole. Because Jesus has been raised from the dead, it can be said with the certitude of faith that never in any way or at any time was Jesus as a person separated from God. This was

---

53. Ibid. 136.

the internal logic of the early Church's christology that led to the idea of pre-existence, as we have seen in chapter four. The truth, then, in the concept of the incarnation is the indivisibility of this man Jesus with the eternal essence of God. "If God has revealed himself in Jesus, then Jesus' community with God, his Sonship, belongs to eternity."[54] While one should not separate Jesus' unity with God from his concrete human existence, still one must distinguish the eternal Son from the man Jesus in order to preserve the truth of the patristic doctrine that the incarnation is in origin a movement from God to man. The God who has revealed himself at all times through the creative and historical process has, in Jesus, himself come out of his otherness into our world, into human form, has become man. Remaining always in the perspective of God's creative and historical activity in the world, Pannenberg summarizes his position: "Only so long as the perception of Jesus' resurrection remains precedent to the concept of incarnation is the Biblical meaning of the idea of *God* preserved in Christology and only so long does Christology also remain related to the Biblical understanding of *man* and of the *world* as history."[55] We now turn to the question raised by Jesus' unity with God, viz. his distinction from the Father, which is the origin of the doctrine of the Trinity.

(3) *Jesus' personal relation to the Father.*

It has been shown—and this remains the point of departure for all further considerations—that Jesus' person cannot be separated from God's essence if Jesus in person is God's self-revelation. However, Jesus understood himself as set over against the God whom he called Father. . . . If Jesus' history and his person now belong to the essence, to the divinity of God, *then the distinction that Jesus maintained between himself and the Father also belongs to the divinity of*

---

54. Ibid. 154. Pannenberg goes on at this point to discuss the mythical thinking of middle Platonism which separates Jesus' community with God and his temporal appearance in order to reunite them through a dramatic process. We referred to this in discussing the thought-world of Chalcedon above, 128–129.

55. Ibid. 159 (italics mine).

> *God.* The relation of Jesus as Son to the Father may be
> summarized with primitive Christianity as 'obedience'.[56]

In terms of our schema above, one might put it this way: God's 'becoming' involves both the identity of the man Jesus with God and
the differentiation of the Son from the Father. Therefore, God's being or essence (as Creator involved in the historical process) is established ontologically as such only at the terminus of the process,
at the point at which there is only identity in the sense of the perfect
unity of Father, Son, and Spirit. Paradoxical as it is, one must affirm
both that God has become triune in and through the creative, historical process and that God is eternally this threefold unity. The differentiation of Father and Son takes place not simply in history but
in God himself insofar as God embraces the whole of creation and
draws it into his own inner divine life in the person of Jesus. The
doctrine of the Trinity raises three interrelated issues: the necessity
of some concept of *Logos,* the differentiation of the Holy Spirit as a
third 'person', and the unity of God who is in essence three. We will
now discuss each of these in turn.

While agreeing with Pannenberg that one cannot simply take
over the *Logos* concept of classical christology with its middle Pla-
tonic speculations that tend to separate the *Logos* as an independent
being from the concrete existence of Jesus and then to reunite them,
I am surprised that he equally rejects Emil Brunner's attempt to understand Jesus as being in his person *the* Word of God. In the light
of his later insistence upon the resurrection as "absolute metaphor,"
the following quote is somewhat surprising.

> This understanding of the divine Word has, however, hard-
> ly any other value than that of a metaphor. It is only fig-
> uratively possible to say that the invisible God speaks. In
> this sense one may, or course, say that God seeks to com-
> municate something through certain events, just as in other
> situations events have a 'language'. Certainly, with respect
> to Jesus a peculiarity is to be noted. Jesus' resurrection

---

56. Ibid. 158–159.

means that God has claimed as his own the promise of salvation made by the pre-Easter Jesus and thus recognized Jesus' word in a definite sense as his own word. Nevertheless, it is still only a figurative expression when the event of God's revelation in Jesus' fate is designated as God's 'Word', an expression that—in order to be true—presupposes a substantiation outside itself for the fact that God is revealed in the person of Jesus. However, this concept of the Word does not have the ontological significance of an independent hypostasis beside God the Father, and thus does not have the significance of the patristic Logos concept. . . .[57]

If the understanding of Jesus as the Word is limited to a phenomenological description, then the above criticism is valid as we shall see in treating the approach of Hodgson. But, for Pannenberg, Jesus' resurrection means more than a recognition of his word or message; it constitutes him as the Son in an ontological sense. If "revelational presence" truly includes "substantial presence," then one must articulate this in ontological terms. All of our language about God has a metaphorical structure. Pannenberg's later concern is to distinguish within metaphor that which tends toward the merely mythical from that which truly speaks to the human condition, to the way things *are*. As noted at the beginning of this chapter, the employment of analogy is an explicit and conscious attempt to move the metaphorical language of the New Testament in the direction of metaphysical discourse. It is the recognition that only identity-in-being can control all *merely* mythological and/or legendary tendencies. Thus, as with Schoonenberg, Pannenberg must take the metaphysical implications of his language with the utmost seriousness if he wishes to propose an adequate christology. If one accepts the enhypostasis of the Word as an explanation for Jesus' ontic identity with God, as we proposed in treating Schoonenberg, then Jesus as *the* Word remains a most appropriate expression for Jesus' personal identity as the self-communication of the Father.

---

57. Ibid. 167. On the resurrection as "absolute metaphor" see 187 (see above, 131).

If Jesus is differentiated from the Father as an 'I' in relation to the Father's 'Thou' because the Word is hypostatized in him, how are we to understand the differentiation of the Spirit? Why do we speak of a Trinity and not simply of a Duality? There are two distinct questions here: one with regard to the divinity of the Spirit and the other with regard to the distinction of the Spirit from the Father and the Son. The divinity of the Spirit is grounded in the fact that the Spirit belongs to the event of God's revelation in Jesus. Throughout the Old Testament the Spirit is primarily God's creative, life-giving power. Jesus in his earthly ministry can be characterized precisely as the eschatological prophet because his whole ministry was in the power of that same Spirit. Finally, the whole history of Israel and the personal history of Jesus culminated in that decisive, eschatological event of God's creative, life-giving power: the resurrection. The resurrection is revelatory of the Trinity because it is the Father who embraces the Son in love. The Spirit as the love between Father and Son is the creative power of God that transforms Jesus in his personal identity. Hence, in the light of the resurrection, Paul stresses the identity of Jesus and the Spirit: *sōma pneumatikon* (1 Cor. 15:44), life-giving Spirit (1 Cor. 15:45), the Lord (*Kyrios*) is Spirit (2 Cor. 3:17). It is in this sense that one could properly develop a 'Spirit Christology'.

But, at the same time, one must keep in mind the fact that the New Testament recognizes a clear distinction between Jesus and the Spirit, perhaps most clearly in John's doctrine of 'another Paraclete' (John 14:16–17, 25–26) as well as in Paul's understanding of the present experience of the Christian community (e.g., Gal. 4; Rom. 8) and in Luke's understanding of the activity of the Spirit in Acts. This differentiation of the Spirit whom the Father sends at the request of the Son should not be understood in terms of yet another hypostasis in history but in terms of the Spirit's activity in drawing *us* into the divine life. The Spirit is God's way of giving himself to us; we know the Spirit as distinct in the experience of ourselves as totally the gift of a transcendent God. Jesus is distinct from the Father as Son through the enhypostasis of the Word; we are distinct from Jesus as sons and daughters through participation in Jesus' Spirit, i.e., the Spirit as the community of love between Father and Son gives to us community with the Father and Son. The Spirit then is the personal center of our lives for that which constitutes us in our humanness, as we have seen, is union with the divine. Thus, if Jesus is an 'I' in relation to the Father's 'Thou', the Spirit is the 'We' of the divine life insofar as the Father in embracing the Son embraces all of us as well and so draws us into his own inner divine life.

The differentiation of the essence of God into three leads, finally, to the question of unity, for we believe in one God. "If Father, Son, and Spirit are distinct but coordinate moments in the accomplishment of God's revelation, then they are so in God's eternal essence as well. But how are they one single God in spite of such differentiation?" Once again, for Pannenberg, the essence of God must be understood in terms of God's creative involvement in the historical process. Hence, he does not look for an answer in the *Logos* speculations of either the Eastern Church (unity of origin in procession from the Father) or the Western Church (unity of relation in the incommunicability of the Persons), but in Hegel's notion of *person* as self-sublimation through being immersed in the other. "Through this profound thought that the essence of the person is to exist in self-dedication to another person, Hegel understood the unity in the Trinity as the unity of reciprocal self-dedication, thus, as a unity that only comes into existence through the process of reciprocal dedication." This must be interpreted in the direction of the New Testament understanding of the concrete, personal existence of Jesus as involving such mutual dedication. Thus, Pannenberg concludes: "In the vital movement of such reciprocal dedication, the unity of Father, Son, and Spirit consummates itself in the historical process of the revelatory event."[58] This dedication of Jesus to the Father and the Father to Jesus and of the Spirit in their mutual relationship, as well as the dedication of the triune God to all of humankind, came to its most critical expression on the cross. If the resurrection is the *decisive factor* as the confirmation of Jesus' whole life in such wise that it constitutes him ontologically as the Son, then the cross is the *critical factor* as that which grounds and gives concrete content to the meaning of *this* resurrection. This is the position of Juergen Moltmann to which we now turn.

58. Ibid. 180–183.

C. Crucifixion (Juergen Moltmann)

The sub-title of *The Crucified God* reads: "The Cross of Christ as the Foundation and Criticism of Christian Theology." Methodologically, Moltmann is in full agreement with Schoonenberg and Pannenberg that an adequate christology must begin and end with the concrete personal existence of Jesus, that the proclamation of Jesus' obedience even unto death (kerygma) is the indispensable basis for affirming his divinity (doxology). The power of his book lies in the fact that he refuses to domesticate the cross, i.e., that he seeks to unveil the cross in all of its scandalous impact as naked and unreligious, as the utterly incommensurable factor in the revelation of God. This is what makes it the critical factor. It calls into question all of our assumptions about the divine and the human and forces us to reinterpret everything through the dialectical experience of its opposite (e.g., life/death), for that is where God is revealed. In the terms of our previous analysis, to take the cross of Jesus seriously as the self-revelation of God is to affirm God's personal self-involvement in the creative process at its most radical, at a level that calls for the 'permanent iconoclasm' of all our christological images.

Moltmann would agree with the two points made at the beginning of our discussion in chapter three, viz. that the death-resurrection can only be properly interpreted in the light of the earthly ministry of Jesus that precedes and of the kerygmatic ministry of the early Church that follows and that the death-resurrection is a single event such that each interprets the other. In explaining his theme, he relates *The Crucified God* to his earlier work:

> *Theology of Hope* began with the *resurrection* of the crucified Christ, and I am now turning to look at the *cross* of the risen Christ. I was concerned then with the remembrance of Christ in the form of the *hope* of his future, and now I am concerned with hope in the form of the *remembrance* of his death. The dominant theme then was that of *anticipations* of the future of God in the form of promises and hopes; here it is the understanding of the *incarnation*

of that future, by way of the sufferings of Christ, in the world's sufferings.[59]

The theme is still hope, but if hope is to be realistic and liberating it must apprehend the pain of the negative not through an abstract theory about suffering but through the concrete experience of God's suffering in the world. Put synthetically, Moltmann's position is that the crucified Jesus is the incarnation of the risen Christ. While the broader context remains important for our understanding, Jesus' earthly ministry and the Church's kerygmatic ministry must always be interpreted primarily in the light of this focal event which continually shatters our assumptions about either. Jesus' question to his disciples, 'Who do you way that I am?', can only be answered in view of his further and final question on the cross, 'My God, my God, why have you forsaken me?'

We have employed a number of Moltmann's insights earlier, both in our discussion of methodology in chapter one and in our discussion of the crucifixion in chapter three, the latter with modifications concerning his notion of a *stasis* within God. Our purpose here, as with Schoonenberg and Pannenberg, is not to deal with all the issues in christology that he raises but to analyze and evaluate the central insight of his approach, the starting point that conditions his conclusions, as a help to us in achieving an integrated christology. Hence, we will focus primarily upon his synthetic chapter six which he entitles "The 'Crucified God'." Prior to that, however, we must discuss a fundamental disagreement with Pannenberg that Moltmann brings to the fore in his fifth chapter entitled: "The Eschatological Trial of Jesus Christ."

In discussing the relationship between eschatology and history, he enunciates a principle with which we would agree: ". . . the legitimate critical question is: does the primitive Christian belief in the resurrection do justice to the life and death of Jesus, or has it put something else in Jesus' place?" It is true that "the true criticism of faith in the resurrection is the history of the crucified Christ." But this seems to imply for Moltmann a dichotomy between the historical understood as ontic (the way things *are*) and the eschatological

---

59. Moltmann, *Crucified* 5.

understood as merely noetic (a source for our *knowledge*), which the following quote illustrates: "If we are to understand the truth about Jesus according to the witness of the New Testament, we must take two courses at the same time: we must read his history both forwards and backwards, and relate both readings, the ontic-historical and the noetic-eschatological, to each other and identify the results we achieve." Pannenberg seeks to resolve any such dichotomy by establishing the resurrection itself as an historical event. In our criticism of that position, we have sought to characterize the decisive, eschatological activity of God as meta-historical. Yet, we agree with Pannenberg that that event is truly ontic in the sense that it is truly transformative of Jesus and so constitutes him in his ontological identity as the Son. Moltmann employs the language of Pannenberg when he goes on to characterize the resurrection ". . . as the beginning of the end of history in the midst of history . . . as the beginning of the eschatological transformation of the world by its creator." But when he then goes on to speak of this as ". . . a prelude to, and a real anticipation of, God's qualitatively new future and the new creation in the midst of the history of the world's suffering,"[60] one wonders if he understands the transformative effect of the resurrection upon Jesus in the same sense as Pannenberg.

His treatment of "Jesus' Resurrection from the Dead" serves only to underline the suspicion that he does not. He correctly emphasizes, over against Pannenberg's stress upon universal history with its inherent danger of claiming anthropological truth independent of the concrete history of Jesus, that the fundamental question is the righteousness of God. The situation of the Easter witness was that Jesus had proclaimed that righteousness and raised expectations that were shattered by the crucifixion. It is true that the notion of resurrection must be interpreted in the context of the general apocalyptic expectation, but what makes it distinctively Christian is the fact that it was this man Jesus—condemned as a blasphemer, exe-

---

60. Ibid. 160–165. Hodgson, *Jesus* 12–18, criticizes Moltmann's category of the *novum* for replacing a vertical dualism with a horizontal dualism insofar as it dichotomizes God's future activity as something completely *new* from continuity with God's activity in the past and present. It is not clear that Moltmann has overcome this objection in *The Crucified God* even though the emphasis is now upon the *remembrance* of the cross.

cuted as a rebel, and forsaken by God—whom God has raised. Thus, the resurrection confirms the message of Jesus and opens up the future as God's future.

But, for Moltmann, this means that the righteousness of God is still referred to the end of history for its confirmation. This is true, but then the question becomes: what concretely *grounds* our hope in that future? Is it only the death of Jesus or is it the transformation of his person as pledge of our own transformation? When Moltmann not only denies that resurrection means 'revivification' (a return to this life) but also asserts that it excludes *any idea* of 'a life after death', when he says on the other hand that it does not deny 'the fatality of death' but rather symbolizes 'the future of the dead', one wonders exactly how one is to conceive that future. Of course that future is open and will be shaped by how we respond to our call to mission in this life, the point perhaps which Moltmann wants to secure, but there is an unnecessary vagueness here that limits too readily the concrete creative activity of *God* in the resurrection event. We agree with Moltmann against Pannenberg that the resurrection is a matter of faith and hope and not a matter of factual historical proof in the modern sense, but when he then seeks to combine his 'language of promise' with Pannenberg's notion of 'anticipatory event' in the expression 'promise event', [61] one can only ask what he means by event or, more fundamentally, by his continued use of 'new creation'. From our perspective, this should mean the ontological transformation of Jesus himself.

Given this qualification on the nature of the resurrection-event,

---

61. Moltmann, *Crucified* 173. See 166–178 for the whole discussion. Also, see above, 77–79, for our notion of continuity in the resurrection as involving both identity and difference. It should be noted that in his discussion of the merely functional christologies (Jesus as representative) of Jean Calvin, A. A. van Ruler, and Dorothee Soelle (256–266), Moltmann protests that they can only be provisional and that they ignore the abiding character of the inner trinitarian life as Father, Son, and Spirit. They ignore the creative and liberating activity of *Jesus* which is a *new* reality in eschatological terms. "Only when, as in Paul, eschatological-functional christology is taken up from beginning to end into a trinitarian christology, is it and does it remain Christian. But conversely, for trinitarian christology that means an alteration in the concept of God. The cross does not bring an end to the trinitarian history in God between the Father and the Son in the Spirit as eschatological history, but rather opens it up" (265). This could be understood in the ontological terms we have employed, though Moltmann does not use such terms.

or at least the need for greater clarity on this point, it nonetheless remains true that it is the cross which is the fundamental expression of the significance of the resurrection, something to which Moltmann thinks Pannenberg has paid too little attention. Thus, while the resurrection qualifies the cross so that it becomes an eschatological event (noetic) because it says *who* really suffered and died, i.e., the Christ (Luke 24:26: "Why did the Christ have to suffer these things?"), it is the historical event (ontic) of the cross that gives material content to that personal identity. In these terms, Moltmann accepts Pannenberg's notion of the "retroactive force" of the resurrection as maintaining, not only for our knowledge but for his being, the unity and identity of Jesus as a person. He remarks: "This is a helpful idea for understanding the resurrection faith which leads to Christian belief in Jesus. But in my view the *person* of Jesus who was identified through the resurrection is not expressed sufficiently clearly in the accord between Jesus' claim and God's confirmation of it."[62] What is needed is to focus on his death on the cross *for us* in order to make sense of his resurrection *before us.* This is to reverse the noetic and the ontic order so that, in eschatological terms (noetic) he is the *incarnation* of the coming God in his historical death on the cross (ontic).

> Through his suffering and death, the risen Christ brings righteousness and life to the unrighteous and the dying. Thus the cross of Christ modifies the resurrection of Christ under the conditions of the suffering of the world so that it changes from being a purely future event to being an event of liberating love.... The cross is the form of the coming, redeeming kingdom, and the crucified Jesus is the incarnation of the risen Christ.[63]

This unrelenting focus upon what takes place in the cross, refusing to domesticate the cross or to relegate it to a mere passing phase in the history of Jesus, has profound implications for our concept of God (what was God *doing* in and during the crucifixion of

---

62. Ibid. 181.
63. Ibid. 185.

Jesus?) and for our understanding of ourselves as well. Hence, in treating Moltmann's synthetic chapter six, we will consider the nature of his starting point and its implications for the experience of God and of human life. This exposition can be reasonably brief since we have already used much of the material in chapter three. With the qualifications made above, the important thing to note is that he confirms the basic approach of Schoonenberg and Pannenberg—particularly the emphasis upon the concrete history of God's dealings with the world as *trinitarian*[64]—as we have analyzed it.

(1) *Starting point.* In the plan of his book, Moltmann has three christological chapters followed by three systematic chapters which are intended to develop "the consequences of this theology of the crucified Christ for the concept of God (chapter 6), for anthropology (chapter 7) and for a critical theory of Church and society (chapter 8)."[65] We are primarily concerned with the first, for the revolution that Jesus has brought into our world is fundamentally in the concept of God and it is this that raises critical questions about our understanding of humanity and society. The question of Jesus (Who do you say that I am?) remains a question for our personal identity, but it can only be answered by personally participating in *this story* of what took place between Jesus and the Father on the cross.

What would it mean to say that God experiences the mystery of death? Moltmann rightly sees that theism, by reason of its 'definition' of God as incapable of suffering and death, must evacuate the cross of deity and that atheism is simply a protest against the indifference of this theistic God in a suffering world. Theism tends to emphasize the divine at the expense of the human and atheism the human at the expense of the divine. Both set up an intolerable dichotomy that cannot be overcome by any 'theoretical' understanding of divine-human relationships as applicable to the question of suffering but only by the concrete, historical experience of a God who personally involves himself in the creative process at that point which is most critical for life, viz. death. But, the 'death of God' cannot be understood from the concept of God as 'simple' but only as '*trinity*'.

---

64. This insight is central to the third book of his trilogy, *The Church in the Power of the Spirit,* which he subtitles: "A Contribution to Messianic Ecclesiology."
65. Moltmann, *Crucified* 200.

The place of the doctrine of the Trinity is not the 'thinking of thought', but the cross of Jesus. 'Concepts without perception are empty' (Kant). The perception of the trinitarian concept of God is the cross of Jesus. 'Perceptions without concepts are blind' (Kant). The theological concept for the perception of the crucified Christ is the doctrine of the Trinity.[66]

This leads Moltmann to speak more properly not of 'the death of God' but of *death in God.*

> ... it is advisable to abandon the concept of God and to speak of the relationships of the Son and the Father and the Spirit at the point at which 'God' might be expected to be mentioned. From the life of these three, which has within it the death of Jesus, there then emerges who God is and what his Godhead means. Most previous statements about the specifically Christian understanding of talk about 'the death of God' have lacked a dimension, the trinitarian dimension. 'On the cross, God stretched out his hands to embrace the ends of the earth,' said Cyril of Jerusalem. . . . This symbol is an invitation to understand the Christ hanging on the cross as the 'outstretched' God of the Trinity.[67]

Earlier we analyzed the resurrection in the image of the Father reaching out and embracing the Son and, in that embrace, embracing all of us as well. It is that mutual embrace of love that pours forth the Spirit and opens up for all of creation the eschatological hope of liberation through participation in the inner life of God himself, an inner life of liberating love. "For the 'history of God', whose nucleus is the event of the cross, cannot be thought of as history in the world, but on the contrary makes it necessary to understand the world in this history."[68] What then is the experience of God on the cross which opens up new possibilities for the experience of human life?

---

66. Ibid. 240–241.
67. Ibid. 207.
68. Ibid. 218.

(2) *The Experience of God.* The christological doctrine of the two natures contrasts the divine (incorruptible, unchangeable, indivisible, incapable of suffering, immortal) with the human (transitory, changeable, divisible, capable of suffering, mortal) and so affirms that God cannot be subject to suffering. Moltmann offers three considerations to the contrary.[69] First, 'God is not changeable' is a simile. It is not an absolute but a relative statement. God is not changeable as creatures are changeable. The intent is not to reduce God to that which is not-God, to the level of a creature, but it says nothing about God's free, creative initiative. Second, 'God cannot suffer' is also a simile. As we saw with Schoonenberg, God cannot suffer as creatures suffer, i.e., out of deficiency. But God can suffer out of the fullness of his being which is love. If God cannot voluntarily open himself to the possibility of being affected by another, then he cannot love. Third, love always involves interrelatedness. Salvation is not merely a negation of human deficiency, such as changeableness and mortality, but is a true fellowship, a dialogic relationship, in which God out of his own free initiative enters into real relations with his creatures as Creator and truly depends upon the free response to his initiative to shape time. Although this is a reformulation of Moltmann's basic insights into my own terms, it is clear that he is in fundamental agreement with our earlier analyses.[70] He strongly agrees with our other authors that the experience of God can only be properly understood and articulated in trinitarian terms. The dimension that he adds to them is his unrelieved focus on the cross, on the experience of the 'crucified God'.

What happened on the cross between Jesus and his *Abbā?* With the modifications noted in chapter three regarding Moltmann's concept of a *stasis* within God, we can repeat: to say "God is love' is to say that 'God did not spare his own Son but handed him over' (Rom. 8:32). This means that God did not spare himself: the Father suffers the death of his Son in the infinite grief of love and the Son suffers dying in response to that same love (which was the fundamental mission of the Son). As with Pannenberg's use of the notion of person as involving reciprocal self-dedication, we are talking about

69. Ibid. 229–231.
70. See above, 73–77 and 146–157.

a relationship between persons, not between two qualitatively different natures (one capable of suffering and the other not). "Here we have interpreted the event of the cross in trinitarian terms as an event concerned with a relationship between persons in which these persons constitute themselves in their relationship with each other."[71] Therefore, God exists as love in the event of the cross, for he takes up death, that which symbolizes the *whole* of human history, particularly its deepest negativity, into his own inner life. That is what salvation means. It is Jesus in his personal relation to the Father as Son who first lives out the drama of salvation and so opens up for all of creation the possibility of participating in his unique relationship to the Father in and through the experience of human freedom as liberating love, which is an experience in the power of Jesus' Spirit (Rom. 8:14–24a, 38–39). Paul's question puts it best: "He who did not spare his own Son, but handed him over for the sake of all of us, how will he not in union with him grace us (*hēmin charisetai*) with all things?" (Rom. 8:32).

(3) *The experience of human life.* The experience of human life takes place, as Moltmann puts it, in the *pathos* of God and that can only mean for a Christian in the trinitarian history of God's dealings with the world, which is the inner mystery of God himself. Only here can one speak of the fullness of life.

> Following Philippians 2, Christian theology speaks of the final and complete self-humiliation of God in man and in the person of Jesus. Here God in the person of the Son enters into the limited, finite situation of man. Not only does he enter into it, descend into it but he also accepts it and embraces the whole of human existence with his being. . . . He lowers himself and accepts the whole of mankind without limits and conditions, so that each man may participate in him with the whole of his life. . . . He humbles himself and takes upon himself the eternal death of the godless and the godforsaken, so that all the godless and godforsaken can experience communion with him.[72]

---

71. Moltmann, *Crucified* 245.
72. Ibid. 276.

As we saw in chapter three, it is God's complete and total identity in the Son with the whole of human life—and especially with god-lessness and godforsakenness—that makes it possible for us to accept the whole of our lives, including death. Such acceptance is an experience of the liberating love of God. But this should not be conceived in individualistic terms. God can save none of us except insofar as he is in solidarity with the least ones in our midst. As long as there is anyone who is oppressed, alienated, forsaken, all of us are oppressed, alienated, forsaken. This places salvation in the perspective of the liberation of creation as a whole. Salvation is our communion with one another in and through Jesus' communion with the Father, but such salvation, oriented as it is to the final consummation of all creation, still leaves the future open and God's love vulnerable to the response of human freedom.

We are commanded to love one another as Jesus has first loved us (John 13–17) and this love reaches its most critical point in the command to love our enemies and to pray for those who persecute us (Matthew 5:44), a prayer that can only be made through the Son to the Father in the Spirit. Yet, in Moltmann's strking terms, such love

> cannot prohibit slavery and enmity, but must suffer this contradiction, and can only take upon itself grief at this contradiction and the grief of protest against it, and manifest this grief in protest. That is what happened on the cross of Christ. God is unconditional love, because he takes on himself grief at the contradiction in men and does not angrily suppress this contradiction. God allows himself to be forced out. God suffers, God allows himself to be crucified and is crucified, and in this consummates his unconditional love that is so full of hope. But that means that in the cross he becomes himself the condition of this love.[73]

But, if God has truly died 'outside the gate', if we have truly forced him out and exiled him from the midst of human life, can he be experienced in any other way than as absent? Is there any legitimate

---

73. Ibid. 248.

sense in which he can still be spoken of as present? This is the question of Peter Hodgson in his book *Jesus—Word and Presence,* to which we now turn.

If for Pannenberg the resurrection is the *decisive factor* in understanding Jesus and for Moltmann the crucifixion is the *critical factor,* then for Hodgson the historical Jesus as the Word of faith, which includes of course the Word of the cross (*ho logos tou staurou:* 1 Cor. 1:18), is the *indispensable factor.* Towards the end of his book he raises the question of how Jesus can be said to be present in the contemporary world. "The fundamental experience of Christian faith is that Jesus *himself* is present in the event called 'resurrection'. The 'presence' in question, then, is a *personal presence,* the presence of a person to persons."

In the course of his discussion he rejects notions of personal presence as involving physical immediacy, effective historical influence, or psychological immediacy and appeals to the resurrection narratives, especially the Emmaus story, as involving *verbal encounters* that evoke *recognition.* "The thesis may be proposed that *personal presence occurs when recognition is evoked by means of word, including also verbal action or enacted word.*" He concludes:

> One of the central functions of the community is to preserve the memory of the Crucified One (cf. 1 Cor. 11:24, 25). For recognition implies some sort of prior encounter, which is recalled by memory. To 'recognize' means to 'know again'. . . . There can be no recognition, and hence no presence, of the risen Jesus apart from memory of the historical Jesus. For the first disciples who experienced the risen Jesus, the relation to the historical Jesus was direct and personal. For us, however, this relation is of necessity mediated by the traditions concerning his historical word and deed. Without these traditions there would be no means of recognizing *who* is now present; in this sense, the risen Jesus is 'identified' by reference to the historical Jesus. Because it possesses spatio-temporal extension, the community is the essential bearer and preserver of memory.[74]

---

74. Hodgson, *Jesus* 266–270.

We return to the point at which we began our investigation: knowledge of the historical Jesus. In chapter one we maintained that such knowledge is a *subordinate but indispensable* dimension in the total process of responding to Jesus in faith. Hodgson maintains that it is indispensable. Does he maintain that it is subordinate? We will now examine how he arrives at the above conclusion in order to complete our christological synthesis.

D. HISTORICAL WORD (PETER HODGSON)

Hodgson's book is an attempt "to move through and beyond interpretations of God's *absence*, of which the death of God theology and the theologies of the future are important recent expressions, to a fresh understanding of his *presence*, definitively so in the words and deeds, death and resurrection, of Jesus of Nazareth."[75] Everything in the book is related to this central theme: "Jesus—Word and Presence." In the course of his discussion of various interpretations of God's absence in recent theology, he offers some objections to Moltmann's category of *novum* and Pannenberg's definition of God as "the power of the future" which will help us to situate his position in relation to our two previous authors. In seeking a new mode of transcendence, these theologians of the future look neither 'above' nor 'within' but 'ahead' toward a qualitatively new future which is truly the end of history because it is a *nova creatio ex nihilo.* Christ is the *anticipator* because he realizes the end of history in the midst of history. Hodgson raises three questions concerning this effort to interpret God's absence as his futurity:[76]

> First, it may be asked whether an *absent* God can still be conceived in any meaningful way to be *alive, active,* and *beneficent* . . . A second difficulty with this interpretation of God's absence is an ambiguity toward human activity and the possibilities of political and social change . . . Finally, the interpretation of God's absence as his futurity

---

75. Ibid. xiii.
76. Ibid. 14–18.

tends to issue in a horizontal dualism—a 'supernaturalism
of the future'—because all continuities between past and
future, history and eschatology, have been exploded.

Moltmann calls for a 'linking' between suprahistorical and intrahistorical transcendence, but he does not offer an adequate analysis of
it in terms of the structure of history or of temporality as such.
Hodgson recognizes that both authors in their more recent writings
have moved closer to the position that he maintains: "In brief, for
both Moltmann and Pannenberg *the futurity of God no longer signi-
fies his absence but his presence, his mode of being present as the coming God, whose power already qualifies the present.*"[77] But he still feels
that neither author satisfactorily answers the question of *how* this future God is present.

Hodgson's thesis, following Gerhard Ebeling, is that God is experienced as absent today precisely because of the failure of language
both in its religious and in its secular usage. "If God is experienced
as absent because of the failure of language, then by implication it
is precisely language that can also become the medium of his presence. God is present, if at all, by means of word." Hodgson maintains that it is in the nature of God to be present *only* by means of
word. What is required today, then, is a rebirth of language. "The
task of this book is to document this thesis and to explore the paths
along which a rebirth of language might occur. These paths lead ultimately, for the Christian, to the one who was the definitive word
of faith and who remains the agent and norm of authentic language
today."[78]

Before outlining the steps that he takes along these paths, it will
be well to situate him not only in relation to Moltmann and Pannenberg but also in relation to our own position, as articulated in chapter one, on the relationship between history and faith. Hodgson
agrees with the position of Moltmann, with which we began, that the
task of christology is to maintain a careful dialectical balance between the Jesus of history and the Christ of faith, between historical

---

77. Ibid. 20.
78. Ibid. 22–23.

quest and present responsibility. His description of the hermeneutical structure is accurate and to the point:

> ... the hermeneutical 'circle' is constituted by the dialectical movement between critico-interpretive and practical-responsive thinking in the total process of historical understanding. Hermeneutic is to be identified with the process of historical understanding as a whole, to which are subordinated two reciprocal and mutually conditioning functions: the critico-interpretive movement from the interpreter (or historian) through the text (or author) to the subject matter of the text, and the practical-responsive movement from the subject matter through the text to the interpreter.[79]

There is a constant inter-action between the truth of the text and our own truth. Not only do we interpret the text but the text interprets us. Within this dialectical tension and movement between critical and practical thinking, we always stand *in medias res.*

Christology, as a hermeneutical procedure, must always maintain the dialectical movement, which characterizes historical thinking in general, between the present responsibility of faith and the quest of the historical Jesus. In speaking of christology's responsible function, Hodgson offers a caution with which we heartily agree, viz. that it "does not permit the substitution of assertions of faith for the realities of history or the avoidance of pursuing historical questions to their limit. Rather faith is to be brought into hermeneutical play with the given of history, and thus is to be corrected and purified in the process of understanding, which it permits." Yet, when he discusses the position, with which we also agree, that the quest of the historical Jesus is not intended as a 'proof' or 'legitimation' of faith but rather as an aid to its interpretation, his understanding of faith seems to be close to that of Van Harvey, which we criticized in chapter one, viz. that faith is reduced to a dimension of historical knowledge.

---

79. Ibid. 31.

Faith is the gift of the word of God, empowering man to a new mode of existence. Although intrinsically related to historical events, it is not 'caused' by such events. Faith involves acknowledging as normatively true and constitutive for one's own existence what is precisely always only probably certain in the historical mode. It involves a recognition of the significance of certain events for salvation that goes beyond any possibility of proof.[80]

Similarly, Harvey describes faith as a response to a disclosure situation, to a certain meaning perceived in an historic event. It is a perspective that the believer has on the same realities that confronts the non-believer.

That this is Hodgson's position is confirmed by his emphasis throughout—not unlike Harvey's "radical historical confessionalism"—upon holding radically to the historical man Jesus as the content and the criterion of christology. He states his position clearly by reformulating the classical distinction between the person and the work of Christ to conform to the hermeneutical structure of christology:

The doctrine of the *person* of Christ (the doctrine of the incarnation) may be understood to direct its attention to the historical Jesus, the one who *was presence* in virtue of God's self-presentation in word. The doctrine of the *work* of Christ (the doctrine of atonement or soteriology) is properly concerned with the one who is *present,* the one who is risen from the dead and 'comes to stand' in the world as the agent of reconciliation. . . .[81]

In this he distances himself from the position of Pannenberg for whom, as Hodgson characterizes it, "the 'humanity' of Jesus corresponds to the critically recovered Jesus of history, whereas the 'divinity' corresponds to the risen Lord." He affirms that the classical distinctions between person and work, humiliation and exaltation,

---

80. Ibid. 42, 45. See above, 18–22, for my criticism of Van Harvey's position.
81. Ibid. 49–50.

earthly Jesus and risen Lord can be reinterpreted to correspond to the two poles of the hermeneutical structure of christology, viz. historical quest and present responsibility, but not the distinction between the human and the divine natures because

> the concept of distinguishable 'natures' in Jesus is a metaphysical abstraction that violates historical experience and does not correspond to the hermeneutical structure of christology, i.e., to the way that we *know* Jesus. Both as past historical figure and as the one who is now present, we know him only in the unity of word of God and word of man, i.e., as the *homologia fidei.*[82]

Of course, Pannenberg and all the authors we have treated offer criticisms of the two-natures doctrine as a metaphysical abstraction. The real issue here is not about a somewhat artificially contrived distinction between history/humanity and resurrection/divinity, but whether the resurrection event—as something that happened to Jesus and that embraces the *whole* of his personal history—is truly constitutive in an ontological sense of his personhood. For all of our authors, the *being* of Jesus must correspond to our *knowledge* of him and vice versa, but for Hodgson the only way that we know Jesus is historically. Therefore, the person of Jesus is identical with the quest of the historical Jesus. This makes historical knowledge the controlling factor in all that we can say about Jesus and so effectively by-passes the developing christology of the New Testament as we have analyzed it in chapter four. This is the obverse of our position which sees the historical quest as a *subordinate* factor. As we sought to show in chapter one, faith and history are both ways of knowing within historical consciousness, and therefore within the structure of hermeneutical understanding as Hodgson describes it, but faith knowledge is not reducible to a dimension of historical/historic knowledge. The Word-faith correlation, while internally related to history, is primarily revelatory in character, something that simply

---

82. Ibid. 49, n. 37.

transcends the inevitable limitation of scientific historical knowledge while remaining intrahistorical.

The value of Hodgson's approach for our own christological purposes is that he offers through a phenomenological description of God's Word in the world profound insight into the structure of history and time as linguistic. We can only applaud his criticism of any christology which would attempt to begin either 'from above' or 'from below' or 'from before' as false alternatives because it is Jesus in the concrete particularity of his own personal existence who reveals to us and so 'defines' the divine, the human, and the future. This has been the constant theme of this book and of all the authors we have treated. Hodgson proposes a contemporary word-christology which seeks to *radicalize* the concept of 'word' by resolutely locating it in the finitude and historicity of human experience as the 'place' of God's self-communication. This corresponds to our insistence upon word as the creative power of God whereby God progressively involves himself in the creative process *qua* Creator. Our principal difference with Hodgson, as already alluded to in chapter three, is that Jesus' uniqueness as the definitive and irrevocable 'place' of God's self-communication in word is not adequately grounded in a description of Jesus as the one who speaks the truth *about* the human condition. Jesus is God's Word because in his personal identity he *is* the truth about the human condition, especially at the moment of death. Only an identity in being with the divine can adequately ground the Christian claim that Jesus is unique among all the savior figures in human history. Therefore, Hodgson's insights, valid as far as they go, need to be grounded in a metaphysics of ontic identity if one wishes adequate grounds for claiming that Jesus is unique.[83]

Given the above qualifications, Hodgson's approach is of great value in understanding Jesus as the Word. We will now look at his

---

83. See above, 81 and 171–172 for our criticism of Pannenberg's rejection of a word-christology. Hodgson, *Jesus* 72, refers to this position of Pannenberg as well. As can be seen, our use of Hodgson's phenomenological description of word is retained but transcended by an ontological understanding of the enhypostasis of the Word grounded in the resurrection event.

christology in more detail by considering the nature of his starting point, the relationship between the Word of God and God, and Jesus as the Word of faith.

(1) *Starting point.* Hodgson begins his construction of a christology with a phenomenological analysis of word as the medium of presence. His approach is principally indebted to the philosophy of Martin Heidegger and the theology of Gerhard Ebeling. Our purpose here is not to engage his argumentation, which is brilliantly done and speaks for itself, but simply to outline his conclusions as an aid to understanding how his approach can contribute to our own integrated christology.

Hodgson sees word in relation to three horizons of presence: temporality, spatiality, and transcendence. His thesis is summarized as follows: "Word is an event or a power—the power of the future—that gathers into presence (or unconceals) both temporally and spatially, transcending human speech while coming to expression precisely there. As such, word is the event of being itself."[84] As the event of being, word or language both constitutes the essence of what it is to be human, human personhood, and transcends human personhood. We will consider briefly the horizons of space and time as constitutive of human personhood and then the horizon of transcendence.

Following Heidegger, *time* is not understood simply as a function of the subjective consciousness but as the unified *event* (which is the event of being itself as temporality) of the future coming through the past into the present. Language is the medium of this 'presencing'. "Historical reality is deeply hidden in space and time. Only by language are we able to retrieve the past (to make it present by bringing it to speech anew) and to grant the future (to open ourselves for it and to let it come near). It is by means of word that

---

84. Hodgson, *Jesus* 84. The 'dianoetic' or unconcealing character and the 'dynamic' or event character of word are what he sees as authentic elements in the *Logos* tradition (Greek *logos* and Hebrew *dabar*). See 74–79. This applies to Jesus as follows: ". . . Jesus himself *is* the word of God, not as the incarnation of a pre-existent divine Person but as the one whose word is the power that brings life, whose word is the coming-to-speech of God himself. The use of 'word' as a christological title does not violate its fundamental sense of living, spoken event but is rather its fullest exemplification" (82).

man's existence as historical is opened up for him."[85] Therefore, word constitutes presence to oneself (which includes one's world) through temporal integration.

Following Walter Ong, *sound* indicates not only the temporal but also the spatial character of word, an aspect somewhat neglected by Heidegger. The spoken word, which is the basic but not the only form of word, is an *embodied* medium that makes encounter possible.

> Word as sound establishes personal presence. The human voice conveys presence as nothing else does; indeed, we could say that voice *is* presence. The reason, suggests Ong, is that sound is a unique 'sensory key to interiority'. Sound has to do with the self-manifestation of interiors. Sight presents surfaces for it is based on reflected light. We are unable to penetrate 'into' a person when we see him. . . . Sound moves from interior to interior and thus is able to open up interiors to each other without destroying their interiority. . . . Sound surrounds us and thus situates us in the midst of a world. We find ourselves *in* the presence of a person rather than 'in front of' his presence. 'Being in is what we experience in a world of sound'. In this sense, word constitutes space as well as time.[86]

Therefore, word constitutes presence to one's world (which includes oneself) through spatial integration. Word is event both in a temporal-historical and in a spatial-bodily sense. "In summary: space and time are co-constitutive horizons of human existence, and full *personal* presence is accomplished by the dialectical movement between presence to oneself and presence to the world. 'Personhood' means presence realized simultaneously in these two horizons. . . . As the medium of presence, word constitutes personhood."[87]

---

85. Ibid. 91. This idea is derived from Gerhard Ebeling, *God and Word* (Philadelphia: Fortress, 1967) 16–25.

86. Hodgson, *Jesus* 93–94. Cf. Walter J. Ong, S.J., *The Presence of the Word* (New Haven: Yale University Press, 1967).

87. Hodgson, *Jesus* 108.

The horizon of transcendence is intended to emphasize that the word which gathers into presence both temporally and spatially is not simply identical with human speaking. As there is an ontological difference between Being and beings (Heidegger), so between language and human speaking. True and faithful word, an authentic coming to expression of Being, occurs within human speaking (which is our 'place' in the event of unconcealment) but is experienced as a *gift* that comes not 'from above' (as a separate, supernatural reality that invades our reality) nor 'from within' (as completely within the control of human capabilities) but from the future (as the power of the future that gathers us into presence with ourselves and our world). Faith can understand this as a description of God's Word: word that gathers into presence both temporally and spatially yet transcends human speaking.

In its most primordial sense, word is the means of the event of creation, of letting *be*: 'God said: Let there be light . . .' (Gen. 1:3). We are talking about the creative power of God *within* the creative process. As Ebeling emphasizes with regard to human speaking, word here means normal, natural, historic word that takes place between human persons; the difference is not between the nature of word as oral speaking but between who is the speaker: God who is *verax* or man who is *mendax*. In a word, wherever truth is spoken, there is God's Word. Hodgson describes this as *homology,* the same word is both human and divine when it occurs as a true, authentic, faithful word. This correspondence is not to be understood as *analogy.*

Analogy (*ana,* up + *logos,* word) suggests a relation of proportionality between words or things that are otherwise different (e.g., exist at different levels of the ontological scale). It is rather a relation of homology (*homos,* same + *logos,* word), a relation of correspondence rather than of proportionality . . . the point is that this correspondence does not involve a 'supernaturalizing' of word but rather a restoration of human speech to its own most proper function. This point is essential for a proper understanding of the relation between the word of God and the word of man. When the latter is brought to authenticity by the former, i.e., when

it becomes word of faith, then it exists in a relation of homology to the word of God, serving as the appropriate instrument or means for the coming to speech of God's
creative, redemptive, and unconcealing word. Rather than
referring to the *analogia fidei*, as Karl Barth does (thus
suggesting the suprahistorical character of the word of
God), we may refer to the *homologia fidei*. Faith means
precisely homologous speaking.[88]

In all of this, Hodgson is concerned not to hypostatize word as
an active, personal, divine agent along the lines of the Logos-flesh
christology. He seeks to avoid this in two ways. First, he speaks of
finite transcendence: word does not violate the finitude of human experience but deepens and preserves it because it happens only *within*
this world. Word is not personal agency but the *means* whereby one
becomes a human person. Second, homology or correspondence re-
quires a dialectical movement between language and human speaking in order to preserve an element of non-identity. These two points
raise the question of the relationship between the Word of God and
God.

(2) *Word of God and God.* Hodgson seeks to identify God and
word dialectically. One can say neither that God is a being behind
his word (as if word were merely an expression of a more fundamental, prelinguistic reality) nor, reversing the predicates in a hyposta-
tizing manner, that the word is God (as if word itself were a personal
agent rather than the medium or power that constitutes personhood). Our position, of course, is that the word is not hypostatized,
in the sense of being a 'Thou' over against the Father's 'I', already
in the inner-trinitarian life but only when the word became flesh,
thus constituting the human personhood of Jesus and so becoming
personal agent as a new and unique reality within the creative process that moves from creation through covenant to incarnation. While
insisting upon the uniqueness of the incarnation, I find Hodgson's

---

88. Ibid. 101–102. In n. 101, he affirms the valid use of analogy in second-order
language *about* God, a reference we quoted above, 136–137, in speaking about the need
for analogy. For Ebeling's views on the nature of God's Word, see his very fine article
"Word of God and Hermeneutics" in *Word and Faith* 305–332.

formulation for the dialectical identification of God and word to be valid and insightful, viz. *"God is the one who has word absolutely and in this sense is the primoridal word-event, the event of being."* This parallels the striking formula of Karl Rahner that God is "the being that 'has being' absolutely." In this one instance being and a being absolutely cohere. This dialectical identity allows for the true ontological difference. Hodgson's use of word rather than being is intended to affirm the personhood of God.

> As *the one who* has word absolutely, God is the one true and perfect person for word is the constitutive power of personhood. As the one who has word *absolutely,* God is distinguished qualitatively from all other beings, which exist only at the disposal of word, serving as the 'place' where it comes to speech. My formula proposes a dialectical identification of God and word in such a way as to discourage the hypostatization of word and to designate the unique personal being of God vis-à-vis all creatures.[89]

Hodgson sees three fundamental implications for an understanding of the being of God, viz. God is presence, personal, and revelation. First, God is presence:

> As the one who has word *absolutely,* God is the *primordial* unity of time. He is not merely gathered into presence by the power of the word, as finite beings are; rather his being *is* presence. 'Presence' signifies the dynamic unity (not identity) of future-past-present accomplished by word. To say that God is 'presence' is a way of affirming that God's being in its essence is being-as-temporality.

---

89. Hodgson, *Jesus* 116–119. The reference is to Karl Rahner, *Hoerer des Wortes* (Muenchen: Koesel-Verlag, 1963) 66, 69. In n. 122 Hodgson explains Rahner's formula: "This formula is based in turn on Rahner's concept of an 'analogy of having being' (*Analogie der Seinshabe*)—not on an 'analogy of being' (the classical *analogia entis*). Being itself is not analogous but the emergence of the difference between being and beings and the degree to which or the mode in which beings 'have' being. This modification is intended to avoid the objectivistic-hypostatizing misunderstanding of being and of the ontological difference."

Although time, especially the notion of futurity, is more easily an image of transcendence than space, it must be remembered that God is not only imaged as the beginning and the end but also as the height and the depth. Hodgson's description of God as presence is, in my terms, a description of God as Creator, as the one who encompasses or embraces the world in such wise that all of creation and especially human history is in him. Thus it is better to speak of the world in God rather than of God in the world. In this sense, one can properly speak of God as the primordial unity of time and space.

Second, God is personal: "As the one who has word absolutely, God is preeminently personal, for personhood consists of the event—the temporal, historical event—that happens by gathering and being gathered into presence through the word. To be personal means to exist in presence. As *the* word-event, God *is* presence." God is the one true and perfect person for word is the constitutive power of personhood. In this sense, it is better not to speak of three 'persons' in the Trinity but of the one person (God) as the word existing triunely in three modes of being (Barth) or subsistence (Rahner) and in a twofold structure of self-communication (self-distinction and self-relation). God, unlike creatures, transcends and incorporates both relativity and absoluteness. As the one who has word absolutely in himself, he is present to himself as 'his own other' and so absolutely independent of creation. As the one who constitutes the world in existence through the creative power of word, he is present to the world as Creator and so relatively dependent upon that creation in becoming God for another. Hodgson's view here agrees with our notion of God becoming triune in and through the creative process, although he would disagree with our notion of God becoming one in being with the person of Jesus.

Third, God is revelation:

As the one who has word absolutely, God is revelation. There is no God other than the revealing, unconcealing, self-communicating God, the God who speaks and *is* in his speaking. God cannot be seen but he may be heard. Visual images have never been permitted of the biblical God. The reason derives from a fact discussed earlier, namely, that sight reflects surfaces but sound communicates interiors without violating their interiority. Since God is not a body, he has no 'surface' and cannot be seen (except metaphorically). But as word he is pure interiority and thus can be heard.

Speech as we know it is necessarily embodied. Thus God can speak to us only by making the world his body, i.e., by embodying his word in the world. I would suggest again that he does this by an ever-deepening involvement of himself as word moving from creation through covenant to his quintessential self-expression in the incarnation. His transcendence is preserved once again by distinguishing his absolute presence to himself from his relative presence to the world. "God's being is a double relational being. Revelation is the outward 'repetition' of God's internal self-relatedness to which it perfectly corresponds because it is God's *self*-communication. In brief: God 'is' the word of revelation both *ad intra* and *ad extra*. Only his revelation *ad extra* is dependent upon embodiment in the world for its coming to speech." Finally, what God reveals is not 'things about himself' but rather the possibility of authentic human existence in the world, in and through which one discovers God himself at the very center of created reality. Therefore, it is better to speak of God's *indirect* self-*communication* in his unconcealment of the world, as we saw in treating Pannenberg's notion of revelation.[90]

So far we have only described the possibility of God's word in the world. Its actuality depends upon the concrete, contingent events of history, particularly for Christians the personal history of one man, Jesus of Nazareth. We live in a world, as did Jesus, in which failure of word has led to a loss of presence to self, to world, and to God. For Hodgson, this is what sin formally means. Christologically, it means unfaith, faithless speech. Thus, he moves to a concrete, exegetical consideration of Jesus as the Word of faith.

(3) *Jesus as the Word of faith.* Hodgson's basic thesis is that Jesus was the definitive and irrevocable (but not exclusive or final) 'place' of God's self-communication in word, i.e., that Jesus was 'presence' in a unique and definitive sense because his word was

---

90. See above, 166–167. The treatment of God as presence, personal, and revelation is in Hodgson, *Jesus* 120–130.

faithful: there was a correspondence or concurrence of his word with the divine word, which is what Hodgson describes as homologous speech. This means that Jesus' person *is* his word. A person is known in and through his words and deeds (and also his fate), a point that we too have emphasized. Hence, there is no interest here in 'psychologizing' Jesus' interior states of mind, but rather in analyzing the impact of his historical words and deeds. Hodgson seeks to show that Jesus definitively realized the three horizons of presence (presence to oneself, to the world, and to God) by correlating these three horizons with three dimension of the concept of 'word of faith', viz. the *quality* of Jesus' speech (a new language), the *content* of Jesus' speech (a new mode of existence), and the *enactment* of Jesus' speech (a new *praxis*). He seeks to integrate these two sets of relations into a common schema which, as he cautions, is a useful organizational schema but should not be construed too rigidly. One must maintain the dialectical character of the relationships in the three horizons and not play one off against the other. For our purposes here, I can do no better than to quote at some length his own summary which he then develops at length in the rest of the chapter. One will recognize great similarity with our own development of the earthly ministry of Jesus in chapter two.

Thus, Hodgson proposes to

> consider the three horizons of presence under each of the three dimensions of Jesus' word, thus arriving at nine qualities of presence by which his being as the word of faith may be characterized. (1) Jesus' word as *faithful word was* (a) an *authoritative* word, discernible especially in the unique freedom of his teaching, by which he liberated men from the constraints of the law, cult, religious piety, social convention, political oppression, and showed himself to be fully constituted as a person at one with himself. His word was (b) a *truthful* word: the parables, as the paradigm of his teaching as a whole, were events of disclosure, opening reality, bringing the truth to bear upon a deceitful world. His word was (c) *homologous,* existing in a relation of correspondence to the word of God—as he himself acknowledged by prefacing some of his sayings with the quite

unique formula, 'faithfully I say to you' (*amēn legō humin*).
(2) Jesus' *word about faith* as the definitive mode of human
existence described faith (a) as *power,* improbable power
like that of a grain of mustard seed, which gathers life into
presence temporally, integrating personal existence, freeing
it from anxiety and powerlessness; (b) as *wholeness,* the
healing of physical affliction and social cleavage, gathering
life into presence spatially, making it whole, 'saving' it in
the midst of estrangement and disintegration; and (c) as
openness for the kingdom of God—the coming 'kingdom of
presence', which means life in the presence of God who *is*
presence, and which is man's final destiny but of which we
now have a foretaste and share by faith. (3) Jesus' *enactment of faith* was marked by the qualities of (a) *freedom* in
the world, his presence to himself as 'radical man'; (b) *responsibility* for the world, his co-humanity or being-for-oth-
ers as the 'brother of men'; and (c) *obedience* to the will of
God, his presence to God as the true 'son of God'. Jesus'
freedom, responsibility, and obedience were climaxed by
the *death on the cross,* which accordingly is to be understood as a word-event, *the* word-event of faith.[91]

I find this to be an admirable summary of the impact of Jesus'
historical presence as the word of faith and have no fundamental
quarrel with it. We have already given our own version of much of
the same material in chapter two. Hodgson's approach is valid as a
phenomenological description of God's word in the world but, as already indicated, I would want to go further and say that Jesus is
God's word because in his personal identity he *is* the truth about the
human condition, especially at the moment of death. Hodgson's insights need to be grounded in a metaphysics of ontic identity such
as we have been proposing throughout this book if one wishes adequate grounds for claiming that Jesus is unique. I can only agree
with Hodgson's attempt to reinterpret the definition of Chalcedon,
but I think his proposal, as also Schoonenberg's, falls short of an adequate reinterpretation. Hodgson succinctly states his position:

91. Hodgson, *Jesus* 151–152.

By substituting *homologia* for *homoousion* I propose to avoid the abstract distinction between 'nature' and 'person', and to find a more adequate way of describing the unity of Christ. The homology in Christ is comprised by the concurrence of the word of God (the power that gathers into presence and constitutes personhood, although it is not itself personal agency) and definitively faithful human speech. Homology describes both the unity and the distinction of God and man in Christ, a unity-in-distinction that is to be understood as an event of language and is fundamentally constitutive of human personhood.[92]

To this I would simply add: if God's word is the constitutive power of all that is, then it must be said that God's word constitutes the personhood of Jesus in a way that is unique to him.

This can be understood only by looking at the *whole* of Jesus' life, as Pannenberg insists. The resurrection, as God's eschatological word about death, is a new creation that is first of all truly transformative of Jesus and only so the realistic ground of our confession of him in faith and our hope from him for the final consummation in love. Thus, the risen Jesus is not 'identified' only by reference to the historical Jesus but realizes his full personal identity as the Son by reason of the Father's creative and transforming embrace in the power of the Spirit at the eschatological 'moment' of raising him from the dead. We confess (*homologein*) this in faith as Jesus confessed his Father's faithful love and associated our confession with his: 'Whoever acknowledges me (*homologein en emoi*) before men will be acknowledged before the angels of God. . . .' (Luke 12:8a). This new homology, which is primarily doxological in character—the praise of God for his new creation in Christ Jesus the Lord—can only be articulated systematically through a proper use of analogy as second-order language *about* God in Christ.[93] Only identity-in-being can control all *merely* mythological and/or legendary tendencies in christology and at the same time adequately ground the tradition-

---

92. Ibid. 147.
93. See above, 130 on the primary of doxology and 136–137 on the need for analogy.

al claim to Jesus' absolute uniqueness. This is the function, primarily negative, of metaphysical language in reference to the story of Jesus. As with the historical way of knowing, such language must always remain subordinate to the metaphor as narrated, i.e., to the concrete, personal story of Jesus as the parable of God. The origin and goal of all christological language, whether it be historical, mythical, or metaphysical, is Jesus. We are always brought back to the primacy of Jesus, a primacy that includes but transcends every attempt to bring to expression the mystery of his personal relation to his *Abbā*.

E. THE PRIMACY OF JESUS

The task of christology is twofold: from within the Christian faith, to demonstrate the intrinsic basis and justification for the claim to Jesus' absolute uniqueness and, from without, to demonstrate the relevance of such a claim for the contemporary understanding of reality and truth, particularly in religious terms for the understanding of God's universal salvific will. Thus, by way of conclusion, we raise the same questions with which we began this book. In the light of all that has preceded, we will comment briefly on these two inseparably related issues: Jesus' uniqueness and universal salvation.

The question of Jesus' uniqueness is the question of what constitutes a fully adequate christology for the contemporary Christian. That question involves both the contemporary understanding of reality in terms of historical consciousness and the traditional understanding of faith in Jesus as involving four interrelated and inseparable dimensions that are essential for that faith-consciousness, viz. that it be rooted in the history of Jesus, centered finally and definitively in the eschatological event of Jesus' death and resurrection, and culminated in the doxological confession of Jesus' oneness in being with the divine. The four authors that we have treated all agree in their attempt to remain within historical consciousness and to employ the kinds of historical-critical tools that we have relied on in our analytical chapters two, three, and four. They have all accordingly emphasized the all-embracing creative activity of God in terms of the concrete, historical processes of a world that is moving in eschatological hope toward the final and definitive liberation of the whole of creation. They, as we, have sought to locate christology within this universal context of God's creativity as the deepest expression of his love for all of creation. Though they have slightly differing starting points, they all seek to integrate the four dimensions of historical Jesus, cross, resurrection, and incarnation by centering upon the concrete, personal existence of Jesus of Nazareth. They all seek to avoid the thought process that first separates and then reunites the divinity and the humanity of Jesus. If for Pannenberg the decisive factor is the resurrection, for Moltmann the critical factor is the cross, and for Hodgson the indispensable factor is the historical word, nonetheless they all agree with Schoonenberg that "Jesus' divine sonship is his human-ness to the utmost." There is a consensus of approach here that points to Jesus in the concrete particularity of his own personal existence. The concrete, personal history of Jesus is basic and essential to the affirmation of his divinity, for it is *only* in his *Da-Sein* that we have access to God's dealings with the world as trinitarian.

Where I have been critical of these approaches is in the *radical* character of the Christian doctrine of the incarnation. Only Pannenberg seems to take seriously enough the ontological depth required for an adequate christology. While the other authors offer emphases much needed in Pannenberg's christology, he alone of the four offers a way of getting at the central core, the root, of the Christian faith. What makes that faith relevant for today is not the use of contemporary methodologies, useful as they are, but the ineradicable because eternally rooted conviction that at a particular point of time in an obscure place called Galilee God became one with his creation in a man named Jesus because his word is faithful. It is the particularity of the incarnation that is essential and distinctive to Christianity. Has any other religion ever made the kind of claim that Christianity makes, viz. that God has come near to us, as near as he can, by identifying himself with a creature, the man Jesus, or that God is personally involved in our human condition in such wise that he is affected deeply within his own divine life by our human response, a response that came to its critical and culminating expression in the personal history of Jesus? We Christians proclaim a truth that is so wonderful and so radical that we dare not believe it ourselves, let alone live out its implications. It is this claim to definitive truth in the absolute uniqueness of Jesus that makes problematic our understanding of Jesus' proclamation of the Kingdom for all human persons.

We maintained in our second chapter that 'Kingdom of God' is Jesus' comprehensive term for the blessings of salvation insofar as it denotes the divine activity at the center of all human life and that 'faith' is his human, experiential term for salvation itself insofar as it denotes the human response, universally valid, of openness, acceptance, and commitment. Further, in the fourth chapter, when we treated the development of christology in the light of the resurrection, we maintained that christology is rooted in soteriology and must always remain so, for it is but the deepest expression of soteriology in that it affirms at its most radical God's creative being-in-the-world *for us*. Hence, we maintain at one and the same time the universalism of God's salvific love as brought to expression by Jesus himself and the uniqueness of Jesus as the final and definitive embodiment of that love. The question in connection with other religions is not so much over the theoretical possibility (however it may be articulated philosophically) of God's word becoming incarnated in some form of human embodiment but over its actuality, i.e., not whether it may have occurred but why only once, why do Christians claim it happened once-for-all (*eph' hapax*) in Christ? The answer, it seems to me, lies in the nature of the claim itself as a claim to truth.

The truth cannot contradict itself. The human quest for unity maintains that as there is only one God who creates one universe, so there is only one truth though we approximate it in a multiplicity of human expressions. Russell Aldwinckle, in a very fine chapter entitled "Jesus or Gotama?"[94] sees the issue to be joined where there appear to be contradictions or irreconcilable differences in regard to truth claims. He notes a number of interesting similarities between the historical Jesus and the historical Gotama, one of the most intriguing being, as I see it, that both proclaimed a kind of a-theism by focusing upon transcendence within this world. There is an emphasis upon human experience, and especially upon the experience of suffering. Yet, it is precisely in their understanding of suffering

---

94. Aldwinckle, *More Than Man* 211–246. See also Moltmann's remarks on "Christianity and the world religions" in *Church* 150–163.

that one can perceive their profoundly different understanding of the reality of God as personal and hence of the reality of human experience. Both recognize the widespread and pervasive reality of suffering but they understand its origins differently.

For Gotama, suffering is rooted in desire which is evil and which can only be overcome by the destruction of the self. Reality is ultimately nirvana, the absence of craving. For Jesus, suffering is rooted in the perversion of personal relationships which can only be overcome by centering oneself in the one relationship that makes all others possible. Reality is ultimately gracious, a loving and caring *Abbā*, and therefore Jesus celebrates life by his parables, his table-fellowship, his healing ministry. Aldwinckle takes note of the seeming paradox of the compassionate Buddha. He recognizes that both Jesus and Gotama were deeply and passionately concerned for the true welfare of their fellow human beings, but he sees their differences as ultimately irreconcilable:

> . . . it is still a fact that the difference between the two remains in relation to the nature and reality of God and the importance of the person as a potentially redeemable child of God. There is no way in which the basic presuppositions of their respective world views can be reconciled or harmonized. Gotama's agnosticism about a personal Creator, even if interpreted as the mystic's caution about using human language to point to the transcendent, his acceptance of karma and the anatta doctrine of the nonpermanence of the self—all these simply cannot be reconciled with a Christian theism rooted in the Hebraic and Christian view of a living, personal Creator-God who fashioned man for an eternal fellowship of love with Himself. The joy in heaven over one sinnner who repents simply does not make sense in the context of the ideas in which Gotama taught and developed his doctrine of nirvana. At this point each man must make his own crucial spiritual choice. In the light of this, it is impossible for the Christian to speak of the divinity of the Buddha where the word 'divinity' would make sense.[95]

---

95. Aldwinckle, *More Than Man* 235.

This comparison of Jesus and Gotama serves to sharpen the problem, for what are we to think of the universalism of God's salvific love in the light of world history—the untold numbers of people who have never had any contact with Christianity and the growing awareness today of the validity of religious experience outside and independently of Christianity? The genius of early Christianity, the decisive difference from Judaism that finally allowed it to become a new religion in its own right and not merely a sect, was its ability to transcend differentiations into Jew or Greek, slave or free, male or female (Gal. 3:28) and to proclaim a higher unity in Christ Jesus that would exclude no one. The news was so good and created such an exuberance and enthusiasm that it was only natural and right to seek to share it with the whole world as it was then known, i.e., to a world primarily circumscribed by the Mediterranean with Rome at its center. But the world has proved to be much larger, both in its geographical extent and in the complexity of its history, than could have been imagined by those early Christian missionaries. The same applies to us today in terms of the galaxy we live in, let alone the universe.

In our contemporary context, enlightened by our historical knowledge of Jesus, we cannot ignore the universalism of Jesus which, in its respect for the gift of life given to each, transcends even Christianity. Here a clear distinction must be made between Christianity as a *religion* which has a particular history and structure that has embodied both good and evil, especially in its influence upon Western civilization, and Christianity as a *vocation,* a mission given in the Spirit of Jesus, that is continually striving to bring to expression the truth that claims all people, Christian and non-Christian alike. In this sense, Jesus stands in judgment on any form of exclusivism, whether it be found in Judaism, Christianity, Buddhism, or anywhere else. But, if this is so, what is the point of christology?

As we noted in chapter four,[96] christology is a very specific and explicit response of *disciples* to the mystery of Jesus' whole life as revealed definitively in the light of the resurrection. Every christology is a very human attempt to bring to expression the mystery of Jesus as a person, a mystery which continually transcends the human ex-

---

96. See above, 107–108.

pression. The purpose of any christology, then, is not to perpetuate itself but to offer a true and valid (though necessarily limited) articulation of the mystery of salvation as embodied in the person of Jesus. This mystery, which Jesus embodies most fundamentally in his relation to his Father, is for all persons. The articulation of it is an attempt to make it available, to bring it into consciousness, but this can take place in a multiplicity of christologies. Not only in the subsequent history of Christianity, but already in the New Testament itself such a multiplicity exists. I am not suggesting that one christology is as good as another—a kind of christological relativism—for Christians must continually discern and differentiate in order to deepen their grasp of the truth. The early confession of faith, KYRIOS IĒSOUS, is a dogmatic assertion that makes a claim about truth, about the way things *are.* But, while one must retain the assertive character of Christian faith, I am suggesting that christology is second-order level of reflection about that truth and hence is always a 'speaking towards' it (*intendere*) without ever fully 'grasping' it (*concipere*). Such second-order level of reflection must always be in service to that which is more fundamental and primary, viz. the offer of salvation to each and every person within the concreteness and particularity of the gift of life that is given to each.

The vocation of the Christian, the mission given in the Spirit of Jesus, is fundamentally the same as the mission of Jesus himself: to help bring the Kingdom to its full realization, i.e., to enable each and every person in the concreteness of his or her own situation to embody that most fundamental human value which Jesus embodied and without which humanness is impossible, union through him with the Father in the power of the Spirit. Christians, if they are to be true to their own self-identity, must always retain the primacy of Jesus in his concrete, personal existence as the unique Son of the God whom he called *Abbā.* This is already a christological statement on a second-order level but its truth may be realized concretely in a diversity of life-situations. The important point, by way of contrast to Gotama's understanding of reality as indicated above, is that it is *this truth* that must be realized, the truth of a loving and caring Father who suffers in our suffering in order to overcome our self-alienation and bring us into the full realization of our selves by drawing us ever more deeply into the personal reality of his inner trinitarian life.

Yet, what Jesus teaches us is to be open to all truth wherever it may be found. We Christians can affirm at the same time the absolute uniqueness of Jesus and the universal salvific will of God only if we do not seek to *control* the revelation given in Christ. Dialogue with non-Christian religions must truly be dialogue, not monologue, so that we fully expect to learn from them as they from us. The primary attitude must be to respect the gift of life as God gives it to each one and to nurture that gift in its authenticity. One who is called to be a Christian, then, is called to proclaim the God revealed in Christ (*kerygma*), to embody that proclamation in community (*koinonia*), and to be in service to the world striving to enable all human beings to embody in their own personal lives the values of the Kingdom (*diakonia*).[97] The Kingdom of God, proleptically realized in the person of Jesus, is still an eschatological concept. The truth of what we proclaim will only be fully realized at the eschaton when Jesus will hand the Kingdom over to the Father and God will be all in all (1 Cor. 15:20–28). In my opinion, it is only in such an eschatological perspective that we can maintain together the absolute uniqueness of Jesus and the universal salvific will of God. Our vocation as Christians is not to control or predetermine the final disposition of all things but to be in service to it by witnessing to the truth that is in us. We can only do this by being true to the Spirit of Jesus. We believe that it was his Spirit that enabled the early Christians to develop christology and that it is his same Spirit that enables us to be in continuity with that faith and to proclaim it anew today. But faith in the Spirit of Jesus demands openness to the freedom of that Spirit of truth who will guide us into *all* the truth (John 16:13). That truth will make us free only when the whole of creation has been set free. It is the same Spirit who moved over the waters at creation (Gen. 1:2), whom Jesus handed over at the moment of his death on the cross (John 19:30), and who cries from the very center of our hearts, from the very center of creation itself, *Abbā!* (Gal. 4:6; Rom. 8:15–16).

---

97. McBrien, *Church* 73–85. See above, 56–58.